Preparing the Modern Meal

NEW AFRICAN HISTORIES

SERIES EDITORS: ALLEN ISAACMAN, DEREK R. PETERSON, AND CARINA RAY

David William Cohen and E. S. Atieno Odhiambo, *The Risks of Knowledge*
Belinda Bozzoli, *Theatres of Struggle and the End of Apartheid*
Gary Kynoch, *We Are Fighting the World*
Stephanie Newell, *The Forger's Tale*
Jacob A. Tropp, *Natures of Colonial Change*
Jan Bender Shetler, *Imagining Serengeti*
Cheikh Anta Babou, *Fighting the Greater Jihad*
Marc Epprecht, *Heterosexual Africa?*
Marissa J. Moorman, *Intonations*
Karen E. Flint, *Healing Traditions*
Derek R. Peterson and Giacomo Macola, editors, *Recasting the Past*
Moses E. Ochonu, *Colonial Meltdown*
Emily S. Burrill, Richard L. Roberts, and Elizabeth Thornberry, editors, *Domestic Violence and the Law in Colonial and Postcolonial Africa*
Daniel R. Magaziner, *The Law and the Prophets*
Emily Lynn Osborn, *Our New Husbands Are Here*
Robert Trent Vinson, *The Americans Are Coming!*
James R. Brennan, *Taifa*
Benjamin N. Lawrance and Richard L. Roberts, editors, *Trafficking in Slavery's Wake*
David M. Gordon, *Invisible Agents*
Allen F. Isaacman and Barbara S. Isaacman, *Dams, Displacement, and the Delusion of Development*
Stephanie Newell, *The Power to Name*
Gibril R. Cole, *The Krio of West Africa*
Matthew M. Heaton, *Black Skin, White Coats*
Meredith Terretta, *Nation of Outlaws, State of Violence*
Paolo Israel, *In Step with the Times*
Michelle R. Moyd, *Violent Intermediaries*
Abosede A. George, *Making Modern Girls*
Alicia C. Decker, *In Idi Amin's Shadow*
Rachel Jean-Baptiste, *Conjugal Rights*
Shobana Shankar, *Who Shall Enter Paradise?*
Emily S. Burrill, *States of Marriage*
Todd Cleveland, *Diamonds in the Rough*
Carina E. Ray, *Crossing the Color Line*
Sarah Van Beurden, *Authentically African*
Giacomo Macola, *The Gun in Central Africa*
Lynn Schler, *Nation on Board*
Julie MacArthur, *Cartography and the Political Imagination*
Abou B. Bamba, *African Miracle, African Mirage*
Daniel Magaziner, *The Art of Life in South Africa*
Paul Ocobock, *An Uncertain Age*
Keren Weitzberg, *We Do Not Have Borders*
Nuno Domingos, *Football and Colonialism*
Jeffrey S. Ahlman, *Living with Nkrumahism*
Bianca Murillo, *Market Encounters*
Laura Fair, *Reel Pleasures*
Thomas F. McDow, *Buying Time*
Jon Soske, *Internal Frontiers*
Elizabeth W. Giorgis, *Modernist Art in Ethiopia*
Matthew V. Bender, *Water Brings No Harm*
David Morton, *Age of Concrete*
Marissa J. Moorman, *Powerful Frequencies*
Ndubueze L. Mbah, *Emergent Masculinities*
Judith A. Byfield, *The Great Upheaval*
Patricia Hayes and Gary Minkley, editors, *Ambivalent*
Mari K. Webel, *The Politics of Disease Control*
Kara Moskowitz, *Seeing Like a Citizen*
Jacob Dlamini, *Safari Nation*
Alice Wiemers, *Village Work*
Cheikh Anta Babou, *The Muridiyya on the Move*
Laura Ann Twagira, *Embodied Engineering*
Marissa Mika, *Africanizing Oncology*
Holly Hanson, *To Speak and Be Heard*
Paul S. Landau, *Spear*
Saheed Aderinto, *Animality and Colonial Subjecthood in Africa*
Katherine Bruce-Lockhart, *Carceral Afterlives*
Natasha Erlank, *Convening Black Intimacy in Early Twentieth-Century South Africa*
Morgan J. Robinson, *A Language for the World*
Faeeza Ballim, *Apartheid's Leviathan*
Nicole Eggers, *Unruly Ideas*
Mark W. Deets, *A Country of Defiance*
Patrick William Otim, *Acholi Intellectuals*
Daniel Magaziner, *Available Light*
Admire Mseba, *Society, Power, and Land in Northeastern Zimbabwe ca. 1560–1960*
Ademide Adelusi-Adeluyi, *Imagine Lagos*
Jody Benjamin, *The Texture of Change*
Benedito Luís Machava, *The Morality of Revolution*
Holiday Powers, *Moroccan Modernism*
Allen F. Isaacman, Joy M. Chadya, and Barbara S. Isaacman, *Elusive Histories*
Devin Smart, *Preparing the Modern Meal*

Preparing the Modern Meal

Urban Capitalism and Working-Class Food in Kenya's Port City

Devin Smart

OHIO UNIVERSITY PRESS

ATHENS, OHIO

Ohio University Press, Athens, Ohio 45701
ohioswallow.com

Printed in the United States of America
Ohio University Press books are printed on acid-free paper ∞ ™

Library of Congress Cataloging-in-Publication Data

Names: Smart, Devin, 1983– author

Title: Preparing the modern meal : urban capitalism and working-class food in Kenya's port city / Devin Smart.

Description: Athens : Ohio University Press, 2025. | Series: New African histories | Includes bibliographical references and index.

Identifiers: LCCN 2024062352 | ISBN 9780821426234 paperback | ISBN 9780821426227 hardcover | ISBN 9780821426241 pdf

Subjects: LCSH: Food habits—Kenya—Mombasa | Working class—Kenya—Mombasa—Social conditions | Urbanization—Kenya—Mombasa—Social aspects | Food consumption—Economic aspects—Kenya—Mombasa | Street food—Kenya—Mombasa

Classification: LCC GT2853.K46 S63 2025 | DDC 647.95096762/36—dc23/eng/20250331

LC record available at https://lccn.loc.gov/2024062352

For my parents, Doug and Irene Smart

Contents

List of Illustrations ix

Acknowledgments xi

Introduction 1

Chapter 1 The Work of the Daily Meal
Cuisine, Labor, and Migration in Early-Colonial Kenya 32

Chapter 2 Comestible Commodities
Food Provisioning and the Commercialization of Daily Life in Midcentury Mombasa 52

Chapter 3 Mealtimes and Modern Urbanism
Kitchen Labor and the Working Day in a Capitalist City 76

Chapter 4 "Making Food Vendors a Regular and Permanent Feature in the Town"
The Politics of Street Food in Late-Colonial and Decolonizing Mombasa 105

Chapter 5 Street Food and Urban Life at the End of the Twentieth Century 133

Conclusion
Working-Class Food and Informality in the Twenty-First Century 158

Notes 173

Bibliography 223

Index 239

Illustrations

MAPS

0.1. Map of Mombasa Island and surrounding mainland, ca. 1848 — 3

0.2. Map of Mombasa Island and surrounding mainland, 1963 — 3

FIGURES

1.1. Laborers of Conservancy Department in Mombasa, early 1900s — 46

2.1. Dried-goods shop (*duka*) in Mombasa, early 1900s — 65

2.2. Women selling dried fish in Mombasa, early 1900s — 70

3.1. Selection of breakfast offerings from Ali Masha — 89

3.2. The port at Kilindini Harbour, first half of twentieth century — 91

3.3. Umazi Mzungu preparing *maharagwe* at her street-food eatery — 95

3.4. *Biryani* — 98

3.5. *Ugali* — 98

5.1. Hamisi Nyoka having *ugali* with *matumbo* (tripe stew) — 145

5.2. Mohammed Omar at his small food stand — 147

Acknowledgments

The idea for this book comes directly out of my time spent in Mombasa. I first went to the city in 2010 and was welcomed into the Old Town home of Mohammed Mchulla and Rukiya Abulerehman. Those who have stayed with or visited their home, which includes a considerable number of scholars of coastal East Africa, can testify to the amazing food that comes across their table, the very best of Swahili cuisine. That I would eventually write a book on the history of food in Mombasa is certainly tied to these initial culinary experiences. It did, though, ultimately take more time before I finally settled on the topic of food. In 2012, I returned to Mombasa for an intensive Kiswahili program and emerged from a morning of class each day in search of lunch. As I enjoyed my midday meals in this cosmopolitan port town, frequenting a large variety of eateries, I came to see that many of the questions I wanted to ask about the history of capitalism and labor could be explored through food. Conversations and experiences at the table with my classmates also shaped my thinking. In particular, my new friend and classmate Luke Myhre invited me to come try his favorite *chapati* vendor, set up in a makeshift structure in a parking lot adjacent to Old Town; watching those cooks at work was among the defining moments that pushed me toward writing this book.

During that summer, I also met Samar al-Bulushi and Caleb Edwin Owen, both of whom became good friends, as well as colleagues in African studies, and during subsequent research trips to Kenya I was roommates with each of them twice. Samar, an anthropologist, helped me to connect Kenya's past to its present, and Caleb, working on his own urban history of Kenya, without doubt fundamentally shaped how I see Kenya's past.

Additionally, the interviews I conducted for this book would not have been possible without the invaluable work of my two research assistants, Onesmus Mutua and Mercy Nyambok. Onesmus organized and attended all the interviews in Mombasa. Most recently, during June 2024, he also took photographs for this project, many of which appear in the pages of this book. Mercy arranged and also attended all the interviews in Kisumu and the surrounding rural areas of Nyanza Province, and the people I was able to speak with provided insights that have proved essential to the conclusions in this book. I must also give great thanks to my friend Oguthu Seth Okumu, who opened his home to me in Kisumu while I was conducting interviews there. Although my research has taken me most often to Mombasa and Nairobi, Kisumu holds some of my best memories from my time in Kenya.

I have also been the beneficiary of the work of many archivists and librarians who have helped me access the written sources for this book. This was especially true of the late Richard Ambani, who during his life helped many historians find sources in the Kenya National Archives, and I was lucky to have worked with him too. In the United Kingdom, Lucy McCann has consistently over the years been a great help in navigating the archives of the Commonwealth and African collections of the Bodleian Libraries at the University of Oxford.

I also owe much to the faculty at Western Washington University and the University of Illinois at Urbana-Champaign who played a key role in my intellectual and professional development. At Western, Louis Truschel piqued my interest in African history as an undergraduate when I took his course on Northeastern Africa, which eventually culminated in him supervising my MA thesis years later, while I also learned much from the insights and advice of George Mariz and Ricardo López-Pedreros. Much of my education in African history at Western also happened in the office of Jonathan Miran, and only now that I have become a professor myself do I fully understand how generous he was with his time. Not only did he run an independent study for me on the history of Islam in Africa, but for countless hours beyond that we sat in his office discussing Africa's past as well as the professional life of the academic historian. I am deeply grateful for his mentorship.

At Illinois, I found an inspiring intellectual community. My adviser Jim Brennan always provided sharp and challenging feedback, and I am a much better writer and historian for it. Jim also introduced me to fellow historian of Kenya Paul Ocobock from the University of Notre Dame. At conferences, over the phone, and in correspondence, Paul has proved a kind and valuable mentor. Additionally, Antoinette Burton has been a great influence in my life (as is true for many other students at Illinois) as a historian, not least of which through the World Histories from Below program she organized during the first years of my PhD, where I encountered questions that I am still working through today. Many other faculty at Illinois influenced me in lasting ways, including Terri Barnes, Prita Meier, Kristin Hoganson, and Tamara Chaplin.

My fellow graduate students there became fast friends as well as scholarly colleagues. During those years, I felt quickly at home in Champaign-Urbana in no small part because I met David Greenstein, Scott Harrison, T. J. Tallie, Megan Russ, Deirdre Ruscitti Harshman, Stefan Kosovych, Stefan Djordjevic, Utathya Chattopadhyaya, Michael Staudenmaier, and Beth Eby. Rob Rouphail and Beth Ann Williams, fellow students of Jim Brennan during my time on campus, became both friends and sources of support as we all embarked on big projects. Rob and I are both urban historians of the Indian Ocean world, and I have lost count of the number of conference panels on which we have both presented. I look forward to many more in the future.

The research that forms the foundation of this book was also supported by several funding sources at Illinois. These include departmental and Graduate College research grants, my time as a Nicholson Fellow at the Illinois Program for Research in the Humanities (now the Humanities Research Institute), and a Dissertation Completion Fellowship from the Graduate College.

I have also been fortunate to be warmly welcomed as a colleague into the Department of History at West Virginia University. I have been honored to join the rich tradition of African history built by Bob Maxon during his fifty years at WVU, and I have learned much from other colleagues working on empire and decolonization in Africa and beyond, including Joseph Hodge, Tamba M'bayo, Sean Lawrence, and Brooke Durham. I have additionally been fortunate to work with many African history PhD students in our department who have been essential to creating a dynamic space for African studies at WVU, including Muoki Mbunga, Paul Banda, Gift Wasambo Kayira, Bright Alozie, Waliu Ismaila, Odunayo Adeojo, Eunice M'biya, Abu Koroma, and Stiffin Ndungu. There are too many other current and former colleagues at WVU who helped make the history department and wider campus a welcoming intellectual home since I arrived in 2017, so please forgive a collective thank you to you all. I must, though, send an individual one to Michele Stephens, who now lives outside London, not only for being a great colleague and friend while she was at WVU but also because she kindly agreed to take photographs at the British Library of the two maps of Mombasa that appear in this book. This project also received financial support from WVU, as I used the research funds from my postdoc and then start-up funding as an assistant professor to finance trips to Kenya and the United Kingdom to complete the final research.

The book is also much improved because of comments on the manuscript from the anonymous peer reviewers and the series editors of New African Histories, especially Derek Peterson, who took the lead on this project. I must also thank Ricky Huard for all his help and guidance over the years in turning this manuscript into a finished book. Additionally, I want to acknowledge that parts of this book draw from two previously published articles, "Provisioning the *Posho:* Labor Migration and Working-Class Food Systems on the Early-Colonial Kenyan Coast," *International Labor and Working-Class History* 98 (2020) and "The Reproduction of Urban Capitalism: Street Food and the Working-Day in Colonial Mombasa," *Journal of African History* 64, no. 3 (2023).

Now, most important to me, my family. Heather was one of the people I met early in my time at Illinois, and I am grateful for the life we have built together. I have also learned much about teaching and creativity from this former classroom teacher, who has since then become a professor of museum studies. We have two amazing children: Lucy, who was born as I was finishing my dissertation; and Elliott, who joined us two years later. They have both grown up alongside this book and become more curious over the years about this project that is now finally complete. I look forward to exploring the past, present, and future with both of you, Elliott and Lucy. My two siblings, Erin and Miles, went in a quite different professional direction than I did, becoming mountain guides in the French Alps, yet I have gained much from the way they inspire me to get outside and explore the world. Finally, my parents, Mom and Dad. I am so fortunate to have parents who provide me with unconditional love and support. I am appreciative of it each day of my life, and they have encouraged me along every step of the process that led to this book. Thank you. I dedicate this book to them.

Introduction

BEFORE MOVING to Mombasa around 1970, Evans Nduati Gitonga spent the first two decades of his life on a rural farm in Kenya's Central Province. All the food his family ate, he recalled in a 2014 interview, came from the fields around his childhood home near what was then called Fort Hall, now Murang'a, a rural area about eighty-five kilometers northeast of Nairobi. They grew maize, millet, sorghum, bananas, beans, arrowroots, and more, and his mother and grandmother worked each day to turn these raw ingredients into the regional cuisine of the Kenyan Highlands. Gitonga, as a male child, did not help in the kitchen or learn any of the techniques necessary to successfully create these dishes. His primary contribution to cooking was to provide the fuel, gathering wood in the surrounding environment to feed the kitchen fire. As for many others in rural Kenya, most days during his childhood started with a fermented porridge made from millet and sorghum, and if he was lucky, leftovers from the previous night's cooking pot would fill out his breakfast. For meals later in the day, Gitonga remembers *githeri* most of all, a Highland staple of beans mixed with maize kernels that he ate from the hollowed-out and dried shell of a calabash, a bulbous gourd that makes an effective serving bowl. Food was personal and local. He walked on the soil that nourished him, gathered the firewood that boiled and roasted his food, and relied on the skill, time, and effort of his mother and grandmother for his daily meals.[1]

In Gitonga's midcentury rural home, cash only occasionally entered the food system that fed his family. In Mombasa, Kenya's port town on the

Indian Ocean, food could not be acquired without it. Rather than growing food in their own fields, people living in urban areas bought it from open-air markets, itinerant vendors, and small grocery stores called *maduka.* Many men like Gitonga also arrived in the coastal city young, single, and without women in their homes. This meant they had to cook their food, usually for the first time in their lives. Gitonga, though, was little interested in preparing his own meals, and fortunately for him the city also made it easier to pay someone else to do the cooking that had previously been confined to the unpaid domain of domestic work. He purchased nearly all his food from Mombasa's fast-growing street-food industry. These roadside vendors offered not only relief from cooking but also the novel flavors of a cosmopolitan urban cuisine shaped by the port town's Indian Ocean culture that drew from both littoral communities and the foodways that up-country migrants like Gitonga brought with them to the city. In the morning, instead of porridge, he bought freshly prepared *chai,* a sugary tea cut with milk, along with *mahamri,* a semisweet fried dough. Later in the day, he regularly purchased *ugali,* a thick staple of boiled maize meal, and complemented it with a vegetable relish like *sikuma wiki,* a dish of cooked-down greens. His reliance on street food waned somewhat when he eventually married. If his wife was in Mombasa, she prepared their meals, making town more closely resemble country. However, she primarily lived back in Central Province and only periodically visited Mombasa. When she was away, which was most of the time, he again bought his meals from street vendors.

Gitonga's experience is a single example of a history both African and global. This book places food systems at the center of two of the dominant processes of modern world history: proletarianization and urbanization. Since 1800, vast migrations throughout the world's societies have brought people from peasant communities into cities where they had to acquire cash before they could access their food. In places like Mombasa—as in New York, London, Paris, Mumbai, and other centers of modern urbanism—a rapidly increasing number of people could no longer nourish themselves from produce grown in nearby soil; instead they had to rely on commercial markets to acquire their daily food.[2] The expanding scale of this still-unfolding process shows no signs of slowing down. In 1960, just under 35 percent of the world's population lived in cities. By 2018, that number had grown to 56 percent in an uninterrupted linear ascent.[3] While examples of urban farming may provide some prospect that city life need not necessarily mean a total reliance on the market for nourishment, the reality is that the overwhelming majority of people living in capitalist cities purchase their daily sustenance.[4] *Preparing the Modern Meal* is a local history of how capitalism and regional

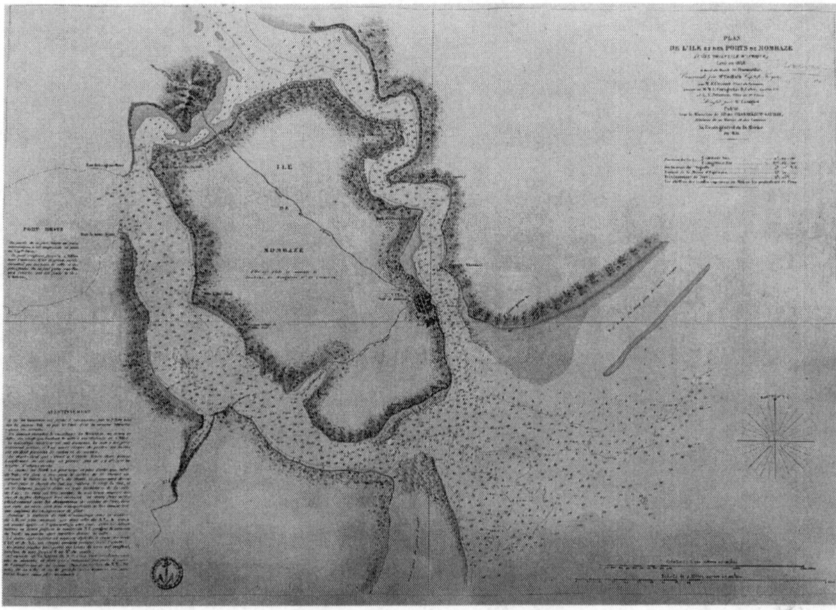

MAP 0.1. Map of Mombasa Island and surrounding mainland, ca. 1848. From the British Library Collection, Maps H.F.SEC.19 (1297).

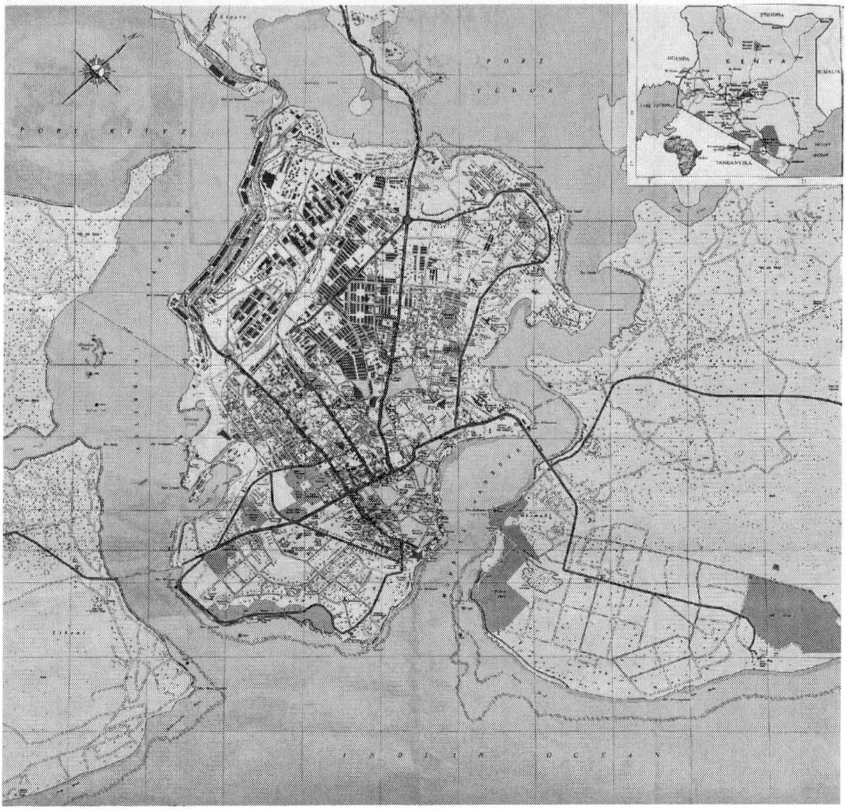

MAP 0.2. Map of Mombasa Island and surrounding mainland, 1963. From the British Library Collection, Maps 66430 (125).

migration transformed the food system of a single city in East Africa during the twentieth century, forming part of the global story about how modern urban life changed the way people access, prepare, and consume food, that most essential of all necessities.[5]

TOWN, COUNTRY, AND THE DIVISION OF DOMESTIC KITCHEN LABOR

Mombasa was Kenya's second city during the colonial era but might have been its most economically important. The port town was the choke point of the colonial economy, the place where the rail transport carrying raw materials from the interior, like coffee, tea, and sisal, met the ocean liners that took these commodities to global markets. The workers who loaded and unloaded this cargo from trains and ships, stored it in warehouses, and built, serviced, and repaired the physical infrastructure of the port and railway were among the most crucial within East Africa's regional economy. If they decided to strike, as they often did starting in the 1930s, they could halt a significant portion of western Indian Ocean trade. Exploring the ways in which such wage laborers worked, collectivized, and protested is crucial to understanding the lives of working people in twentieth-century Africa and is a topic well covered in Mombasa's as well as the continent's historiography.[6] *Preparing the Modern Meal* is also a labor history, but it does not focus on the wage-earning worksite. Instead, this book is a labor history of social reproduction, the necessary work that sustains life by sheltering, educating, clothing, healing, and, indeed, feeding people. As feminist scholars underlined in the 1970s and 1980s, this kind of work, done largely by women, is essential to the continual reproduction of capitalist societies. Without it, there is no working class. Socially reproductive labor provides the care and nourishment that people need to expend the effort to work each day.[7] There are many dimensions to social reproduction, but this book focuses on how food fits into the systems that maintained working classes on a daily basis in capitalist cities.[8] Indeed, the biological need to eat means that food is the most important aspect of daily social reproduction, a point Jane Guyer underlines by noting that food systems form the "most fundamental aspect of the material basis for social life."[9] Put another way, as Mombasa street-food vendor Agnes Gome told me, "A person must eat; it's not a must to dress."[10]

In both peasant and capitalist societies, food systems revolve around growing crops and raising livestock, processing and preparing these raw ingredients into eatable cuisine, the social distribution of these comestible resources, and then, finally, after all that work, consumption.[11] Though the specific character and scale of these processes have varied widely across time and space, there was also much continuity in the thousands of years from the agricultural revolution until the dawn of the industrial age. The rise of the Atlantic economy after 1500 certainly began to circulate new ingredients into the cuisines of both the Americas and Afro-Eurasia, but most people, in most societies during the centuries that followed, continued to eat food produced in the immediate vicinity of their home, consuming meals that were almost always prepared inside their household. Modern capitalism and urbanization, though, produced a radical rupture in the way people accessed food, the nature of their cuisines, and social and economic dynamics of *kitchen labor*, that daily work of converting raw ingredients into a consumable dish and then cleaning up the mess that is made.[12]

The gendered structures organizing the domestic division of kitchen labor have proved enduring across time and space, as women have been principally responsible for food preparation inside their households.[13] In recent decades, images of men cooking have become ubiquitous in mass media and social media alike, which suggests a greater social acceptance of the idea that men too can prepare the family's food. However, sociological data show that, however much men are more interested in cooking now than in the past, this has not to date translated on a social level to anything close to a revolution in the household division of labor in heterosexual families. For example, between 1998 and 2009, data gathered on Organisation for Economic Co-operation and Development (OECD) countries and China, South Africa, and India showed that women spent four times as much of their day on household kitchen work as men did. This is a function, as Michelle Szabo and Shelly Koch argue, of the broader "'unfinished' gender revolution," as women continue to do the majority of unpaid household work.[14] Thus, for all the gains of feminism, the idea, and indeed the practice, that women cook and clean in the kitchen has been remarkably durable.

This should not, though, lead to the conclusion that the gendered organization of domestic cooking remained stable during the modern era.[15] Globally, proletarianization, labor migration, and the demands of urban life have created novel households and routines where prior assumptions about kitchen labor and gender could not always be maintained. Indeed, one of the common features of labor migration in Africa and other parts of the world has been that migrant men often found themselves living in homes without women. Even when women and men lived together, wives often regularly worked jobs that pulled them away from the home kitchen during mealtimes.[16] Moreover, in East and Southern Africa especially, many "urban" women only lived in the city part of the time, what Teresa Barnes calls "marital migrancy," often living more permanently in the countryside, where they worked family land and raised their children.[17] These urban households required new divisions of domestic labor. Drawing from evidence on recent rural-to-urban migration in China, the largest such movement of people in world history, Susanne Y. P. Choi and Yinni Peng argue that the adjustments that men have made within the spatial and political-economic realities of urban life have created a condition they call "masculine compromise." No longer able to consistently rely on the unpaid work of female relatives, men must make "pragmatic adjustments" in the division of household labor.[18] Similarly, Deborah Cohen, in her study of peasant men from Mexico who migrated to the United States during the mid-twentieth century, observed that in these households without women, male migrants "could not maintain even the appearance of [the] staunchly entrenched demarcation between 'women's' and 'men's' work. . . . Food needed to be prepared, soiled pants washed and ripped shirts sewn."[19] However, drawing on their evidence from China, Choi and Peng stress the provisional nature of these adjustments, as such "masculine compromises are the product of pragmatism rather than a transformation in cultural values and ideals," which means that a patriarchal division of household work may be reinstated "when the conditions that forced men to compromise disappear."[20]

What the research of Choi and Peng underlines, above all, is that the domestic division of labor in the modern world cannot be understood in static terms, as the shifting dynamics of geography, demography, and the working day have shaped who has done the labor of reproducing households. However, while some Africanist historians have taken an interest in the gendered work of cooking, the existing literature has not pushed much beyond James C. McCann's generalization that "Africa's cooks, who built distinct repertoires of methods, processing, and presentation, were women."[21] This conclusion holds if one's analysis remains spatially grounded in rural communities, as evidenced in McCann's survey of African food history as well as in focused studies on the agrarian foodways of Mali, Ghana, Gabon, Malawi, and South Africa, along with the research done for this book on Kenya. The historical record does consistently show that women continued to do nearly all the cooking in these rural African societies throughout the nineteenth and twentieth centuries.[22] However, the history of gender and cooking must also account for the fact that vast numbers of men and women across the African continent were in motion during the twentieth century, moving between town and country, sometimes permanently but often for only a temporary period. McCann does concede exceptions to his general conclusion about gender and kitchen labor but only to foreclose further study, noting that "in African societies bachelors do cook—but not creatively and rarely well."[23] However, by stopping there, the social history of gender in modern Africa remains incomplete, leaving untheorized how that most essential form of household labor, which for most of human history was culturally rendered as the work of women, became the daily task of men on an unparalleled scale in African cities like Mombasa during the twentieth century.

Preparing the Modern Meal, therefore, connects town and country to examine the gendered division of kitchen labor in modern Africa, along with other aspects of East Africa's food system. Such a spatial approach to urban working-class history has deep roots in the historiographies of Africa and other parts of the world. From E. P. Thompson writing about industrializing England to Keletso Atkins's research on migrant Zulu workers in nineteenth-century Natal, labor historians have stressed how workers in emerging capitalist societies need to be understood through their agrarian origins, that working-class people in fast-growing cities continued to draw on the moral economies of their rural homes even as they were making these new and "modern" urban communities.[24] Frederick Cooper made this very point in his research on Mombasa, writing that to study "the diverse meanings that dockwork had, one must do research not just in Mombasa, but in western Kenya, in Kwale, in Taita, and in central Kenya, for that is where many dockers originated" and subsequently returned. Therefore, Cooper concludes, "To do urban labor history, in other words, is also to do rural history."[25] By placing migrants in their rural and urban communities, this book offers a historically and geographically contingent understanding of the way the gendered division of kitchen labor changed in modern Africa. This spatial approach also opens up additional questions about how urban capitalism transformed food provisioning, cuisine, and the relationship between cooking, eating, and the structure of the working day.

CUISINE AND TASTE IN AFRICAN HISTORY

Many of the people who migrated to Mombasa during the twentieth century came from the Kamba-speaking communities located in the semiarid hinterland between the Indian Ocean coast and the area that became Nairobi. Though livestock figured prominently in their domestic economies, they were above all agriculturalists who created a cuisine from the products of the soil. For the daily meal, Kamba women most often prepared the staple *isio,* a dish that combined the soft, malleable texture of beans with the crunchy sweetness of whole-kernel maize.[26] Farther west and to the north in the Kenyan Highlands were Kikuyu-speaking communities, who came to represent a large proportion of those who migrated to Mombasa during the twentieth century. The Kikuyu did not have quite as many livestock as the

Kamba, at least in part because their better-watered region could sustain more agricultural production, and from their fields they cultivated ingredients that women prepared into *irio,* a dish so ubiquitous that its name was also the word for "food." It started with a base of boiled and mashed bananas and took on extra flavor and texture as the cook added maize kernels, legumes, salt, fat, and sometimes greens.[27] Isio and irio, the primary staples from two of the rural societies most represented among Mombasa's migrant communities, complicate the way that historical anthropologist Sidney Mintz has theorized peasant cuisines. Mintz, who was drawing on Audrey Richards's ethnography of rural Bemba foodways during the 1930s, argued that the world's agrarian cuisines have been principally organized around a carbohydrate-rich staple that is then complimented by a separate meat, fish, or vegetable "relish" that adds flavor, nutrition, and general palatability.[28] This "staple-and-relish" framework does go a long way in establishing the general features of peasant foodways, like those of the Bemba and other agrarian societies in Africa, but it does not fully explain rural cuisines in Kenya or provide a basis for understanding how diets changed during the twentieth century. Staples like irio and isio, the latter "eaten practically every day without anything being added to it," could stand on their own, combining different flavors and textures into a single dish.

Among the Kamba and Kikuyu, the staple-and-relish framework was not an enduring feature of their rural cuisines. Instead, it was a modern phenomenon that only began to take root in their foodways as a consequence of labor migration after 1900. The relationship between migrant wage labor in colonial Kenya and a newly emerging working-class cuisine developed, in part, from the wider history of social reproduction in Britain and its empire. In industrializing Britain, urban workers were largely dependent on cash to purchase their food in an expanding range of retail shops and eateries, but exceptions were made in some factories staffed by women in which a paternalist ethos led male industrialists to provide food to their female workforce.[29] In the empire, this gendered industrial paternalism turned into, in the phrasing of Patrick Harries, a kind of "racial paternalism."[30] As with the notion that British women should be directly fed by their male employers, migrant African men were seen by colonial authorities as a vulnerable population. Colonial labor theory during the nineteenth and early twentieth centuries held that migrant Africans were not ready for the impact of a fully proletarianized life and thus concluded that they could not be trusted to procure necessities like food with their cash wages in a market economy. Instead, the British introduced "master and servants" laws that required employers to not only pay cash wages but also provide migrant workers with in-kind payments of shelter, medical care, and food.[31] With these laws in place in Kenya, employers of migrant laborers during the early-colonial era provided their workers with a daily ration of food, referred to as *posho* (the Kiswahili word for "ration") by Africans and Europeans alike. At the end of a workday during the first decades of the twentieth century, after shoveling coal in Mombasa or harvesting sisal on a nearby plantation, migrants picked up their posho, which usually consisted of 1.5–2 pounds of maize meal, along with small quantities of supplementary ingredients like salt, vegetables, meat, and fish. Most of these migrants were men, and so not only were they cooking consistently for the first time, but they had to prepare a meal with few ingredients at their disposal. Most boiled the maize, creating a thick porridge, uniform in texture and mild in flavor. Such a dish, similar to plain rice, crusty bread, or other kinds of starchy staples, was best when accompanied by foods with contrasting tastes and textures.

For the Kamba and Kikuyu, this combination—a large plain starch complemented with a relish of meat, fish, or vegetables—was a genuinely novel experience. There were migrants who came from rural communities with dishes analogous to this milled-grain porridge, like the Luo from western Kenya, but even for them this new working-class food system presented a stark change from their cuisine in the countryside. For the Luo migrants, the radical novelty came from eating maize-meal porridges almost every day, month after month, a strong contrast to the diversity of ingredients and dishes they had at home.[32] For the agrarian foodways of Kenya, variety was driven by the wide range of crops that people grew and the dynamics of seasonality, as the daily meal changed when the available ingredients shifted based on what could be harvested or gathered and as the grain stores dwindled over time. However, for the labor migrants, rationing tied workers' diets to the steady supply chains of commercial grain markets and other commodified foodstuffs. This new food system, as in other parts of the world, flattened the cyclical time of seasonality into the temporal regularity of capitalist supply chains, as the new African working class came to eat the same milled grain nearly every day, year-round.[33] This continued even after rationing came to a close. Like workers elsewhere, those in Mombasa after the 1930s earned cash that they then converted into food in the city's market economy, but even though the posho rationing system had ended, maize meal maintained its paramount place in working-class cuisine. By midcentury, it had become the most widely available cheap grain in the city and, not insignificantly, was among the easiest to cook after a long day of manual labor on the docks or at the railyard. In Mombasa, maize meal first as rations and then purchased with cash from small, dried-goods stores was routinely prepared into a grain porridge, which the African migrants complemented with a relish if they had additional money to spend. Readers who are familiar with Kenyan food today will have already recognized this maize-based dish, *ugali* (also called *sima*), which has come to dominate the country's cuisine. Labor migration and urbanization took a dish that had been one item among many in some of East Africa's rural cuisines, and was entirely absent in others, and turned it into the ubiquitous staple of modern Kenya. Thus, certainly in East Africa and perhaps elsewhere too, cuisines structured around a plain starchy staple with an accompanying flavorful relish have, historically, been less than universal and as modern as they are traditional.

Tying rural to urban food history in this way also allows us to reconsider how historians have understood the history of taste in Africa. When analyzing rural African culinary cultures, some scholars have argued that the sensation of fullness was prized above taste. For example, Diana Wylie, examining Zulu foodways during the nineteenth century, concludes that their cuisine's "outstanding characteristic . . . was its variety" but also that "taste was associated more explicitly with beer rather than solid food." Moreover, even though "many prized the sweetness in sweet potatoes and sugarcane and sometimes added honey to sour milk to counter its sour taste," they nonetheless "ate mainly to feel full."[34] McCann, considering rural cuisine across Africa more generally, has written that the continent's ubiquitous starchy grain porridges have been grounded in "the concept of fullness, what it feels like to have 'eaten.'" Pushing the point further, he emphasizes that "cultural preferences for what constitutes a proper and filling meal" were "based more on texture of a particular glutinous starch than on its taste, and far more than on a meal's meat, fish, vegetable, or spice component."[35] These conclusions, though, cannot be sustained after a closer examination of the historical evidence or as a theoretical matter.

It is not clear why peasants, such as the Zulu, with diverse cuisines who showed ample desire for variety and balanced opposing tastes like sour and sweet should be characterized as preferring fullness above all. Additionally, the idea that the texture of a dish could be assessed separately from its taste, or to cordon off plain filling staples from their more-complex relishes in a hierarchy of preference, is to compartmentalize components of the total eating experience that cannot be isolated from one another. The plain staple and contrasting relish are inseparable, a point underlined by Richards in the 1930s when she observed (using a singular pronoun but in reference to the Bemba collectively) that "while he declares he cannot live without *ubwali*," a thick millet-based porridge, he "is equally emphatic that he cannot eat porridge without a relish (*umunani*), usually in the form of a stew. Both constituents of the meal are essential." The relishes, along with making the thick ubwali easier to swallow, also "give the porridge taste and . . . lessen the monotony of the diet." Maintaining the proper proportion between the tastes and textures of umunani and ubwali (ideally a ratio of 2:5) was also fundamental to the enjoyment of the meal, and people would eat less of the porridge if sufficient relish was not available, as one Bemba woman explained: "When we have little *umunani,* then we cook little porridge."[36] Indeed, whether in rural Zambia, Kenya, or anywhere else, people consume and assess their food in multisensorial process in which different components form an irreducible totality, as tastes (sweet, sour, salty, bitter, and umami) interact with each other and combine with smells, sensitivities to chemical reactions (e.g., spiciness from peppers) inside the mouth, and the auditory and physical experience of texture produced by chewing (called "mouthfeel"). As Ole Mouritsen, a food scientist, and Klavs Styrbæk, a professional chef, conclude in their recently coauthored research, "Taste impressions from various sources are not independent or experienced in parallel; they interact and are combined in a manner that is not merely cumulative but to a great extent synergistic—the integrated impression is more than the sum of its parts."[37]

People in agrarian as much as modern industrial societies have sought food that best embodies this synergistic experience, if conditioned by the resources they are able to command at any given moment of hunger. That is, in rural and urban Africa, people certainly wanted to eat foods that made them feel full, but, to the extent that circumstances allowed, they also desired pleasurable combinations of different smells, tastes, and textures in their daily meals.

Recent research in African food history demonstrates this in a rural context in West Africa. Laura Ann Twagira, in her study of foodways in agrarian communities in Mali, shows that among female cooks "it was the quality and not simply quantity of available food" that mattered, and "for local men and women, quality was . . . measured by the taste for specific textures, smells, flavors, and the sensation of fullness." Twagira focuses on cuisines that fit rather neatly into Mintz's starch-and-relish framework, as the principal staple was *toh,* a thick millet-based porridge, followed by rice, each of which was always preferably consumed with a "sauce," prepared variously from vegetables, meat, or fish. Indicating the value placed on the relish, one of the ways that poverty and famines were experienced was through having only a small amount of sauce, or lacking it entirely, to enhance and change the flavor of the staple. In contrast, relative prosperity was defined as the opposite, the time when people were able to invest surplus resources into the ingredients necessary to prepare "more appetizing" sauces to complement staples like toh.[38] Thus, eating food mainly to feel full was more a response to scarcity than a defining feature of culinary preference, as the integration of complex flavors and textures with a staple and contrasting sauce was the ideal to which people aspired. Indeed, as we look closer at the migrants who left rural East Africa and made new lives in the fast-growing port city of Mombasa, it becomes clear that the way their food tasted mattered enormously to them as well.

During the first decades of the twentieth century, the people who migrated to the Kenyan coast as wage laborers brought with them rural expectations that the daily meal should consist of both filling food and contrasting flavors and textures. Thus, the simple rations they were provisioned by their employers during the early-colonial period were a stark disappointment.[39] During the 1910s, workers were provided with little more than a daily ration of 1.5–2 pounds of grain, a stultifying monotony that shocked even some colonial observers. Writing about Kenya's labor system more generally, a government report published at that time noted the "unsuitability and monotony of the diet" offered by the rationing system and observed that "sufficient care is not taken to provide labourers with the various kinds of grain and vegetable foods to which they are accustomed," ignoring how people in the region were used to "a very mixed diet."[40] However, though intensely exploited, these workers also held considerable power in Kenya's early-colonial economy because of the general scarcity of labor, leverage they used to improve the quality of their daily meals. By the mid-1920s, workers had managed to pressure their employers to both increase the quantity and improve the quality of their rations, as many now received 2–2.5 pounds of maize meal per day, along with vegetables, meat, fish, and sometimes supplementary cash to purchase additional ingredients. Moreover, though rationing represented a minimum base of food security for migrants, they still chafed at a system that limited their decision-making over what they ate. Indeed, after rationing ended, people continued to demonstrate the importance they placed on a diet that corresponded to their taste preferences, even if this came with some risk. During the 1940s, wartime conditions led to the reintroduction of a ration scheme for certain workers in Mombasa; even though this guaranteed a supply of bulk calories in a time of high wartime prices, many opted to receive cash instead, taking their chances in the hope of purchasing food more in line with their culinary desires. In search of taste as much as bulk, Mombasa's migrant working class rejected the idea that food was simply a means to an end, a way to satisfy hunger and acquire energy. Food was also a source of pleasure.

However, as workers drew on what resources they could to improve their daily meals, they did not simply aim to reproduce rural cuisines in an urban context. Instead, they looked for comforting flavors in the food markets of a cosmopolitan port town and created new foodways through ingredients that were available in the city's commercial economy. In Mombasa, familiar foods from the countryside, like maize and meat, were consumed with far greater frequency while other truly novel items such as wheat, sugar, and tea became routine.[41] Household cooks prepared much of this food inside domestic kitchens, creating meals that sustained themselves and their family and friends. However, the dynamics of urban capitalism also led to the commodification of cooking on a scale with no precedent in the region's history, a process driven by new consumer markets for prepared food in a town with a working class that increasingly had the need, desire, and (at least some of the time) the money to pay others to prepare their food. Feeding thousands of people each day, these commercial cooks, alongside those in households, performed the intellectual and physical labor that created Mombasa's new urban cuisine over the course of the twentieth century. These professional cooks also became an integral part of how urban capitalism transformed the nature of space, time, and nourishment in modern East Africa.

STREET FOOD, URBAN SPACE, AND THE WORKING DAY IN KENYA'S PORT CITY

For most of human history, kitchen labor had largely been unpaid domestic work done inside the household, but rapid urbanization throughout the world after 1800 commodified cooking on an unprecedented scale.[42] While eateries that cater to poorer city residents have an antique history, the globalization of urban capitalism during the nineteenth and twentieth centuries exponentially expanded the demand for these services and led to the proliferation of cafés, saloons, cafeterias, bakeries, street-food vendors, and innumerable other such institutions that sold prepared food to proletarianized urban residents.[43] The expansion of these working-class eateries was driven not only by the more general commodification of daily needs and wants under capitalism but also by the way that modern urbanism created new spatial relationships between home and work. Scholars have observed how the growth and sprawl of cities that came with the Industrial Revolution expanded the geography of urban life in ways that made purchasing the midday meal a new necessity for workers. During early phases of industrial urbanism, employees often lived close to work and returned home for lunch or had family members bring them cooked food. However, the widening sprawl of cities increased the distance between residence and worksite to the extent that accessing food from home during a lunch break became challenging or nearly impossible.[44] To sell their labor during a long working day, people needed to pay someone else to prepare their lunchtime meal. Historians of Europe and the United States have detailed how the making of working classes in these regions required new eateries on a vast scale, but we still know comparatively little about how urban capitalism transformed the work of cooking in modern Africa.

In twentieth-century Mombasa, working-class consumers came to rely especially on street-food vendors for their daily meals, above all at lunchtime during the working day. These eateries expanded in concert with rapid urban growth, emerging in a city that went from a population of 25,000 in 1900 to over 665,000 by the end of the century.[45] Spatially, Mombasa in 1900 was a collection of neighborhoods on an agricultural island. By 2000, the island was fully urbanized and was also surrounded by large suburbs on the nearby mainland.[46] This process turned a small port town into a vast city of commuters, as people began to travel significant distances to work each day. When they departed their homes in the morning, they also left their domestic kitchens behind. Like workers in industrializing Chicago for whom, as Perry Duis observes, "the search for something to eat at noon became an urgent necessity," Mombasa's laboring classes needed someone to prepare them food halfway through the working day. Street food filled this role because it suited the needs of petty entrepreneurs and consumers alike. These eateries were part of what development scholars would come to call the "informal" economy, a sector composed of comparatively small businesses that tend to provide everyday goods and services and often operate in a state of legal ambiguity.[47] Common throughout twentieth-century Africa, Asia, and Latin America and during the industrialization of Western societies, these forms of petty commerce have expanded when "formal" waged employment cannot sufficiently absorb the number of people looking for work, and so many try to earn their living by opening small businesses.[48] For prospective street-food vendors with limited resources in Mombasa, this kind of business required minimal capital start-up costs: cooking pots, utensils, plates, and cups, with optional add-ons like tables and chairs and perhaps a small structure. For customers, street food was cheap and often conveniently located. The prices were comparatively inexpensive because vendors, like others in the informal economy, kept overhead costs low by avoiding the payment of rent, either to a commercial landlord or as a fee for a spot in a municipal market.[49] Moreover, with their businesses not tied to registered rental properties or city markets, people running street-food eateries could set up in the alleys, parks, and streets close to centers of mass employment, allowing people to buy a meal and then quickly return to work.

By providing these services, street-food vendors became essential to the reproduction of the working day in twentieth-century Mombasa. Since the 1980s, scholars have produced numerous studies on the social reproduction of laboring classes in urban Africa, examining the new social structures that emerged in cities to provide the necessary care, rest, and nourishment to enable people to show up at work each day. However, we still know little about how these workers, once on the job, were able to labor from the early morning until the late afternoon. That is, the existing literature focuses on residential space as the site of social reproduction in African cities. For example, the work of Frederick Cooper, Lisa Lindsay, and others shows the lengths to which the late-colonial state went to turn male migrant laborers into a more permanent and regularly employed urban proletariat, living in homes with wives whose unpaid domestic work reproduced their labor.[50] Other scholars like Luise White have demonstrated how sex workers sold a range of domestic services, which included cooking food for their clients. Their commodification of social reproduction, though, including the preparation of food, was tied to the residences where many sex workers ran their businesses.[51] Even research on "market women," which has gone the furthest in explaining how the laboring classes in African cities acquired their daily food, mostly examines traders who sold produce, ingredients that had to then be prepared into meals at home.[52] All of this domestic and commodified labor in and around households was crucial to sustaining urban working classes in modern Africa. However, by late morning in a town like Mombasa, hunger began to build for those doing manual labor in humid heat for the port, railway, and other urban employers. Many of these people had also commuted a long distance from their residential neighborhoods. Therefore, during working hours, they depended on nearby vendors who had spent their mornings chopping, boiling, and frying food so that a variety of dishes would be ready for the lunch-hour rush. Once satiated, customers could then return to their jobs. These working-class eateries bridged morning to afternoon and thus held together the long working day of Mombasa's economy.

The history of street food and the working day in Mombasa also illuminates how urban capitalism transformed the culture of time in modern African societies, as these businesses were integral to how a regularly scheduled lunch break became part of the routines of African workers. For decades, Africanist historians have drawn on the work of E. P. Thompson to explore the ways that colonial capitalism transformed agrarian notions of time. Much as Thompson did, historians of Africa examined these temporal changes through a vertical framework of conflict, resistance, and negotiation, struggles waged as European employers and missionaries attempted to impose the time-discipline of industrial capitalism onto Africans who came from societies structured by preindustrial work rhythms and other epistemologies of time.[53] These scholars have provided far-reaching insights into how new ideas of time, work, and leisure emerged in modern Africa, but this approach does not fully explain how midday culinary cultures changed as people moved from rural to urban societies. Some scholars have found time-discipline conflicts at work in the development of new eating patterns in colonial Africa, like Keletso Atkins, who observed an increasing "regimentation" of when people ate in nineteenth-century urban Natal, as "monthly workers were obligated to alter their meal patterns to authorized intervals of breakfast, lunch and supper, a practice contrary to the traditional custom of eating twice a day."[54] Jeremy Rich, in his study of food history in colonial Libreville, situated mealtimes as part of a larger missionary project to instill work discipline into African congregants, using a range of tactics from church bells to more-coercive measures to penalize people for not eating at "fixed times."[55] However much time-discipline may have shaped the development of new temporal patterns of eating in these circumstances, such a framework has only limited use in understanding why lunch became part of the regular routine of Mombasa's working class. The new forms of commerce enabled through urban capitalism were more decisive.

Through rural-to-urban migration, the relationship between the working day, commercial life, and geographical space changed significantly. In rural East Africa, as Atkins indicated for the Zulu in the southern part of the continent, there usually were only two meals per day. In up-country Kenya's agrarian communities, this routine was tied very much to the spatial dynamics of their working life. During the morning before work began, people had access to their household kitchen and consumed a hearty breakfast before setting off for a day of labor. For those engaged in cultivation, some crops were grown close to home, but many agricultural fields were a considerable distance away. In these rural areas, most men spent much of their time herding livestock, which meant they often had to travel quite far from their household each day to find grazing lands. Thus, whether farming or herding, rural work regularly took people prohibitively long distances from their household kitchens, and so returning for lunch was not practical. Instead, they made do with small snacks throughout the day, consuming portable items they could bring with them or berries and other edible plants they could gather from the landscape. Crucially, though, these cultural eating practices were contingent on particular spatial circumstances, rather than any concrete preference about how meals ought to be structured throughout the day. Kenyan farmers did like to eat a more formal lunch when it was possible. That is, when people happened to be working closer to home, they often did eat lunch.[56] The commercial geography of the city changed the underlying relationship between mealtimes, space, and the working day. People in both rural and urban communities traveled long distances to work, but the difference was that those in the city gathered into dense concentrations in industrial, commercial, and other high-employment neighborhoods, and then all became hungry around the same midday hour, creating mass consumer markets for prepared food. The scale of this urban demand, the kind of market formation not possible in dispersed rural geographies, facilitated the more regular routine of eating a midday meal, as it stimulated the formation of the street-food industry. While rural agriculturalists could eat lunch only when working close to home, someone from that same community who had migrated to Mombasa had the option to purchase lunch from a street-food vendor every day, if they had the money to pay for it.

The archival evidence also complicates the idea that European employers in Kenya's busy port town were particularly interested in imposing a version of time-discipline that included an extended break from work in the middle of the day. For example, at the docks, Mombasa's most important employer, the rush to load and unload ships was intense, and nothing ground the workday to a halt like the lunch hour. Indeed, during the late 1930s, some wharfage companies did not have formal lunch breaks. Food was instead brought to workers while they were on the boats; workers then took a brief break to eat their lunch and returned straight to work after they finished. As Shariff bin Mohamed, a leader of a group of dock workers, explained to a labor commission in 1939, they took only five minutes for their meal "if a man ha[d] any work to do," and people ate "while . . . standing."[57] This was the case not only at the fast-paced port but also places like the Mombasa plant of the Texaco Oil Company, where there were no set lunch breaks, which meant work continued nearly unabated. Alfred William Tulk, a representative from the company, told the same 1939 labor commission that workers "are allowed to bring their own food but the work is not stopped." He continued that most just "eat [their food] while at the machines. They definitely have no specific time off for eating it."[58] Over the long term, formal lunch breaks did become the norm, but there is no indication that this was because employers pushed to create a workday that conformed more closely with the routines of the factory system in Europe. That Africans became accustomed to taking a break at midday for a meal had much more to do with the fact that there were convenient and affordable options a short walk from where they worked, creating the material circumstances that facilitated the development of a new cultural practice.

These street-food eateries that became central to the daily routines of Mombasa's workers can also be understood as part of the history of *restaurants,* a new and distinctly modern institution. Historians have argued that restaurants in Europe began to emerge at the end of the eighteenth century and were distinguished from other eateries in the way that they individualized the eating experience. In contrast to inns and taverns, which often served a single meal to all the diners at a set time, customers in restaurants chose their food from a menu with a list of dishes, and they ate on their personal schedule because food could be ordered on-demand as long as the restaurant was open.[59] With some important distinctions compared to the European experience, street-food eateries in Africa also individualized the daily meal in clear ways. Africanists have pointed not only to how people in rural communities often ate from the same pot but also that the food itself was seen as a communal resource, that there was a reciprocal obligation to share food with the wider community.[60] Such forms of reciprocity continued in the city and indeed were often key strategies for survival in harsh urban economies, but urban food sharing was largely limited to the people within a household. Street-food businesses operated outside of these dynamics, as they were organized around a different type of exchange relationship. They were commercial businesses that interacted with customers as individualized market consumers. Amity, trust, and mutual dependence did develop between street-food vendors and their regular customers, relationships that formed the basis for extending credit to people when they did not have the cash to buy a meal. These transactions, though, were not made of the implicit promises of rural reciprocal obligations, that the receiver of a gift would eventually repay the favor in some way. These were legible credit-debt relations. Customers owed a certain amount, and they were expected to pay back it back within a bounded duration of time. Indeed, some street-food vendors in Mombasa only extended credit if they knew where their diners worked, as then they could go to the employer and get what was owed.[61] As individuals, with cash or the promise of cash through credit, working-class consumers in Mombasa could, at their convenience, stop by a street-food eatery and choose their meal from a variety of choices.

The expansion of eateries in Mombasa also led to the creation of new culinary professions in ways reflective of how commercial cooking has been gendered historically throughout the world. Jack Goody has observed how, as far back as antiquity, cooking tended to be gendered as exclusively female work when done inside the home, but men regularly took up kitchen labor when done in a professional setting.[62] In Mombasa, men have been actively involved in running street-food eateries since at least the 1950s, when steady data on the gendered structure of the industry started to be recorded. However, at midcentury, there was also a clear gendered division within the industry. Male street-food vendors, who came from communities where they did not learn to cook at home, tended to run food carts with simple menus, offering tea, beans, grilled meats, and various types of fried dough that they bought in bulk from women who prepared the menu items in their homes. Female vendors, drawing on their expertise, often ran the larger roadside restaurants, which offered a greater selection and more-complex dishes. By the final decades of the twentieth century, such gendered distinctions faded as a masculine culture of professional cooking became institutionalized in the city, and men increasingly opened bigger eateries with expansive menus. Thus, in Mombasa during the twentieth century, both women and men made steady incomes by selling prepared food to the city's laboring classes. Some also earned reputations for the quality of their dishes, and the most fortunate even managed to accumulate small amounts of capital. Though men tended to prepare food at home only when there were no women in the household, many of them cooked every day as a way to earn a living in Mombasa's urban economy.

THE WORK OF STREET FOOD IN THE POLITICAL ECONOMY OF MOMBASA

This book provides a business history of Mombasa's street-food vendors. However, it is also a labor history of the city's informal economy. Incorporating informality and other forms of "wageless" work into labor history requires, as Michael Denning wrote in a 2010 essay, that we see how "capitalism begins not with the offer of work but with the imperative to earn a living." The subject of labor history remains the proletariat, but, as Denning continues, "we must insist that 'proletarian' is not a synonym for 'wage labour' but for dispossession, expropriation, and radical dependence on the market."[63] Mombasa's street-food vendors were small-scale entrepreneurs but also part of a larger class of proletarianized urban dwellers looking for a way to earn income in an economy where wages were only one and often a quite unreliable option. Over the past two decades, a small number of Africanists, including Emily Lynn Osborn, Abosede A. George, and Lisa Lindsay, have resituated African labor history by placing informal economies into the same analytical frame as waged work.[64] These studies, along with this book, are advocating for a new labor history that accounts for the reality that by 2013, outside of agriculture, around 53 percent of Africa's workers operated in the informal sector.[65]

This new labor history, though, must also explain how informality changes the dynamics of class conflict, given the frank differences in how wage earners and petty traders earn income. Indeed, there are limits to explaining class struggle as the battle between capital and labor over the distribution of surplus value when workers have no employer but instead are independent entrepreneurs. The conflicts that shape the political economy of informality have often been over the rights of people to earn a living as entrepreneurs. Because they run businesses, the political claims of informal workers have sounded less like those of wage laborers and more like larger capitalists seeking liberal economic policies to facilitate greater profits. To conflate the two, though, is to study political economy absent the dynamics of power. While the claim-making language and political strategies of the waged and the informal are on the surface rather different, their underlying purposes converge in a shared effort to force powerful classes to make concessions that allow them to earn enough to live under capitalism. This book will examine how one group of informal workers, Mombasa's street-food vendors, struggled to create the conditions under which they could survive, and sometimes thrive, in Kenya's port town.

For most of Mombasa's colonial history, street-food vendors operated largely beyond the view of city officials. During the 1930s, municipal authorities wrote down laws that effectively made these kinds of businesses illegal, but in practice the town's inspectorates were understaffed and hesitant to disrupt the flow of socially reproductive products and services that vendors provided to the city's laboring classes. Starting in the 1950s, though, street-food eateries began to be consistently and at times violently harassed by state authorities who saw their illicit businesses as impediments to making Mombasa into a particular kind of modern city. This coercive turn most directly affected vendors, but it also threatened to increase the cost of labor because, in strictly economic terms, these eateries and other informal traders were quite useful to Mombasa's employers. By keeping prices and therefore the living expenses of the working class down, they ensured the continual reproduction of a low-wage economy.[66] However, as Bruce Berman and John Lonsdale, along with Frederick Cooper, have argued, unrestricted accumulation was not the only principle that shaped Kenya's political economy. The colonial state often enforced policies against the interests of individual employers and specific sectors of the ruling class to serve the broader project of creating a controlled and stable capitalist society.[67] As with striking workers who received higher pay and new social provisions, the assertion of control at the expense of increasing costs underlay the postwar shift in urban policy toward the informal economy.[68] Street-food vendors may have helped to preserve a low-wage system, but they also stood in the way of a modern city in which building, sanitation, commercial licensing, and property laws were strictly enforced. By squatting on private and government land without title or rental agreements, they complicated the relationship between land and private property. Their lack of running water and toilets created concerns about foodborne diseases. Their structures made from mangrove poles (*boriti*) and thatched roofs (*makuti*) that covered dirt floors violated restaurant building and sanitary bylaws and, not insignificantly, offended the aesthetic sensibilities of the governing elite.[69] Certainly, the political economy that colonial officials wanted to foster in late-colonial Mombasa was designed to ensure accumulation by private capitalists and produce revenue for the state, but this, they felt, was not sustainably possible without a particular kind of urban society. To create this city, during the late 1950s, government officials initiated large-scale campaigns in which they arrested vendors and tore down informal structures. The state had determined that employers' profits on the margins, and certainly the income-earning strategies of petty entrepreneurs, were worth sacrificing in the service of making Mombasa a modern capitalist city.

Such uses of coercive state power to reshape unruly cities into controlled urban spaces was not unique to Mombasa or colonial Africa. As David Harvey points out, drawing on his work on nineteenth-century Paris but theorizing globally, during such "bouts of urban restructuring . . . violence is required to build the new urban world on the wreckage of the old."[70] Harvey's analysis describes well the intentions of Mombasa's municipal officials at midcentury, but his portrayal of such processes as unfolding in an inexorable fashion does not account for how the dynamics of social reproduction and the desire to maintain a stable society constrained elite urban initiatives. These kinds of modernist urban development projects create contradictions that cannot be easily resolved. In Mombasa, no matter how much the authorities disliked the improvised architectures of vendors, desired to control urban space, and wanted to regulate trade, they could not ignore the needs of working people to be provisioned with affordable food while on the job. Moreover, as formal wage labor failed to keep pace with a rising urban population, these kinds of informal businesses became increasingly important to the social stability of African cities like Mombasa, staving off more-severe unemployment crises with unknown political consequences for the government. Thus, street-food vendors were usually poor and often viewed with disdain by Kenya's ruling classes, but they also played an indispensable role in the city's political economy.

The contradictory politics of street food emerged during the late-colonial era and endured through decolonization. The end of colonial rule did create genuinely new and meaningful forms of security for food vendors in the city, but precarity nonetheless remained a constant feature of their working lives. After independence, the late-colonial idea that street-food vendors did not belong in a modern city remained a premise of elite thinking, but changes to Kenya's political system and political economy also led to officials, at times, becoming more open to the operation of these kinds of businesses in Mombasa. As citizens rather than subjects, street-food vendors were able to exert more pressure on elected officials who relied on their votes, while deepening unemployment also meant that the political cost of clearing vendors from city streets was steadily increasing, as an ever-greater number of people came to rely on the informal sector for their livelihoods. However, the security that some vendors achieved was highly contingent and could be quickly lost when the political dynamics of the city changed.

Thus, the experience of street-food vendors in Mombasa since midcentury reveals a history that has been less linear and more a crooked path of fluctuating gains, losses, and uneven access to economic opportunities. These dynamics have placed informal workers onto a somewhat different historical trajectory than the way that historians of Africa and beyond have periodized the fate of wage-earning working classes since the end of World War II. Though many scholars have complicated the picture of relative midcentury working-class prosperity, pointing especially to how race and gender limited access to stable employment and its associated benefits, the dominant narrative nonetheless remains one of steady erosion following this postwar moment, driven by the neoliberal transformation and, in the West especially, deindustrialization. This overarching narrative does effectively capture the experiences of wage workers in African and Western societies, as the prospect of achieving economic stability through a well-remunerated job did markedly decline during the last decades of the twentieth century.[71] However, informal workers like street-food vendors do not fit neatly into this periodization, in part because their economic stability comes not through whether they can find a desirable job with an employer but instead from their ability to secure a location closely adjacent to potential customers and, crucially, by avoiding fines, arrests, and having their makeshift structure destroyed by demolition crews. Indeed, the era of state-led capitalist development immediately after independence, a time of rapid growth in public-sector jobs that came with wages that outpaced inflation, was also a period of intensifying campaigns to clear informal vendors from the streets, as high-modernist urban planners aimed to create a city where food vendors could operate only in municipal canteens.[72] The first decade of independence came with gains for vendors too, as by the early 1970s they had successfully pressured officials to ease some of the legal restrictions against their trade in the city. However, these achievements were quickly lost when a new cholera pandemic arrived in East Africa, putting the sanitation of street-food eateries under intense scrutiny and culminating in a 1978 campaign that aimed to shut down every vendor in the city through fines, arrests, and wide-scale demolitions. Such extreme measures, though, could not be sustained for long, especially in a city where working people were not able to easily afford the prices of brick-and-mortar restaurants and as a building economic crisis was pushing more people into the informal sector.

Driven by these local dynamics in Mombasa, as well as by global shifts in economic theory, state policy toward the informal sector changed during the final decades of the twentieth century. Informal businesses, once seen as symbols of "urban disorder," were becoming part of Kenya's official economic development plans. This was partly because informality provided a release valve that lowered the political pressure of unemployment and also because the small-scale entrepreneurialism of street vendors was compatible with the increasing liberalization of Africa's political economies.[73] In Mombasa, the deepening austerity of the late twentieth century also meant that the city government had abandoned any pretense of financing new infrastructure like canteens to house street-food vendors, and so the sidewalks, alleyways, road reserves, and other open spaces in the town became the only places these businesses could reasonably operate. Thus, fitting the ideological climate and representing a solution to pressing economic and political concerns, street food was legalized in Mombasa during the 1980s. However, this process of legalization was also contradictory, as it generated new forms of inequality within the street-food industry itself. Selling prepared food on Mombasa's streets had become an officially legitimate trade, but only if one had a license and permission to occupy public space, which required developing connections with powerful government officials. Those able to establish such relationships could build long-term successful businesses, but others who were unable to cultivate these connections remained as exposed to being arrested, fined, or having their makeshift structure destroyed as they had been before liberalization. Thus, neoliberalism in Mombasa, as elsewhere in the world, did not mean the state played a less active role in the economy, but more that its purpose had changed.[74] The ambitious infrastructural projects were largely off the agenda. Instead, the city government regulated the legal and physical terrain on which certain individuals were able to accumulate capital, while others were excluded from this process.

However, the ways that liberalization intensified social differentiation among street-food vendors should also not obscure the larger conclusion that all of those working in the informal economy remained vulnerable. Even vendors who managed to accumulate capital and gain prestige within their communities faced a kind of insecurity that their counterparts in formal industries did not. This was because many late-twentieth-century officials, in the final analysis, still saw street food and the informal sector generally as a "temporary" feature of the urban economy, a stage the city would one day move beyond in a linear process of economic development. In the short term, the employment and services these businesses provided were undeniably essential, but Mombasa's future was imagined as one in which they did not exist, replaced by more "permanent" forms of urban commerce located in licensed brick-and-mortar buildings. This idea, the underlying assumption that informality was ultimately undesirable, created an administrative logic that authorities were able to draw on when the removal of vendors became politically expedient. This could be during a public health crisis, when private investors or the government wanted access to the land where vendors operated, or when the political inclinations of these traders became inconvenient to those in power. Most of the time, the people who ran Mombasa's street-food eateries simply went to work and earned their income by nourishing the city. However, each day also portended the possibility that they could be fined, arrested, or have their business quite literally destroyed.

OUTLINE OF THE BOOK

Preparing the Modern Meal is organized into five chapters that examine the formation of a new working-class food system in Mombasa during the twentieth century. In structure, it is bookended by chapters 1 and 5, which cover, respectively, the early and late twentieth century, while chapters 2 through 4 each focus on different themes from midcentury (roughly the 1930s to the 1970s), the decades during which the city's modern food system was made. As an urban history focused on migration, chapter 1 begins not on Kenya's coast but instead in the rural interior at the turn of the twentieth century. This first section of the chapter examines the ways in which these communities produced and prepared diverse and seasonally changing agrarian cuisines. In up-country Kenya, as elsewhere in Africa, gender shaped the production and preparation of food, as women played a considerable role in agriculture and did nearly all the work of cooking. During this same period, thousands of men left these rural societies and migrated as wage laborers, with many arriving in the port city of Mombasa and to work on nearby sisal and rubber plantations. On the coast, food provisioning, cuisine, and the gendered division of labor changed as these men had to rely on the food they acquired through wage labor, which during this period consisted primary of the rations (*posho*) they were provided by their employer as part of their pay. The demographic realities of labor migration meant these men had to prepare their own food, working with the bulk grain ration from their employer and any supplementary ingredients they could acquire. Chapter 1 closes by examining how these migrants, accustomed to rural cuisines defined by variety and seasonality, drew on various means to make the daily meal more enjoyable in a colonial system that otherwise imposed a monotonous and bland diet.

Chapter 2 focuses on the commercialization of Mombasa's food system as rationing largely ended during the 1930s and the city's migrant workers became market consumers dependent on cash to acquire their daily meals. The reality in this unequal urban economy was that people very often did not have sufficient cash to purchase the food they needed, and so they had to develop strategies to survive, which included food sharing within large working-class households, developing credit relationships with retailers, and other such methods. Chapter 2 also explores the businesses that were rapidly expanding at midcentury as the demand for vegetables, meat, and various dried goods like grain, sugar, and tea grew during this period. The chapter concludes by considering how access to fuel and water, necessary components for preparing most dishes, changed as people moved from their rural communities to this coastal city. Up-country, these resources were mostly gathered from common land and watersheds, but, like grain, vegetables, and meat, they became commodities for purchase in Mombasa, whether fuels that included firewood, charcoal, and paraffin or the water that people bought by the jug, filled at one of the municipality's centralized taps.

Chapter 3 shifts the focus from the way people provisioned raw ingredients to how these foodstuffs were prepared into palatable cuisine. As part of this, the chapter considers how urban capitalism transformed the temporal experience of eating, from rural time where breakfast and dinner were the primary meals to an urban setting where lunch became incorporated into the daily routine. Chapter 3 demonstrates how street food fit into and structured these mealtime routines in Mombasa, from its essential socially reproductive role at lunchtime in a commuter city to the way it shaped household dining patterns in residential neighborhoods. Inside these working-class homes, when meals were not bought from street vendors, the division of kitchen labor stemmed from the generational and gendered demographics of the household. Men of the same age shared the work of cooking, rotating among themselves, but more-established and often older men could take on male dependents who, in exchange for food and shelter, would do more domestic labor like cooking. However, for all the cooking that men did in the city, in their homes and commercially, women always cooked when they lived in a working-class household. This chapter, therefore, explores the dramatic transformations in the gendered division of kitchen labor generated by rural-to-urban migration, as well as how, ultimately, the idea that domestic cooking was the work of women continued to shape urban households.

Chapter 4 is the last of the three chapters on the mid-twentieth century, and its focus shifts from social and economic to political history. During the first half of the twentieth century, street food had become an integral part of social reproduction in Mombasa's urban economy, but chapter 4 explores how these informal businesses, operating extralegally in alleys, parks, sidewalks, and elsewhere, were at odds with how late-colonial and early-independence officials wanted to modernize the city. The chapter explores how these officials envisioned a future in which vendors would be removed from the streets and relocated into municipal canteens but also how the speed at which the number of these roadside eateries grew and the insufficient financing of the canteen system meant that this was never fully realized in practice. However, the existence of the project, and the general idea that informal street-food eateries were undesirable, served as the policy basis for mass campaigns during which vendors were arrested, fined, and had their businesses demolished. However, the chapter also shows the considerable power that street-food vendors had in the city because of the key role they played in the reproduction of the working day in Kenya's Indian Ocean port town. Thus, both colonial and early-independence officials had to make significant concessions to vendors and, ultimately, were unable to enact totalizing campaigns to rid the city of these informal eateries. The government went the furthest in its effort to drive vendors off the streets when cholera cases were confirmed in the city in 1978, but even then, as the crisis subsided, a vibrant street-food industry reemerged soon thereafter.

Chapter 5 moves into the final decades of the twentieth century, examining how commercial cooking and eating outside the household changed in a city undergoing dramatic demographic, spatial, and political-economic transformations. The first section of the chapter explores how suburbanization, as well as the rise of tourism, created alternatives to street food for the midday meal. As part of the workplace culture of the hospitality industry, the employees of the many new high-end hotels and restaurants opening in Mombasa received prepared food at work as part of their shift, while practical necessity drove some companies with factories located on the edge of this sprawling coastal city, situated too far from concentrations of street-food eateries, to build canteens where their workers could eat an on-site meal. However, while significant, these new cultures of workplace eating were still exceptions to the rule that most Mombasa residents acquired prepared food as market consumers, and for the working class this meant going to a street-food vendor. Chapter 5 also further develops the business history of street food, examining the pathways people took to enter the industry, the divisions of labor within these eateries, differentiation between vendors as their restaurants expanded in scale and complexity, and the role of credit with their customers. Finally, the chapter considers the political economy of street food in Mombasa as the city entered the neoliberal era, and the contradictory history of this period in which some vendors achieved far greater stability in their lives, but also how new inequalities shaped who was still exposed to insecurity during this time of liberalization.

The conclusion of the book offers not only a summation of arguments but also an epilogue that speaks to how Mombasa's twentieth-century history left all vendors, no matter their social status, vulnerable. Between December 2001 and February 2002, Mombasa (Mvita) MP Shariff Nassir led the largest campaign in the city's history against the people working in the informal economy. Except for the clearances of the late-colonial era and the cholera campaigns of the 1970s, arrests and demolitions were usually localized to a few people or groups of vendors in a particular neighborhood, generated by disputes over land, complaints from neighbors, or small-scale government efforts to "beautify" an area. However, in Mombasa and elsewhere in urban Africa around the turn of the century, governments began carrying out clearance campaigns on a far greater scale for overtly political reasons, often aiming to displace opposition voters in the lead-up to elections. This concluding chapter analyzes how Nassir used ideas about the informal economy with deep roots in city policy to justify what was plainly a cynical attempt to clear potential opposition voters in the run-up to the 2002 election. Remarkable damage was done to the street-food industry, but the effort was ultimately unsuccessful. Nassir had destroyed the physical structures of the informal economy but not the underlying forces that made pursuing these kinds of businesses, despite the risks, a common way that people tried to secure their place in the city.

SOURCES AND METHODOLOGY

Preparing the Modern Meal covers approximately one hundred years, and the sources best suited for researching the themes covered in this book changed considerably across the course of the twentieth century. The research was done primarily in Kenya during numerous trips there, the longest in 2014 and 2015, when I gathered the bulk of my archival and oral evidence. Most of the archival research was done in the Kenya National Archives (KNA) in Nairobi and Mombasa, but I also spent significant time examining written materials at the McMillan Memorial Library and the library of *Daily Nation* newspaper, both in Nairobi. I also conducted more than seventy oral interviews, primarily in Mombasa but also with people in Nyanza Province who had returned there after living on the coast. The research in Kenya was supplemented by sources in British archives, including the National Archives at Kew, the Commonwealth and African Collections at the University of Oxford, and the British Library, as well as with published materials available from American university libraries and other digital resources. Given how the nature of the evidence changed so markedly from one period to the next covered in this book, I will explain my sources and methodology by giving an account of the way historical context, patterns of record keeping, and memory shaped what I used to reconstruct the history of working-class food in Mombasa.

At the turn of the twentieth century, the British were in the first phase of the conquest and colonization of East Africa, and they sent large numbers of academics cum administrators into rural communities to document the societies they sought to conquer. Not only ethnographers but also geographers and general "explorers" detailed varying aspects of African environments and social structures, and this included a detailed record of East African foodways. For an era that oral histories struggle to reach, these studies, found largely in old academic journals and other published volumes, provide the basis for chapter 1's analysis of the gendered structures of food provisioning and preparation in rural Kenya at the start of colonial rule. For the history of the migrants who went to the coast, the records for this period were shaped by the context of labor scarcity. Because colonial authorities were concerned about the availability of a migrant workforce on plantations and in Mombasa, they wanted European employers to maintain (quite) minimum standards to ensure that they would not further damage their reputations among African workers, which could disrupt an already precarious "labor supply." Found especially in the KNA in Nairobi, the records for the Coast Province during the 1910s and 1920s are full of labor inspection reports with both qualitative and quantitative data on living and working conditions, including steady documentation about the food that people ate on a daily basis.

The documentary sources for the three chapters on midcentury Mombasa differ from the ethnographies, geographical studies, and labor inspection reports that inform chapter 1. As the Great Depression and other structural factors effectively ended labor scarcity during this period, the inspection reports that were tied to concerns about the "labor supply" effectively disappear from the archive. However, new forms of documentation that began during the late 1920s proved an enduring source of evidence about urban working-class life. The Municipal Board of Mombasa, later the Municipal Council of Mombasa, was formed in 1927 and in the following decades produced detailed records on those aspects of the city that authorities deemed part of their administrative purview. Among the municipality's responsibilities was regulating petty trade, which consequently left behind extensive documentation on the small food businesses that were rapidly growing in the city. Moreover, while labor inspection reports disappeared, by the end of the 1930s the growing protests by African workers initiated a new phase of state documentation on working-class communities, records particularly important for chapters 2 and 3. After the 1939 general strike in Mombasa, which followed numerous smaller strikes, the British colonial government began commissioning a bevy of large reports on working and living conditions in the city. Frederick Cooper has used these reports to examine how colonial thinking and policy toward African workers changed during the late-colonial era, but they are also among the most detailed records available for urban social history, providing rich data on households, wages, benefits, the geography of urban employment, and how food fits into all these aspects of working-class life.

From chapter 2 onward, the book also relies more heavily on evidence from oral interviews. I interviewed two primary groups of people: migrants from up-country and street-food vendors, two categories that sometimes overlapped. I also spoke with some brick-and-mortar restaurant owners and workers. In Mombasa, these interviews were conducted with my research assistant, Onesmus Mutua. He found people and scheduled interviews, initially drawing on his contacts in the city and then further expanding this network through snowball sampling. Efforts were made to distribute these interviews as evenly as possible between people from Nyanza Province, Central Province, and Ukambani (located in Eastern Province), the areas that had the largest number of up-country migrants who went to Mombasa. However, Mutua's contacts were best among people from Ukambani and Central Province, and a higher proportion of the Mombasa interviews come from these communities. I was, though, able to better balance the sample by spending February 2015 in Nyanza Province interviewing migrants from Mombasa who had returned. These interviews were set up by Mercy Nyambok, my research assistant who attended all the interviews.

I also strove for as equal a distribution as possible of interviewees across time, but fewer people now have firsthand memories of the colonial era. Because most of these interviews were conducted in 2014 and 2015, the late-colonial period of the 1940s and 1950s was the earliest time for which I could find people with direct experience living and working in Mombasa. Even for this period, interviewees who were in their twenties when they lived in Mombasa are in their eighties, nineties, or older. Some still have sharp recollections, but locating a significant number of people at that age who can sit for interviews is challenging. Those with memories of the 1960s and 1970s are far more numerous, and more still the people who lived in the city during the 1980s and 1990s; consequently, these latter two periods account for a larger balance of my interviews. However, while I was limited in the number of people I could find to speak about colonial Mombasa, many more were able to tell me about rural food systems before independence. This is because people who migrated as adults during the 1960s and 1970s grew up in rural areas during the colonial era, and many could recall with great detail the routines of breakfast, lunch, and dinner during their childhoods. This provided important evidence for the changes that came when people migrated to the city.

The interviews were done mostly in Kiswahili and English, and often a combination of the two. I conducted the interviews, but my research assistants would on occasion help with translation when my phrasing failed to capture the essence of what I wanted to say or if I could not understand a response, the latter being most common when surrounded by the cacophonous sounds of Mombasa's or Kisumu's crowded streets. This allowed the interviews to continue smoothly whatever our surroundings and their auditory features, from people's homes to markets to alleyways and the side of the road. Most interviews ranged from forty-five minutes to an hour in length. I had a different set of questions for migrants and street-food vendors, though I asked both when someone was an up-country migrant and ran an eatery. When speaking with migrants, I began with a series of questions about the food system in their rural homes, including the extent to which they grew or purchased their food, what the common ingredients were, who cooked the daily meals, and which meals were served when, among other topics. Then, to establish continuity and contrast when they became migrants, I asked similar questions about their time in the city, covering provisioning, preparation, and consumption. With vendors, I asked questions about how they entered the business, where they worked in the city and under what conditions, what food they sold and at what time of day, and their relationship with governing authorities.

These interviews form a major basis of the evidence for my analysis of independence-era Mombasa, but I also draw significantly on written sources. In a recent article, Nana Osei-Opare has pushed back against what he calls "postcolonial African archival pessimism," arguing that the conditions of these archives are not as dire as they have often been characterized.[75] Certainly, this is a contingent question, as the state of postcolonial archives varies across time, space, and topic. For Mombasa, though, the archival record after 1963 bears out Osei-Opare's point, as it is both extensive and accessible. Documents on the city's colonial history are located primarily in the KNA in Nairobi, but the bulk of government sources on the independence period are held in its regional depository in Mombasa.[76] Still underutilized by historians, this small archive contains substantial holdings of municipal minutes; annual reports of city, district, and provincial departments; and a large number of incredibly detailed files with mixed documentation on a variety of urban topics, many in excess of three hundred pages.[77] Not only do these files contain observations by officials, but many low-income city residents also wrote to the government to express their concerns, part of the wider practice of petition writing in twentieth-century Africa. Other historians have found thick records of petitions for the colonial period, but these did not become common in Mombasa until the independence era when people seem to have felt emboldened to stake claims in a state that was now supposed to represent their interests.[78] These archival sources, paired with oral interviews, newspaper articles, and published government reports, provided a rich body of evidence to write the postcolonial history of Mombasa's working-class food system. Altogether, *Preparing the Modern Meal* combines these sources with those on the colonial period to show the ways in which changes in the daily practices of food provisioning, cooking, and eating can reveal much about how urban capitalism transformed East Africa's societies.

1 ⁓ The Work of the Daily Meal

Cuisine, Labor, and Migration in Early-Colonial Kenya

AROUND 1900, following a day of work in the fields, women in East Africa's agrarian communities began gathering wood and water. They brought these supplies back to open-air kitchens just outside of their circular, wood-framed homes that were covered with long grass and sticky insulating materials collected from the local environment. Once there, they built a fire in between three rocks arranged in a triangle, creating a stove where they placed a clay pot full of water. Ready to cook, they then used varying combinations of millet, maize, sweet potatoes, bananas, beans, and other foodstuffs grown in their fields to prepare the diverse cuisines of rural East Africa. In a daily, repeating routine, these women cooked the food that nourished their communities. By the 1910s, thousands of men regularly left these agrarian societies to migrate to plantations and cities throughout the region to work for wages. The Indian Ocean port town of Mombasa and its surrounding rubber and sisal plantations were among the major destinations for this new migrant working class in colonial Kenya. Upon arriving at the coast, migrants entered a new food system and developed novel routines to prepare their daily meals. After a long, humid day of manual labor, in the late afternoon workers picked up a food ration called *posho* from their employers, which overseers doled out with a *kibaba,* an often not very precise measuring cup. During the 1910s, posho consisted of 1.5 pounds of maize meal or rice, sometimes with a small amount of salt and beans. After collecting firewood and water, the migrants returned to the encampment and started cooking. While their grain boiled away over the fire, they might also prepare a relish of vegetables, meat, or fish to add flavor to their thick, starchy staple. These migrant men could only make this relish if they had something other than rice or maize meal to cook, which they often did not.[1]

This chapter examines the new food system that emerged during the first decades of the twentieth century to feed a growing class of migrant workers on Kenya's coast. Many of these workers came from rural communities in the interior of East Africa. These societies certainly traded a variety of foodstuffs like salt, butter, and dried fish, but people primarily ate food that they or a close relative had grown in nearby fields. In these communities, the labor that produced, processed, and prepared their food was also gendered. Both women and men participated in agricultural work, but women ultimately did significantly more. Moreover, once the crops were harvested, women did the labor of turning these raw ingredients into palatable cuisine. This included processing certain foods, like grinding grain or turning milk into butter, and the washing, chopping, cooking, and cleaning required to prepare foodstuffs into a meal. Women, therefore, were principally responsible for the socially reproductive work of rural Kenya's agrarian food systems. Put another way, men ate food that came primarily from the labor of their mothers, wives, sisters, and other female relatives. However, when these men became migrants, they would never meet the people who grew their food, and they accessed these ingredients by selling their labor to an employer. Once they had their ration, they also had to cook it themselves.

The new working-class food system that migrants entered on Kenya's coast had its origins in Britain's empire. In the metropole, most employers during the nineteenth and early twentieth centuries paid their workers with wages and their obligation ended there. Wage earners in Britain took their cash and directly converted it into food, buying ingredients from grocers, markets, and itinerant traders or prepared food from vendors and other small eateries. The only real exceptions were factories with large numbers of women where a gendered industrial paternalism convinced management to provision female employees with food.[2] While industrialists in Britain saw women as dependent and in need of direct support, in Southern Africa during the nineteenth century, employers viewed African male workers as subordinate, juvenile dependents. This idea was the premise of what Patrick Harries called "racial paternalism," the racialized notion that African male labor migrants were not ready to deal with the disruptions of a fully proletarianized life. As a result, the South African colonial government passed masters and servants ordinances in which employers, in essence, became responsible for the social reproduction of their workforce. They were required to directly provide migrant workers with housing, medical care and, indeed, food.[3] As government and private employers sought to create a laboring class in Kenya, the state drew on the South African model and passed its own masters and servants laws. Consequently, employer-provided rations became the foundation of how Kenya's migrant workers acquired their food during the early-colonial period.

The migrant-labor rationing system transformed how food was provisioned and prepared. It also changed East Africa's culinary culture. In up-country agrarian communities, people ate a varied and seasonal diet. Certain staples were dominant, but even those changed as stores ran low and new crops were harvested and worked into the kitchen. In Mombasa and on nearby plantations, though, migrants were consigned to eat nearly the same meal every day, year-round. With the ration, the best hope for variety was if one's employers offered both maize meal and rice in a rotation, but many only provisioned maize. The other strategy to make the daily meal more enjoyable was to find extra vegetables, meat, or fish to prepare into a relish that could be eaten with the primary grain, adding texture, viscosity, and flavor to a uniform starch. However, this too was a new experience for many of Mombasa's migrants. Anthropologist Sidney Mintz argued that agrarian peasant cuisines globally have been built around this starch-and-relish framework, the latter making the former more palatable and nutritious.[4] However, many of the migrants who came to Mombasa were from Kamba- and Kikuyu-speaking communities where their main staples were not eaten with relishes. Instead, they combined multiple ingredients, textures, and nutrients into single dishes and did not count grain-meal porridges, complemented with a relish, as a large part of their diet as other African societies did.[5] For the Kamba and Kikuyu, the staple-and-relish combination was not an enduring feature of their agrarian cuisines but instead was how they ate as labor migrants.

On the early-colonial coast, then, migrant workers were paid partially in food and made to eat a monotonous diet quite different and unsatisfying compared to what they had back in their rural homes. Given the way they valued variety and taste in their cuisine, it is not surprising that food became an important site of conflict between workers and their employers.[6] In their struggle to improve the daily meal, migrant workers were able to use the leverage that a scarce labor market provided. When looking for a labor force for the coastal region, the British first tried to recruit local Mijikenda peasants and the formally enslaved who lived there. However, these communities refused to work in both the numbers and the regularity to satisfy the demands of colonial planters and urban employers.[7] Consequently, up-country migrants became a large proportion of the coast's laboring classes, but during the 1910s and into 1920s, employers still felt they did not have nearly enough workers and thus were concerned with maintaining a "good" reputation among the employees they had, lest they risk losing their workforce. Migrants used this opening in a highly exploitative labor system to successfully pressure their employers to improve not only their wages but also their rations. By the middle of the 1920s, migrant workers not only had higher wages but also rations that were more substantial and had a greater variety of ingredients.

To explore these transformations in food provisioning and cuisine and how they shaped labor politics, the chapter begins not on the coast but in Kenya's up-country agrarian communities. We will examine the labor process that created the daily meal, as well as the cuisine this produced. From there, we can better understand the changes that the food system of labor migration presented to the people who went to the coast to work for a wage and how they interpreted this experience.

AGRARIAN FOOD SYSTEMS IN EAST AFRICA

Many of the people who migrated to Mombasa and the wider coastal region during the first decades of the twentieth century came from an area often referred to as "up-country," or *bara* in Kiswahili. Most were from three subregions: the semiarid savanna east of present-day Nairobi (Ukambani), the lush highlands northeast of the capital city (Central Province), and then to the west along the shores and hinterlands of Lake Victoria (Nyanza Province). These people were mainly from societies that came to be called the Kamba, Kikuyu, and Luo. Smaller numbers of migrants came from Luhya, Taita, Embu, and Meru communities, among others.[8] The food systems of these societies were part of a larger political economy of labor and resource distribution in which gender structured work and membership in the community granted access to resources. Elsewhere in East Africa, Great Lakes kingdoms and Indian Ocean plantations produced large surpluses of food, but the more decentralized Highland societies were focused primarily on feeding those who lived within them. These certainly were not "closed" subsistence economies, as complementarities between and beyond created regional trade in foodstuffs, as with the Kikuyu, who had "successful crops year in and year out and produce[d] a surplus for sale and exchange."[9] However, most of what was produced was consumed within. The food people ate, the majority of the time, was grown, slaughtered, or caught by themselves or a relative.

These agrarian cuisines at the turn of the twentieth century were largely vegetarian, and so agricultural labor formed the core of food production.[10] As the Swedish ethnographer Gerhard Lindblom observed of Kamba-speaking communities, with whom he lived for more than a year during 1911 and 1912, "The products of the field form the basis of the Kamba people's food."[11] In these societies, women did most of the agricultural work, and therefore their labor produced the majority of the food that they and their communities ate. However, men contributed to agriculture in certain contexts. For example, during the second half of the nineteenth century, Kikuyu and Kamba societies were expanding the areas they had under cultivation, and men played a key role in clearing forests for planting.[12] Noting this process in 1894, C. W. Hobley wrote that "the Wakamba are gradually extending the area under cultivation, clearing away thick woods in a most patient and preserving manner."[13] However, after this initial clearance of land, women became central to agricultural production, as among the Kamba where the work was "carried on almost exclusively by women." The men had "done their part of the work and the women . . . [would] proceed." After a brief respite following planting, "the women ha[d] little leisure from the field work" because the growing crops required weeding, pruning, scaring off fauna from the fields, and finally harvesting.[14] The evidence for the Kikuyu is somewhat more ambiguous. From his travels during the 1890s, Hobley noted that "Kikuyu men work in their fields quite as much as the women." An observer in 1902, though, concluded that men did the "heavier" agricultural work but women did the "planting, weeding and harvesting," and a year later a geographer similarly noted that "women work in the fields, but the men clear the ground, cut wood and build houses."[15] Decades later, Jomo Kenyatta's ethnography of the Kikuyu presented agriculture as labor largely shared by men and women, if often in different roles, though by then land expropriation and labor migration had radically transformed the conditions under which these central Kenyan communities grew their food.[16] The record, therefore, is inconsistent but suggestive that Kikuyu women were more actively involved in the production of their community's food after the clearance of new land, although men also contributed labor at certain points in the process.[17]

Among the Luo along Lake Victoria, the record also contains ambiguity, but women seem to have done most of the agricultural work. G. A. S. Northcote reported in 1907 that men and women cultivated their own individual fields and then contributed to a collective pantry from which the family's food was prepared. Northcote noted that "each adult male and female marks out and tills his own piece" but that "the family in practice shares the produce."[18] About five years later, a visiting British scientist observed that "on the whole," Luo men "share the burdens of life with women . . . and they will even join [them] in tilling their fields of millet."[19] However, during research conducted in 1970, Janet Hay was still able to interview people who had lived in the region at the turn of twentieth century, and they characterized male engagement with agriculture at that time as an attempt to generate trade goods with which to replenish cattle herds that had been devastated by the rinderpest. Therefore, both men and women engaged in agriculture, but male labor may have been done as much for individual accumulation as to contribute to the family's food supply, the latter gendered more as "women's work."[20] Indeed, in 1898, Hobley wrote that "cultivation [among the Luo] is mostly in the hands of the women"; more than thirty years later, two colonial researchers observed that "the hardest part of the work on the land . . . [is] done by the men, but the routine hoeing, etc., is left to the women."[21] As among the Kikuyu and Kamba, Luo men varyingly contributed to the work of producing plant-based foods, but women did the majority of agricultural labor.

One area of food production in which men consistently did most of the work was the raising and hunting of animals, which were gendered as male activities.[22] However, though people enjoyed eating meat when the opportunity arose, it was a peripheral part of these communities' diets at the turn of the twentieth century. At times, hunters caught considerable amounts of meat, but it was often eaten by the men during the hunt.[23] Livestock like cattle and goats were also rarely slaughtered for daily consumption because they were valued more as capital and as a form of insurance in the event of a famine.[24] The most common way meat was eaten within a village was when livestock were killed as part of a ritual, but this was a periodic rather than regular feature of these societies' diets.[25] The communities that diverged most from the vegetarian pattern were the Luo who lived along the shores of Lake Victoria. Both Luo men and women fished from the lake and the many streams and rivers from the watershed that fed into it, with catches ranging from small fingerlings (*ningu*) to more substantial tilapia (*ngege*). These waters were productive enough that Luo counted fish as a regular part of their diets, and they sold dried surpluses throughout the region. These trade networks, though, did not reach the Highlands where Kikuyu and Kamba communities lived, where fish played no role in their regional cuisines.[26]

However, flesh is not the only way to acquire animal protein, especially from livestock. The Luo, Kamba, and Kikuyu regularly milked cattle and goats. Without refrigeration, fresh milk was less common, and women more regularly took the raw cream and transformed it into sour milk and butter.[27] Among the Kamba, for example, women fermented the sour milk in a dried calabash gourd that had been fumigated with smoke. Once ready, the sour milk could be consumed or turned into butter. To do so, women added rocks to the calabash to increase agitation inside the gourd, which they shook and hit against their thighs, creating butter at the end of this laborious process. So important were these fats to their cuisine that those without enough cattle to make butter produced a similar product from castor oil beans, which the Kamba referred to as "the poor man's cattle." Overall, Kamba production of butter was prodigious enough that it was an item they commonly sold to South Asian traders in "considerable quantities."[28] In addition to dairy products, like East Africa's pastoral communities, the more agricultural Luo, Kikuyu, and Kamba also consumed blood, which they acquired by bleeding live cattle. Blood could be consumed as a beverage, but it was also a common ingredient in other dishes, adding salt and rich flavors, as well as nutritionally contributing iron.[29]

Therefore, in the labor process of food production, men cleared fields for agriculture, a labor-intensive event, but women largely did the more continuous work of planting, weeding, harvesting, and processing. Men contributed more to the care of cattle and goats, from shepherding to milking, but women did all the work of converting milk into commonly consumed and marketed dairy products. Consequently, women and men were both involved in the production of foodstuffs but in an unequal way. However, when it was time to cook, women did all the work.[30] As observed in 1902, among the Luo, "all the cooking is done by women," a comment that equally applied across East Africa's agrarian societies.[31] At the turn of the twentieth century, cooking was an extended process in rural East Africa. As a Kamba man interviewed at the time explained, "The woman's work is to powder maize, grind flour, chop wood, fetch water, look for vegetables and cook them."[32] Kenyatta, writing decades later, sought to affirm a similar gendered division of labor in rural Kikuyu communities, observing that "the entire housework naturally falls within the sphere of [women's] activities." Like the anonymous Kamba man from the early 1900s, Kenyatta explained that Kikuyu women "cook, bring water from the rivers, wash utensils and fetch firewood in the forests or bush." Should men attempt to do this kind of work, he continued, they would be socially censured because "if he could perform women's work, what is the use of getting married, for how can a wife and husband be doing the same thing at the same time."[33]

Each day, women prepared the diverse, seasonal, and regional cuisines of rural East Africa. Their kitchens were usually outside, adjacent to their homes, and they cooked over fire in clay pots balanced on three stones. Most cooked dishes were either grilled, boiled, or stewed.[34] In these agricultural communities, their diets were dominated by cereals, along with various legumes, plantains, tubers, and other cultivated plants. For the Kikuyu, their most important dish was *irio,* a word that also simply meant "food." To prepare irio, Kikuyu women began by boiling and mashing bananas, and then they added whole kernels of maize to the mixture. Thereafter, the cook boiled peas or beans in a different pot to the desired consistency; this was then added along with salt to the banana mash. Men would usually eat irio at this point in the preparation, but women commonly also mixed in greens to their final dish. This created a staple that could stand on its own, combining heavy and starchy bananas with crunchy maize kernels and protein-rich legumes. Underlining the centrality of this dish, a British health official in Central Province observed in 1926 that irio was "by far the most frequently and generally used food of the country."[35] For the Kamba, their cuisine was also organized around a staple that could be eaten on its own. Kamba women prepared *isio* by combining and boiling maize kernels with beans, which they ate "practically every day without anything being added to it."[36] The flavors of this dish were much desired, as is illustrated by the effort that the Kamba made to acquire *nzu* (pigeon peas) that were common in isio when away from home. If traveling "to a place where this bean is not cultivated . . . they miss this food more than anything else, and their friends sometimes send them some of the longed-for food."[37]

Thus, the preferred staple of the Kamba was isio, a mixture of maize kernels and pigeon peas, while for the Kikuyu it was the mash-based irio. The Kikuyu also regularly ate a dish quite similar to isio in which maize kernels were "boiled, being at the same time blended with some of the different sorts of bean."[38] Today, this dish is called *githeri,* which is now also the name in English and Kiswahili for both the Kikuyu and Kamba versions. The foodways of these two Highland societies were also similar in that they did not regularly eat the thick porridges made from milled grains that were common in many other rural African cuisines.[39] For the Kikuyu, though maize was a common ingredient, it was rarely consumed in a ground form.[40] Women in these communities did spend considerable time pounding grain, but the resulting product was used most often to prepare a filling drink. The Kamba regularly made *usu* by boiling water or sour milk with ground maize or millet; this drink was "very well liked," featuring a "sour taste," and was "very refreshing." Thin in consistency, usu "thus serves as both food and drink."[41] The Kikuyu had a similar beverage, *uchuru,* though for this drink, flour was mixed only with water and not sour milk. Usually taken cold, uchuru was a drink, not a meal. As observed in the 1920s, "A person who has consumed a couple pints of *uchuru* will not consider that he has had a meal, any more than an average Briton considers that he has fed after two pints of sour-ale."[42] For the Kikuyu and Kamba, their primary staples—irio and isio—both included grain, but in its original shape rather than as milled flour.

The cuisine of the Luo, though, did include a thick porridge, *kuon,* that resembled those of other rural African societies, and this dish fits more closely within Mintz's starch-and-relish framework. Luo cooks prepared kuon by bringing water to a boil and slowly adding millet meal. When it reached a "doughy consistency," more hot water was mixed in, the pot was covered, and then it was left to cook on the fire for an additional thirty minutes. Thereafter, the mixture was removed from the heat, stirred, and finally ready to serve. Uniform in flavor and texture, kuon was eaten with fish or vegetables, the latter cooked in butter, milk, or blood. On certain occasions, the Luo also took kuon with grilled meat.[43] However, though this grain porridge was the preferred staple, the seasonality of the Luo agrarian cuisine meant that kuon dominated their diets only when millet was plentiful after the long rains harvest and the stores were still full. Also, when millet was in short supply, it was reserved for the preparation of a grain-based beverage, like those common among the Kikuyu and Kamba. During those months, many other foods that need not necessarily be combined with a relish became mainstays. As a health officer observed in 1926, "When mtama [millet] is scarce, sweet potatoes and beans are used at the principal meals." Sweet potatoes were sometimes consumed within a staple-and-relish framework, boiled and then eaten with buttermilk to add viscosity and a tart flavor. However, sweet potatoes could also be turned into a stand-alone dish by being fermented in milk and buttermilk, afterward becoming "sour" and "ready for use." The Luo also ate beans in a similar fashion to the Kamba and Kikuyu, combining them with maize kernels to create a dish called *nyoyo.* Dietary patterns changed again when maize was harvested fresh from the fields, as boiled cobs of green maize became the "principal meal."[44]

Therefore, grain porridges complemented by relishes were at the center of Luo diets only for part of the year, and they were not common among the Kikuyu and Kamba. Moreover, no ingredients or dishes were singularly dominant for the entirety of the year. Instead, the main feature of these cuisines was variety shaped by seasonality. Indeed, this was expressed in how the Kikuyu language described the rains that brought their two growing seasons. The rains from March to May were called *mbura wa bembi* (maize rains), and those from October until December named the *mbura wa mweri* (millet rains).[45] Certainly, these millet and maize crops were foundational ingredients to the cuisines of up-country East Africa, but so too, depending on the season, were sorghum, cassava, bananas, sweet potatoes, yams, sugarcane, and varietals of black, red, and green beans, along with other crops.[46] Seasonal hunger when stores were low and the risk of catastrophic famine built precariousness into these rural food systems, but when the crops came these agrarian cuisines offered a great diversity of tastes and textures. The monotonous routine of a daily, year-round diet composed of milled grain, especially maize meal, was a radically new experience in twentieth-century East Africa. Moreover, the staple-and-relish framework was neither a uniform nor, especially for the Kikuyu and Kamba, long-standing feature of the region's rural cuisines. Instead, its wide-scale adoption occurred in cities and on plantations, driven by migrant men who tried to make their bulky rations of grain taste a little bit better.

FOOD RATIONS AND LABOR ON THE COAST OF EAST AFRICA

Thousands of people from these up-country communities, most of them men, migrated to Kenya's coastal region to work during the 1910s and 1920s.[47] Upon arrival, they entered not only a new geographical setting—a city or commercial plantation in a humid, tropical climate situated along the shores of the Indian Ocean—but also a new political economy. As wage earners far from their rural homes, they could no longer rely on their domestic food systems to feed them. If they wanted to eat, they had to first sell their labor. However, cash was only part of the wage they were paid. Much of it also came as an in-kind food ration, posho, which formed the basis of a new migratory cuisine.

For much of the remainder of the chapter, we will explore this new working-class food system on the early-colonial coast and how it represented an economic, social, and culinary departure for up-country migrants. However, in certain ways, it was not radically different from the one that had existed on the coast during the precolonial nineteenth century. During the 1800s, coastal patriarchs extracted labor from enslaved Africans and other dependents, but they were also obligated to "maintain" them, provisioning them with the necessities of life, including food. These food rations, the origins of the Kiswahili word *posho,* were central to a labor system premised on reciprocal obligation.[48] During the middle of the nineteenth century, vocabularies gathered near Mombasa by missionary and linguist Ludwig Krapf placed the meaning of the term *posho* within the patriarchal household. Posho were the "rations, maintenance . . . the portion of food given daily, or from time to time, to a wife . . . or to a child, soldier, or stranger." These people were dependents of the head of the household, and in exchange for labor and loyalty, they were provisioned with food. Similarly, the verb form, *possa,* was defined as giving "one a daily allowance of food, to provide one with food, clothing, etc., to give rations to." Krapf, providing an illustrative example, situated this reciprocal obligation as part of marriage: "He gave his bride maintenance (as the natives do after they have betrothed a young girl)."[49] Enslaved people were also provisioned with food. Sometimes it was rather indirectly, as with those who worked plots on the plantation to grow their own food. However, enslaved Africans in coastal ports were provisioned more directly with actual food, like the *mahamali,* who worked the docks, and the *vibarua,* who ranged from day laborers doing the odd jobs of a port town to highly skilled artisans.[50]

Precolonial food rationing also changed with transformations in the wider labor system and economy in East Africa during the second half of the nineteenth century. As the region became more commercialized through plantation slavery and regional and global trade, posho was essential to the social reproduction of the transport labor force that ran the expanding caravan system between the coast and the interior. These workers, some enslaved and others free, needed food while they traveled as far as Lake Victoria and even to what is today eastern Congo. Such changes in the economic geography of posho also became embedded in language. In vocabularies gathered in Zanzibar during the later nineteenth century, the verb form of *posho* still broadly meant "to give a ration to, to maintain, to habitually feed someone," but also, more specifically, the noun *posho* indicated that it was food given "to porters and sailors . . . a road ration."[51] By the final decades of the nineteenth century, European missionaries and explorers joined Arab and Swahili caravans in organizing large expeditions into the interior, and they were as bound as coastal patrons were to the obligation to provide their porters with food.[52] As these caravans traveled throughout East Africa, road rations became part of the rhythm of the workday. Stephen Rockel, in his social history of the caravan trade, details how these mobile laborers received their ration when they camped at the end of a day's march, provisioned with one kibaba (1.5 pounds) of sorghum, millet, maize, or rice. Depending on where the laborers stopped, these starchy rations would be supplemented with the purchase of vegetables and meats from local communities near the campsites, drawing rural producers into the new food system needed to feed laborers working far from their homes.[53] A starch-and-relish framework may not have dominated Kenya's Highland cuisines during the 1800s, but it was starting to take hold in the food system that reproduced the transport workforce of the caravan trade.

At the start of the twentieth century, as the British accommodated themselves to the realities of making an African working class in East Africa, they too had to face the necessity of social reproduction. While the food system they built was similar to the one that sustained precolonial laboring classes, down to borrowing the word *posho,* the origins of the British-run system in colonial Kenya lay mostly in their southern African colonies, where they had already been providing rations to migrant workers for decades. With new masters and servants ordinances passed in Kenya, people working close to home could legally be paid simply in cash, and often were. However, migrants, or "contract" workers, had to be provided with actual food rations.[54] The contract workers who came to Kenya's coast found themselves laboring in numerous sectors in the emerging colonial economy. In rural areas of the coast, they lived and worked on large commercial plantations that grew a variety of crops, like rubber and especially sisal, a coarse and sharp-leafed plant that was manufactured into twine. In Mombasa, these migrants provided labor for the building, maintenance, and running of the port and railway, as well as for public works projects, sanitation, and other jobs needed to operate the city. Rations were at the center of what these workers ate each day.

During the 1910s, the rations were basic. In Mombasa and on nearby plantations, they usually contained 1.5 pounds of grain each day, either maize meal or rice. Workers were also sometimes issued salt and/or beans once per week. This new rationing system changed the way migrants accessed food, by requiring them to sell their time to acquire it, and it separated them from the production process. In their rural homes, as we have seen, gendered family labor produced most of the food they ate, grown in fields only a short distance from where they ate and slept. Now, workers consumed food that arrived through abstract global and regional networks of commodity exchange. The supply chains that the Uganda Railway, one of Mombasa's and East Africa's largest employers, used to acquire grain provide an insight into the emerging system of food provisioning on the coast. For much of the 1910s, the railway found importing rice from India to be the most reliable source of grain and bought only a small amount of maize locally. However, by 1920, Kenya's maize production had developed to the point that railway managers felt they could rely on local supplies to ration to their workers. This would, these officials argued, both save money and provide a large market for the new colony's commercial agricultural economy. By 1921, the railway stopped importing rice entirely from India and acquired all its rations from local maize producers with "the advantage of this change . . . from a financial standpoint" being "considerable," representing a "saving of several thousand pounds sterling annually." Over the three years leading up to that announcement, the railway had increased its annual purchases of

East African maize from 341 to 2,303 tons.[55] From rice grown in South Asia to maize produced by cash-crop farmers in East Africa, migrant workers' diets were being shaped by managerial decisions about which commodity chain best suited employers, the state, and the wider colonial economy.[56]

Rationing, therefore, changed how these migrants fit into systems of food production and exchange. It also transformed what they ate. Rather than being characterized by variety and seasonality as in their rural homes, the cuisine of labor migration was defined by monotonous regularity. The steady supply of maize meal from commercial markets ensured that it went from being one grain among many, as in their rural cuisines, to the principal food that migrants ate. The experience of eating the same food, day after day and throughout the year, was radically new. While laborers lived in Mombasa or on a plantation, staples no longer changed from one season to the next. The only variety possible under this new food system was preparing different relishes to make boiled maize meal more attractive, and during the 1910s rations offered little more than the occasional issue of beans. The sharp contrast between the agrarian cuisines that migrants left and the food they ate while in waged employment was clearly apparent to colonial observers at the time. In 1915, W. J. Simpson, in his survey of sanitation and urbanization in East Africa, noted that in rural communities Africans had "a varied diet, which [was] well cooked," but as migrants "the food [was] of a different kind, monotonous."[57] Later, in 1926, R. A. Procter wrote in the *Kenya Medical Journal* that "in spite of the common fallacy that two pounds of maize meal is a sufficient ration for a native, maize is by no means the principal food of the Kikuyu." He added that Kikuyu cuisine "is a varied and rich one, and . . . the diet offered to the Kikuyu in European employ must be dull and uninteresting."[58]

Posho, therefore, led to a profound change in what migrants ate. The demography of migration, in turn, transformed who prepared their food. As the previous section details, women did nearly all the cooking in Kenya's upcountry rural communities. In Mombasa and on nearby coastal plantations, most migrants during this period were men, and they cooked their own meals. The affective history of how these men felt about doing labor gendered as female in their rural societies during the early-colonial era remains absent in the archival record. However, the evidence is rather clear that migrants were indeed doing much of their own cooking during these decades. According to labor inspection reports, only one employer on the coast had hired a cook for its employees.[59] Instead, workers were generally supplied with pots and cooking utensils to prepare their posho, as "each man does his own."[60] Among migrant working-class communities on Kenya's coast, the daily labor of social reproduction, in contrast to up-country rural communities, came most often from the labor of the men themselves.

These migrant cooks faced a paltry ration, but many were able to eat a more varied diet. However, their options were shaped crucially by geography. Contract workers in Mombasa paid partially in rations also had access to vibrant urban food markets from which they could purchase additional fruits, vegetables, meat, fish, and much else.[61] Additionally, the city featured illicit food traders who engaged in "the promiscuous sale of fruit in Native Shops and Houses," which the city government tacitly allowed because of insufficient space in its public markets.[62] Therefore, Mombasa workers, if they had enough surplus cash, could purchase supplementary ingredients to prepare a relish to accompany their grain-based staple. Some plantation workers could also access nearby food markets, but many others could not. For example, at Powysland Estate near the town of Kilifi, African workers "could buy what food they fancied," but at the more-isolated Gazi, well south of Mombasa, "they had to depend on the rations supplied."[63] Moreover, migrants had daily and periodic expenses beyond food, and many were also saving money for taxes and bridewealth. Thus, with low wages stretched thin, workers were limited in their ability to spend much money buying more foodstuffs. In these conditions, with a bulk of grain provided as posho and a small amount of cash used to buy additional ingredients, we see the creation of a working-class and migratory cuisine in which the plain starch was complemented by a small dish to add flavor and different textures. "Starch and relish," in East Africa, became the cuisine of labor migration. Very often, this meant boiled maize meal eaten with a small serving of beans.[64]

THE STRUGGLE FOR THE DAILY MEAL

Understandably, African migrants found this diet unsatisfying. During the 1910s and the 1920s, they pressured their employers to improve the rationing system, a struggle in which their most significant point of leverage was a broader labor market defined by scarcity.[65] Throughout this period, Europeans on the coast complained that there were not enough African workers and were acutely aware of how this affected their businesses. Among them was J. J. Lory, manager of a sisal and rubber plantation in Gazi, who told a labor commission during the early 1910s that he had less than half of the total workforce he needed. There were more than one hundred acres of cleared land that they could not plant because of a lack of workers, and of those areas already under production, "unless some means of obtaining labor were evolved, it would mean either abandoning a portion of the cultivated area, or very badly cultivating the whole."[66] Already an issue, labor scarcity on the coast only increased once World War I started, which initiated the mass impressment of Africans to work as porters in the campaign against Germany. Working conditions on the coast were intensely exploitative, but labor scarcity provided workers a measure of power. To consistently find workers, employers had to maintain a "good" reputation among migrants because they had established rumor networks that communicated which worksites should be avoided.[67] As C. W. Hobley, during this period the provincial commissioner of the Coast Province, observed in 1916, "Every plantation has its own reputation among the natives and I consider that a good reputation is only lost by conditions changing for the worse on the plantation itself."[68] These circulating reputations shaped where African workers signed contracts, as the "personality of the employer" could determine why one plantation had too few workers "whereas their neighbors seemed to have all the labour they required."[69] The ability of migrants to make employers feel the effects of labor scarcity provided them space to make demands about how they were compensated, both in cash and in kind.

In this context, contract workers on plantations and in Mombasa were able to gain access to a more diverse diet, but the geographical setting of

FIGURE 1.1. Laborers of the colonial government's Conservancy Department, a common employer of migrant workers in Mombasa. Undated, ca. early 1900s. From the Herskovits Library of African Studies, Northwestern University Libraries, the Humphrey Winterton Collection of East African Photographs: 1860–1960.

their employment shaped the options available. On plantations, workers often succeeded in convincing their employers to provide them land on which to grow their own food, all the more feasible because some plantations did not have the labor to put all their land under commercial cultivation. This meant that people could diversify their diet by regaining access to the means of subsistence. Some were so productive that they were able to sell surplus crops for cash, opening even more flexibility in their budgets.[70] At Gazi-Gogoni Estate, a government inspector in 1917 noted that "the employees have in addition the advantage of cultivating their own shambas [farms]," and they were "quick to take advantage."[71] Steven Stoll has shown how, in the Appalachian coalfields in the United States at the end of the nineteenth century, employers likewise provided their workers with small garden plots, which he sees as having been explicitly exploitative. Instead of paying their workers higher wages to buy food, this allowed mining companies to force their workers to reproduce themselves and their families through their own unpaid agricultural labor.[72] A similar strategy was also employed in the mines of the Zambian Copperbelt during the 1930s.[73] In East Africa, however, these garden plots were more a concession to labor than a strategy of capital to suppress wages. Prior to increased attention to nutrition science in the later 1920s, the racialized assumption of colonial employers during the 1910s was that the maize meal, salt, and perhaps beans that they were legally required to supply as food rations were sufficient to feed their African workers. Plantation owners and managers believed that had already supplied the material basis to reproduce their labor force. Anything workers gained beyond that baseline, like land on which to grow food for consumption and cash, had to be acquired through struggle.

The availability of farmland, though, was unique to plantations. Elsewhere, workers used strategies like desertion to push their employers to diversify their rations.[74] During the 1910s, such tactics were making Europeans increasingly uncomfortable with a labor and food system that tied them so intimately to their workers. Being directly responsible for provisioning workers exposed employers to criticism, which could in turn could cost them their workforce. This was made clear in 1916 when a group of Kamba deserted their employ with the Public Works Department (PWD) in protest "of the quality of the food (unga flour [posho]) supplied." During the controversy, an official underlined that this was also a more "general complaint" from other workers.[75] The following year, the PWD—which apparently was only rationing their workers with maize meal and nothing else—again found that a different group of 123 workers had deserted and that "their chief grievance [was] in their posho," in particular its lack of variety. Asked what they wanted, the workers replied, "A daily issue of some vegetables in addition [to maize meal], and particularly requested chiroko [pigeon peas]." Officials investigating the issue clearly concluded that if workers were "more properly fed there would be less discontent and consequently fewer deserters." Provincial Commissioner Hobley added that "it is next to impossible for my District Commissioners to continue indefinitely to replace desertions; this being so I would beg of you to spare no efforts to make the men contented." The PWD added beans to its rations.[76]

In dealing with both these desertions, Hobley began to question the entire premise of rationing in a commercial food economy. Rather than having employers directly provide food, after the first desertions he simply asked, "Why not give cents and let them buy their own food?"[77] When faced with the second desertions the following year, Hobley reiterated the point.[78] By providing them cash to buy their own food, this change would still adhere, theoretically, to the Masters and Servants Ordinance, as these would be characterized not as wages per se but as a stipend that workers would use to buy their own food. Employers would still be legally provisioning food to their workers, but indirectly, diverting any blame for inadequate food away from management. That a full monetization of the food system did not happen is instructive to how African workers used their leverage to shape this process to their advantage. During the 1910s and 1920s, few employers paid contact workers only in cash. Instead, some employers offered workers the option to either take rations or be paid extra cash. This included the PWD, which by 1919 provided its nearly three hundred Mombasa workers, most of them Kikuyu, either rice or a stipend to buy their food. The choice here is key. Workers had the option to purchase a more varied diet in the city's vibrant markets, but if food prices rose, then workers could fall back on the ration their employers were required to offer them. Rations became a form of insurance. This system operated not only in the city with its vibrant commercial food economy but also in rural areas where there were nearby markets. For example, at the Sokoke Estate near Kilifi, workers received "Rs. [rupees] 10/- without posho or Rs. 8/- with posho," a ration composed of rice and maize meal on alternating days. While the coastal Giriama preferred cash to rations because they had access to food produced by their nearby villages, up-country migrants were more cautious about entirely relinquishing their employers' obligation to pay them partly in food. In 1915, during a period of wartime shortages, migrants chose to have their posho rations because food was scarce. However, when food was abundant, migrants preferred the ten rupees without posho, which allowed them to purchase a more varied diet from local growers.[79]

Rather than end posho, then, contract workers used the leverage of labor scarcity to make the system work more in their favor. In this context, they were able to both improve their rations and push up wages.[80] During the 1910s, the grain portion of the ration was usually around 1.5 pounds per day, with little else other than salt or beans once per week, and sometimes not even that. By the 1920s, though, the grain portion, which had become most often maize meal, had increased to 2–2.5 pounds per day, and it came with a greater variety of additional ingredients.[81] Powysland Estate near Kilifi provides an example of both wage increases and improving rations. In 1920, migrant workers there received between 7 and 12 shillings (Shs.) per month, and were provided with 2 pounds of maize meal, plus twelve cents per week to purchase fish, already better compensation than almost any worker received during the 1910s. However, by 1923, the base pay had risen to Shs. 12/- per month, and the ration was 2 pounds of maize meal daily and 4 pounds on Sunday, plus 2 pounds of cowpeas, salt, bananas, or pawpaws once per week, with extra cash to purchase fish. The next year, the food changed but remained a diverse selection, while the wages increased to a floor of Shs. 14/-.[82]

Trends were similar in Mombasa, albeit with features unique to an urban environment. In the city, at the end of the 1910s, migrants working in ancillary port and railway industries usually made little more than Shs. 9/- per month and received 2 pounds of maize meal per day with no additional food. By 1923, people working in similar employment made between Shs. 16 and Shs. 24 per month and were provided with pigeon peas and salt. A year later, other migrants in the industrial area made Shs. 14/- and received 2.5 pounds of maize meal per day, plus a daily stipend of fifty cents to buy more ingredients. Some Mombasa employers violated the Masters and Servants Ordinance and paid migrants only in cash, but they had to pay significantly higher wages. This included the Conservancy Department, where most workers made between Shs. 20 and Shs. 26 per month; those willing to do "nightsoil," or sewage, work made Shs. 34/-.[83] Posho remained central to Mombasa's contract wage system during the 1920s, but workers were at least as interested in receiving additional money to buy food in the city's markets as they were in receiving more-diverse rations.

Ultimately, food rationing was a constituent part of an exploitative labor system in early-colonial Kenya. Legally required to provision their workers with food, European employers provided migrants a minimalist diet of basic calories, just enough so they would keep working each day. Such a system of social reproduction rested on a racialized and classed vision of society in which colonial authorities saw Africans as a servile labor force needing little more than dense carbohydrates to fuel their labor. Compensating their workers in a way that would have allowed them to acquire a diverse and nourishing diet, one that would provide sustenance and health, not to mention the pleasure of a good meal, was not part of how these European employers viewed Kenya's colonial society. For them, Africans simply needed sufficient calories to work. Even at the end of the 1930s when African labor protests forced the British to recognize the profound deprivation that the city's workers faced, colonial reforms were still conceptualized through race and class within a system in which white Europeans were accorded comfort and African workers were structurally consigned to a lower standard of living. As Frederick Cooper observed about debates on minimum living standards for Africans in Mombasa during this time, "Welfarism took the form of pronouncements by experts who would not have dreamed of living the life for which they were budgeting."[84] As this section illustrates, though, African workers in the 1910s and 1920s used the leverage they had to forge a food system that was better than the one Europeans had tried to impose upon them. Indeed, during these decades, coastal workers were already engaged in forms of class struggle that ensured that employers could not simply dictate the terms of compensation, a reality that the coming strike waves of the 1930s and onward would only make clearer.

* * *

Today, *ugali* is Kenya's ubiquitous national dish, found on most restaurant menus and cooked daily in peoples' homes. Modern ugali, made of boiled maize meal and regularly consumed with cooked meat, fish, or a vegetable on the side, certainly had antecedents in East Africa's agrarian cuisines, like the Luo staple kuon. A similar dish was also part of foodways of the coast, where the term *ugali,* along with its synonym *sima,* originated in the Kiswahili language. In Krapf's dictionary, based on vocabularies gathered in the mid-nineteenth century, *ugali* was defined simply as "porridge," but *sima* was a "porridge made of Indian corn [maize] or millet meal, boiled with water and the milky juice of the cocoa-nut, eaten with any kind of mtúzi [relish]."[85] This chapter, therefore, does not argue that the food system of labor migration wholesale invented ugali or the practice of eating staples with relishes, though for male Kikuyu and Kamba migrants the regular consumption of maize-meal porridges with a side dish during the early twentieth century did represent a genuinely new culinary experience. However, for other communities like the Luo, such dishes were not so new. The radically novel experience that all migrant workers in Kenya shared during the early twentieth century, therefore, was the way this working-class food system removed seasonality from the daily meal. Agrarian foodways in which changing seasons created rotating staples were replaced by the unflinching regularity of commercial supply chains that facilitated a consistent ration of maize meal, day after day, month after month.[86] Coming from rural cuisines with diverse ingredients, textures, and flavors, African migrants found this new monotony unsatisfying and used the power they had to make their daily meal taste better. Those growing their own food on plantations reintroduced literal seasonality, while migrants taking "cash in lieu" of rations engaged in commercial consumption to provide greater variety to their diets.

By the mid-1920s, workers' demands for a better food system intersected with changes in Britain and its wider empire, in which shifts were under way in thinking about the relationship between nutrition and the "efficiency" of labor. During the first decades of the twentieth century, researchers worried that the poor diets imposed by structural poverty on the British working class were leading to declining health and thereby making workers less "efficient." Driven as much by concerns about the economy as by humanitarianism, officials became acutely focused on the nutrition and diet of British workers.[87] During the mid- to late 1920s, the improvement and diversification of East African diets was similarly becoming an official priority.[88] Considering a 1926 improvement in railway rations, Kenya's labor report observed, "It is evident that deficiency in rations is responsible for much disease and loss of man power. There is no doubt that health cannot be maintained, or a proper output of work expected, unless laborers are provided with a varied, liberal, well cooked and properly constituted diet."[89] R. A. Procter, in his 1926 article about Kikuyu diets, wrote that "there would seem little hope of the Kikuyu ever becoming a regular and steady worker until there are radical alterations in the way in which he is fed when out at work."[90] African working-class diets had already improved significantly because of pressure from below, and during this decade, colonial elites were realizing that a better food system was necessary to create the kind of working class they desired. However, these changes were tied to a contingent moment in the history of labor in Kenya. During the 1930s, the economy of Kenya, and the wider world, changed dramatically, and so too did the colony's working-class food system.

2 ⁓ Comestible Commodities

Food Provisioning and the Commercialization of Daily Life in Midcentury Mombasa

UNTIL THE 1930s, the incentives to open a food business in the fast-growing coastal city of Mombasa were limited. The port town drew in large numbers of migrant workers from Kenya's agrarian societies, but many people in this new consumer class, as discussed in chapter 1, did not buy most of the food that they ate. Instead, they were provided rations by their employer. During the 1930s, though, the rationing system largely ended. Its steady maize rations had hardly been popular among migrants, and employers themselves did not particularly like the responsibility of providing their workers with food. The *posho* system exposed management to criticism from employees unsatisfied with their diets, while also creating the extra work of organizing food supplies, the cost of which became more expensive as rations improved during the 1920s. For employers, paying migrants only in cash was becoming an attractive option. Equally important was that for all that workers had done to improve the rationing system, they seemed little inclined to use their collective power to keep it in place. As posho was phased out, workers in Kenya's port city became more like urban proletariats elsewhere, dependent entirely on cash for the acquisition of daily necessities like food. This drove demand, and new businesses emerged across the city to sell comestible commodities to a rapidly expanding consumer class.

For Mombasa's migrant community, the transition to a food system based on monetary exchange was a contradictory process. Individualized consumption promised greater variety in their daily meals because it released people from the crushing monotony of institutionalized food rations. The city's diverse retail options presented people with more choice over what they ate, as they could prepare food more in line with their actual rural cuisines and try the new flavors of this Indian Ocean port town. However, consumer "choice" exists under capitalism only to the extent that people can afford to choose what they buy. Just as workers were acquiring more power over their food decisions, wages were cut during the 1930s, first during the early years of the Great Depression and then extending well beyond the "recovery." By the late 1930s, with wages still stagnant, food prices rose and so the standard of living for the laboring classes fell. In this context of increasing deprivation, strikes began to regularly occur in Mombasa, punctuated by general strikes in 1939 and 1947. In response, as Frederick Cooper has argued, the colonial government pursued a policy of "labor stabilization," raising wages along with introducing other social benefits.[1] Food prices kept rising, though, and wages did not always keep up. Consequently, the city's working classes had to develop strategies to convert inadequate cash incomes into calories that would sustain them. This chapter examines how people managed to acquire their daily meals in Mombasa's unequal political economy.

In this commercializing city, working-class consumers came to buy nearly all their food from an expanding system of grocers, markets, street traders, and eateries. Indeed, food systems based exclusively on monetary exchange have been more possible in urban areas because of the way cities create dense concentrations of commercial activity. In a dynamic port town like Mombasa, workers were able to rely on cash for their food because they could expect to find a variety of businesses eager to sell them raw ingredients and, as discussed in the next chapter, prepared food. Compared to the industrialized world during the mid-twentieth century, and especially the United States, where centralized supermarkets were taking root, Mombasa's food system was decidedly decentralized.[2] People bought their grain from innumerable small grocery stores, called *maduka*, and fresh vegetables, fruit, meat, and fish from open-air markets and itinerant street traders found throughout the city. Today, development scholars have observed that African cities do not have the same problem of "food deserts" found in urban America in its racially marginalized neighborhoods with limited access to diverse grocery offerings. In Kenya, and Africa more generally, the ubiquity of mobile, small-scale traders marketing produce throughout the city, especially in working-class communities, has ensured that fresh food is available in low-income neighborhoods.[3] Nonetheless, inequality still determined what kinds of food people could access, as the key question in Mombasa was whether people had the money to buy the food they needed and desired. Quite often, they did not.

This chapter, therefore, examines how Mombasa's modern and distinctly urban food system was made during the middle decades of the twentieth century. During this time, people in rural areas continued to rely on subsistence agriculture as the primary way they acquired their food, while those in the city became entirely reliant on cash. In the countryside, maize, beans, greens, and other produce came from the fields, while the firewood and water necessary to prepare them into a meal were gathered from the surrounding environment. In the city, these items, as well as other consumables unique to an urban economy, were purchased from maduka, open-air markets, and traders who worked on the streets.

FOOD, MONEY, AND URBAN LIFE

Jackson Nthuli arrived in Mombasa in 1972, taking up a job with the Kenya Ports Authority, but for more than two decades prior he had lived up-country in a rural community in the Machakos District of Ukambani. His parents were commercial farmers, and with access to land they did not need to purchase food on a regular basis. In a 2015 interview in Mombasa, Nthuli recalled that "our food, for the most part, we farmed it."[4] His experience was a common one across rural Kenya throughout the twentieth century. With few exceptions, interviewees who lived in up-country agrarian communities from the 1930s until the end of the century primarily ate food that they grew in their own fields.[5] This included people like Benike Owuir, who lived in Siaya near Lake Victoria from the time she was born in 1945 until the mid-1970s; she explained that "their food was grown on the shamba [farm]. Mboga [vegetables], wimbi [millet], maize, almost everything came from the shamba."[6]

In these agrarian communities, therefore, subsistence agriculture remained at the center of how people provisioned food. However, in rural Kenya, new forms of commercial exchange were also emerging over the course of the century that shaped kitchen pantries and peoples' diets. Maduka shops run mostly by South Asian traders became common in these areas, carrying a variety of dried goods, but their impact on what people ate was limited. The core of the daily diet—grains, fresh produce, and dairy—came most often from the farm, while maduka provided only a small number of shelf-stable ingredients, above all dried tea leaves and sugar.[7]

However, tea was not an everyday beverage, as it was enjoyed only irregularly during those times when people had extra cash to spend. Rather than tea, the grain-based beverages examined in chapter 1 were consumed more frequently, and they were made with products grown in the family's fields.[8]

In the countryside, commercial exchange in foodstuffs also happened beyond maduka, reflecting longer precolonial trends in regional markets that became amplified as the scale of the economy and population grew during the twentieth century. For example, in western Kenya, adjacent to Lake Victoria, rural trade in fish was common.[9] James Hunnington Ogola, who grew up in Maseno about twenty kilometers inland from the lake, was part of a family that had more access to cash than most because of his father's job running a small store for the Church Missionary Society. Nonetheless, they still produced most of their household food in their own gardens. Ogola remembered helping his mother cultivate maize, millet, beans, peas, potatoes, pumpkins, and other vegetables, while they also got dairy products from their cattle. So productive was their farm that they converted their surpluses into fish. Twice per week, fishers from Lake Victoria traveled up the hill to Maseno's market, and Ogola's mother traded their produce for fish.[10] Of course, people who lived close enough to the lake did not have to trade for their fish, as they could just catch them. Vitalis Owiti, who grew up near Lake Victoria around midcentury, told me his family ate fish that his father caught by setting traps in the late afternoon and then pulling them up in the early morning before he went to work.[11]

Thus, in rural Kenya throughout the twentieth century, subsistence and commercial food systems overlapped, but most of what people ate they still grew, or caught, themselves. However, land consolidation and population growth also meant that proportionally fewer Kenyans could sustain themselves in these communities, and people looked to cities like Mombasa as places where they could earn more-consistent incomes.[12] As discussed in chapter 1, those who arrived in the city entered a radically new food system in which they had to perform wage labor to acquire their food. However, by the 1930s, the rations that had shaped the experience of labor migration during the first decades of the twentieth century were coming to an end. Mombasa was becoming a city in which cash was the only way to access food.

The history of how Mombasa's food system transformed during this period is connected to the shifting dynamics of power between labor and management on the East African coast. At the start of the twentieth century, employers in the region had difficulty adequately staffing plantations and urban industries, as well as finding government laborers, but the Great

Depression, combined with longer-term and growing migration to Mombasa, changed the nature of class struggle in a city where a previously tight labor market became saturated with job seekers. Suddenly, a tactic like desertion that had so troubled employers and senior government officials before was of little concern to authorities who were able to report, as in 1937, that "the labour position [in the city] gave no cause for concern during the whole year." A study the following year also concluded that "there is a large surplus of labour in Mombasa which cannot expect to get either regular or semi-regular employment."[13] The city's municipal engineer underlined just how much the labor market had changed, explaining that "when we want 20[,] literally hundreds of boys [African men] come after the job."[14] By the late 1930s, Mombasa's increasingly powerful class of employers, who had never particularly liked the responsibility of rationing, could more easily dictate terms to their workforce. Moreover, with labor scarcity no longer an issue, the colonial state suddenly lost interest in regularly inspecting whether employers were actually following masters and servants laws.[15] In this context, posho rationing in Mombasa mostly ended during the 1930s, and workers were paid only in cash.

However, the city's labor market was neither centralized nor uniform, and so the move away from in-kind payments of food was uneven across job sectors and space. For government employees, who represented nearly 40 percent of Mombasa's African workers, food rationing did decisively end during the 1930s.[16] For example, in 1926, the railway paid its workforce a base wage of 16–20 shillings (Shs.) per month along with two pounds of maize meal each day and a weekly supplement of one pound of beans and one pound of *cheriko* (pigeon peas).[17] By 1939, the minimum wage had risen to Shs. 20/-, except that by then no rations were provided. With the Masters and Servants Ordinance still in effect, the railway tried to stay within the law by claiming that the minimum wage was actually Shs. 15/-, which then came with a stipend of Shs. 4/- for food and an additional shilling for cooking fuel.[18] Similar changes were under way with city government employers like the municipal engineer and the Public Works Department (PWD).[19] As with the railway, a manager at the PWD in 1939 reported, "We do not give them posho in Mombasa at all. We give them 6/- [shillings] a month which we reckon as the value of their food."[20] Many large corporate employers also did not ration their workers; these included the oil companies Shell, Texaco, and Vacuum, which had operations in Mombasa.[21]

The area of employment where food rationing remained strongest during the 1930s was in domestic labor in the city's middle- and high-income homes. In the context of a household, where paternalist overtones were stronger than in overtly commercial sites of wage labor, many domestic workers were provided food as part of their pay, though not universally. In-kind payments were most common in Swahili and Arab households, which had lower wages of 6/- to 8/- per month, but this also included food along with clothes and housing. In South Asian homes, such forms of non-cash compensation were less common. For domestic work, the rule was the lower the wage the more food was included as part of the pay. Indeed, the South Asian households that offered the highest wages neither housed nor fed their workers. Additionally, Kenya-wide data suggest that Europeans mostly did not provide their domestic workers with food, which was likely the case in Mombasa too.[22]

Off the island on the nearby mainland, there is some ambiguity in the record, but workers in these more rural, peri-urban environments seem to have also been buying most of their food by the end of the 1930s. Speaking to the labor commission formed after Mombasa's 1939 general strike, a representative of the employers of the Vegetable Growers Association, R. K. Desai, claimed that these farms followed the Masters and Servants Ordinance by providing workers with posho and allowing them to have "vegetables from the shambas [farms]."[23] However, this testimony does not square with other evidence. There was minimal oversight of these businesses on the distant mainland, and rising food prices after 1935 would have also incentivized the owners of these agricultural estates to pay their workers only in cash, which they appear to have done.[24] Indeed, Kabatha wa Washomba, who worked on one of these mainland farms, purchased nearly all his food. To the same labor commission in 1939, he explained that he and his coworkers together bought a large bag of maize meal each month along with meat. Washomba did indicate that he occasionally supplemented this with some "Indian vegetables" that he picked from his employer's field, but he also added that "they do not belong to us they belong to the owner. . . . I take a little vegetables but the owner shouts at me a lot." Pushed that he may have been stealing them, Washomba replied, "I take it in the presence of the owner, I do not steal it," yet his employer would always express displeasure when he did.[25] On this farm, there were no rations, and any vegetables the workers received had to be taken, pushing the employer to be more of a patron than he wanted to be.

Therefore, pockets of in-kind payments of food still existed in Mombasa's wage-labor economy, but an increasingly large proportion of the city's working class purchased almost all the food they consumed, especially if they were employed by Europeans or South Asians. The existing archival record does not indicate exactly when this change occurred, only that it was in effect by 1939. If rations ended during the early 1930s, this likely would not have been a large concern for African workers. In Kenya, the price of maize, the core of the urban diet, declined by 50 percent during the first years of the Great Depression, and so food remained comparatively cheap.[26] However, food prices along with general inflation began to rise from the mid-1930s onward, and the fact that by the end of the decade most employers had shed the obligation to ration food to their workers is suggestive.[27] Whenever rations ended, their absence was shaping the tense labor politics of Mombasa by the late 1930s. As Frederick Cooper underlined, worker militancy in the city was fueled by an economy in which "few employers . . . offered either housing or rations," and so "workers faced overcrowding and inflation together."[28] Here, Cooper identifies how workers were radicalized by the mounting pressure they faced trying to house and feed themselves on inadequate wages, but we also need to see this vulnerability to the vagaries of a market economy as a new feature of the city's food system. Workers had only recently lost the insurance of being able to choose rations when consumer prices rose. By the late 1930s, they were entirely reliant on poverty wages to purchase food that was becoming increasingly expensive.

Nonetheless, African workers did not view the quite basic insurance that rations provided as enough reason to long nostalgically for the system's return. During the late 1930s and for the remainder of the colonial period, reinstating food rations never materialized as a demand of striking workers. Rather, they wanted higher wages to purchase better food of their own choosing. Indeed, even when World War II presented the opportunity to reinstitute the rationing system, this elicited little interest from Mombasa's wage-earning classes. In 1942, poor crops and the colony's emerging role as a breadbasket for Britain's war in the Middle East combined to create food shortages in Kenya, and consequently the government began a new food-rationing scheme for workers in Mombasa.[29] In an effort resembling the rationing system for migrant workers from the early-colonial period, the state again enforced the requirement that employers provide food directly to their workers. Beginning in 1942 and extending beyond the war to 1949, Africans on monthly contracts could receive employer-supplied rations, often mixed meal in which scarce maize was cut with more widely available grains.[30] Like before, workers had the option to either take these in-kind payments or keep their full cash wage and purchase ingredients in controlled shops in the island neighborhoods of Shimanzi, Makupa, and Mbaraki.[31] However, during this period, African workers generally chose not to return to a system in which their employers controlled their food.

As rationing began in 1942, the collective memory of Mombasa's working class elicited concern over the reintroduction of posho. Indeed, as labor researcher S. V. Cooke reported, "railway employees [were] very suspicious of issues of food in kind owing mainly to the inferior nature of rations often issued in the past." He continued that "in the opinion of the great majority of witnesses who appeared before [the committee of inquiry]," Africans "[did] not want relief in kind." This was particularly tied to the issue of taste and the oppressive uniformity of rations. Cooke found "evidence of the difficulty of arranging that each tribe . . . and there [were] men from many different tribes in employment . . . [got] the foodstuffs to which they [were] accustomed."[32] In 1945, another labor study similarly observed that "the standard ration [left] no room for the variety which [was] increasingly desired by town-dwelling Africans" and that in Mombasa "the monthly issue of 60 lbs. of *posho* [was] an anachronism." Of course, this desire for variety, as we have seen, was tied to rural tastes as much as it was the product of new consumer preferences in the "modern" city. Most of these contract workers, then, prioritizing choice, took their full monthly pay and bought their groceries from controlled stores. In 1944, officials noted that "African employees in Mombasa have so far failed to appreciate the advantage of taking rations rather than cash," while in 1945 "comparative few" railway workers drew available rations from their employers.[33] Railway workers still felt this way in 1947, preferring "to take their ration allowance as cash" owing to "the many different tribes represented in Mombasa, each with its own habits of feeding."[34]

Rations provided a low bar of food security, and one that people did not find to be worth sacrificing control over their diets. At any rate, wartime food-supply measures, the basis for reinstituting employer-based rations, mostly ended in 1948 and were completely wound down in 1949. From that point forward, there is no evidence that workplace rationing on any large scale continued in Mombasa for the remainder of the colonial era or thereafter.[35] The end of food rationing was uneven but ultimately far-reaching. In the city, in contrast to the countryside, the only way to access the daily meal was with cash.

WORKING-CLASS CONSUMERS AND THE BUSINESS OF FOOD

Capitalism is full of contradictions. Understandably, African migrant workers did not mourn the demise of the food-rationing system that had placed decisions about their diets into the hands of employers. As the daily issue of maize meal ended, migrants became individualized consumers, purchasing their own food in a market economy. In some ways, they had been liberated from the tyrannical monotony of rationing. However, social inequality also constrained the "choices" that African consumers had in this emerging commercial economy. The limits of this new consumer society became quickly clear. As rationing declined during the 1930s, freeing up workers to choose their own food, employers also took advantage of a slackening labor market to lower wages. This was not an abstract economic process but the result of particular decisions that individual employers made as their position strengthened. In 1939, during testimony to the labor commission, Mombasa's municipal engineer bluntly admitted to active collusion in suppressing wages, explaining that other employers had complained that his department paid too much, and so the department "came down to . . . [its] figures, the same figures as the Public Works Department and the Railway." He also conceded that such tactics reduced the standard of living for workers, lowering wages for people who no longer received rations. Previously, his workers made higher wages and had been provisioned with a posho of "two pounds of maize [daily]" and "2 pounds of beans, salt, [and] ½ pound of meat" on a weekly basis. Consequently, in the past, his workers "did not spend anything on food" and saved significant sums for when they returned to their rural homes. Pushed by the interviewer to admit that his employees were "not nearly so well off now," indeed "very much worse," the municipal engineer reluctantly replied, "Yes, perhaps it was a little worse."[36] Migrants were free to choose their own food, but only what they could afford.

The economic precarity of Mombasa's workers can be underlined by the fact that even comparatively higher-paid people struggled to make their budgets work. Giddeon Harrison, a clerk who was part of the city's small African professional class, was paid Shs. 90/- per month, while many Africans made only a small fraction of that amount. However, Giddeon's food budget still felt tight every month. In 1939, living with his wife and children, he spent Shs. 70/- per month on food. When he was testifying to the labor commission that year, his interviewer suggested that this seemed an enormous amount, to which Harrison replied, "But what can I do? If I do not get good food my family will get sick."[37] As a higher earner, he spent more than most others did, like a Kamba family of three that put Shs. 21/10 (i.e., 21 shillings and 10 cents) per month toward food or the two single workers who reported their monthly food expenditures at Shs. 17/70 and Shs. 15/75, respectively.[38] Personal tastes, family size, income, and other considerations determined the amount of money that people allocated to food, but everyone certainly needed more than the range of Shs. 13/- to 23/50 that employers, officials, and other colonial elites debated as a "reasonable" standard of living for African workers.[39] Crucially, though, during the late 1930s, many earned even less than that. The average worker was paid around Sh. 13/- per month, and some as little as Shs. 6/-.[40] To put these wages in perspective, Mombasa's district commissioner in 1930 had estimated that an income of no less than 40/- per month would barely cover basic rent and food costs in the city, this at a time when food prices were lower than they became by the end of the decade.[41]

The math did not add up. Most workers were not being paid enough to survive. One effect of this was that credit became an essential part of the new consumer economy and the businesses that marketed to these working-class communities. As rations ended, workers in the city bought most of the carbohydrate-rich grain in their diet from maduka, shops that were much the same as the small dried-goods grocers that were expanding into rural areas, though in Mombasa they were owned by both Arabs and South Asians. At these urban maduka, credit was central to their business model. From the point of view of grocers, Mombasa's working-class consumers represented an expanding market for maize meal and other dried foodstuffs, but because their spending was so depreciated, credit was a necessary financial instrument to keep commerce moving. From the perspective of workers, quite simply, without credit they would not be able to purchase enough food. As James R. Brennan writes about Dar es Salaam during the same period, so in Mombasa "credit . . . was the very lifeblood of urban commerce, without which no trader and very few consumers could survive."[42] Indeed, John Josiah Stevens, the senior supervisor for the Kenya Landing and Shipping Company, a major employer, described in 1939 how some Africans had to "go to the dukas and say if you provide me with food I will pay you at the end of the month and then they spend more than they earn and get into debt with the duka and have to keep going to him."[43]

Abdulla Mohamed, a Digo man who lived in the Majengo neighborhood at this same time, employed such a strategy. He was more fortunate than many because he was able to acquire enough casual shifts at a petroleum company to earn around Shs. 40/- per month. However, drawing from this income to also feed his family, which included his wife and two children, he spent nearly all his money on food, between Shs. 30/- and 40/- per month. To make his budget work, Mohamed established a debt relationship with a duka in which half his store expenses would be carried over each month. He explained, "I pay half and then I pay the other the following month. . . . I am always in debt. . . . If I owe 30/- I pay 15/- . . . and if I can I give him more."[44]

The situation was much the same nearly two decades later, as inflation cut into the wage increases workers had gained through strikes. According to the African Retail Price Index, the cost of consumer goods in Mombasa, including food, more than tripled from 1939 to 1953, while the price of maize meal specifically, the most significant source of calories for many urban Africans, increased by nearly 340 percent from 1939 to 1958.[45] Facing these price increases, workers remained dependent on credit to access enough food. In 1957, Nabwera Burudi, a researcher working for the *Mombasa Social Survey,* spoke with numerous African workers who told her they "were heavily in debt to shopkeepers from whom they bought their foodstuffs on credit." Burudi explained that "the average wage received by the menial staff of the Municipality was found to be Shs. 100/- per month," but that this "did not appear to be commensurate with the present cost of living, particularly when the wage earner is a family man."[46] One migrant, a single Mkamba man who ate a relatively simple diet of cheap carbohydrates and earned a somewhat higher salary of Shs. 130/- per month, had nonetheless accumulated a debt of Shs. 400/- after living in Mombasa for only six months.[47] Once in debt, people found it hard to escape unless they had access to outside capital to pay it down, especially because shopkeepers coordinated among themselves so that workers could not play them off one another. If people tried to leave their debt at one shop and buy from another, they would be unable to acquire credit there because "most traders had a working arrangement with others to prevent this from happening."[48]

However, as challenging as it was for people to escape these cycles of indebtedness to urban retailers, that was better than not having a line of credit at all, the situation of the very poor.[49] During the 1940s, labor investigators found that despite the "evidence before [them] that many [workers were] . . . in debt to shopkeepers," there also was "little . . . to suggest that indebtedness to shopkeepers was common among the lower-paid workers," as they found "it difficult to obtain credit from a [duka] nowadays."[50] That is, those least able to afford Mombasa's high cost of living were most dependent on their meager wages. Having to draw off this small quantity of cash for their food, the poor experienced cycles of (relative) plenty and want tied to their pay schedules. The same labor investigation in 1945 reported that the working poor ate "well for a short period after . . . wages have been paid but [fed] inadequately for a variable period before payday."[51] With little cash that quickly ran low, people made do by eating a diet consisting mostly of dense carbohydrates, reminiscent of the posho ration of earlier decades, or by simply eating less food overall.[52] In a 1947 survey of working-class life in the city, N. M. Deverell found that Africans still felt "compelled" to eat at the "'posho' standard," as their lack of income meant they were not able to eat "a great quantity of food other than *ugali* or rice and other more filling foodstuffs such as cassava." When money was especially tight, people ate when they could. An unnamed Mkamba migrant explained, "If I eat a larger quantity of *ugali* in the evening I do not even require a cup of tea in the morning." Another man who was a casual dock worker similarly explained that "he never [had] breakfast but if working [he took] a cup of tea @ 15 cents at the dock canteen."[53]

Although maduka only extended credit to some customers, they did sell their inventory in ways that marketed it to poor consumers. People who are more economically secure can purchase some of their items in considerable bulk, such as a large bag of grain, a gallon jug of cooking oil, and so forth, which often allows them to save money by buying in volume and time by limiting trips to the store. However, the poor can often not employ such strategies for the simple reason that they do not have adequate funds to make large expenditures on a single trip to a grocer. To accommodate the financial constraints of their customers, like retailers in other African cities, maduka owners would "break bulk" by taking products meant to be sold in larger containers and offering them in smaller quantities.[54] H. S. Booker, a sociologist working for the government during the 1940s, observed that poorer Africans in Mombasa "usually bought in quantities sufficient only for the next meal."[55] In Deverell's survey as part of the same investigation, she wrote that cooking fats like groundnut oil and ghee were purchased "in small quantities at a time according to whether it [was] required to fry fish or use a little ghee for *chapatti* [flatbread] or stew," in amounts "usually sold by the spoonful." Additionally, spices and the supplies for morning beverages were bought in a similar fashion, as "few persons [bought] more than 10 [cents] worth of tea at a time." If tea was purchased in larger quantities, this was likely done by a trader who would in turn repackage it, "making [them] into small 2ct. packets for resale."[56] Bulk breaking emerged in the unequal urban political economies of colonialism, and it has endured, remaining a common retail practice in urban Kenyan and other African cities.[57]

The considerable role of bulk breaking, as well as credit and debt in Mombasa's consumer economy, speaks to the low-spending power of the city's working class. Migrants went to Kenya's port town in the hope of earning surplus income, some of which they meant to send home to their cash-poor rural communities and perhaps to enjoy the excitement of a cosmopolitan city, but many found that they instead subsisted on the margins of survival. Facing such circumstances, workers built networks of solidarity and support among themselves so they did not have to confront poverty as a solitary individual. Closed off from credit at maduka, the working poor established borrowing networks between friends, thus creating informal safety nets from which they could acquire cash when needed.[58] Personal relationships also helped stave off extreme physical deprivation. The casual dock worker from above who did not eat breakfast and took only tea at lunch could lean on family at times when he might otherwise starve. He explained that "if he [was] short of cash he expect[ed] his brother to feed him and he [did] the same for his brother."[59]

Food expenditures are also not made in a vacuum, as they are determined as part of a larger household budget. Given that food together with housing accounted for most working-class spending in the city, people in Mombasa had to make difficult decisions about nourishment and shelter.[60] In this context, the extensive overcrowding in colonial Mombasa's working-class neighborhoods was not merely a strategy to access housing but also can be understood as a way in which people arranged their budgets so they could afford food. In 1930, Mombasa's district commissioner observed that "five or more natives hire[d] a room and each [paid] his proportion of the rent," while they would also take on additional daily people who "required a night's lodging," with "as many as ten . . . sleep[ing] in one room."[61] In 1939, labor officials observed that "as many as eight single men [would] share a room," and later in 1945 that it was "a common practice for a single man living in the Majengo area to join with one or more of his friends in renting a room."[62] These patterns are exemplified in the experiences of Rastas Koshoki, a dairy worker paid Shs. 17/- per month, who lived on the streets when he first arrived in Mombasa. By 1939, Koshoki had found consistent shelter, sharing a room that he said felt "like a hospital ward, about 30 men sleep[ing] in one room." However, he also reported being able to afford three meals a day.[63] Living in crowded housing, poor migrants stretched their wages, utilizing the little cash they had to acquire food.

Sharing a room not only reduced housing costs but also allowed people to pool their resources for food, creating more security with multiple sources of income. Washomba, the Kikuyu migrant who worked on Mombasa's periurban gardens during the late 1930s, was doing just this when he and his fellow workers combined their earnings to buy a bag of maize meal and meat for their meals.[64] Similarly, a man who had migrated to Mombasa during the 1940s from Tieta lived in a single room with a friend, and they shared expenses. As recorded in the 1947 social survey, they were "noticed having tea and bread for breakfast, ugali and stewed liver at midday and Ugali and stew in the evening." In another home at the same time, a man from Ukambani shared "his evening meal with three other Wakamba," while another day there was "3 lbs. of mixed meal . . . being prepared to be eaten by 5 men with one very small fish for 'relish.'"[65]

During the first decades of colonial rule, many of these households were composed of single men like the five Wakamba above who ate their ugali with fish together. However, by the 1940s, considerable demographic change among the migrant community was already under way. By that point, the "single male migrant" that so concerned British policy makers during the late-colonial era represented only part of the up-country African community in

FIGURE 2.1. A dried-goods shop (*duka*) in Mombasa during the early 1900s. From Oxford, Bodleian Libraries, MSS. Afr. S. 1607/1.

Mombasa, as many people were in fact living in conjugal families. In 1943, the more than 23,000 African contract workers in the city, almost all of them male and the majority being migrants from up-country, had registered over 22,000 "dependent" wives and children living with them in the city.[66] In a 1947 survey, a sample of Mombasa's working-class households showed that 38 of 107 men lived with their families, while another survey of 215 African wage laborers working for major employers reported that 134 lived with their wives.[67] The migrant community was becoming less male, and the percentage of women living in the city grew from 34 percent to 40 percent by the end of the colonial period.[68] Certainly, not all migrant women lived with male partners, but many did. In 1947, government sociologist H. S. Booker concluded that many of the women moving to Mombasa were the wives of men who had been there for some time and had decided to live at least semipermanently in the city.[69]

British policy in late-colonial Africa, as Frederick Cooper and Lisa Lindsay have argued, aimed to make such African men into breadwinners, but the reality was that their wages could not sustain an entire household. As

Lindsay showed for colonial Nigeria, so women in Kenya's port city became crucial to income generation in conjugal African households and therefore also to their ability to purchase food.[70] However, women in Mombasa were largely excluded from wage labor. In 1954, only 909 African women were registered as waged workers in the city, representing 2.6 percent of the formally employed. By 1961, the number had risen to just 1,063, even with a surge in Mombasa's overall African population.[71] Without access to wages, women earned cash through petty trade. They sold food, cutlery, clothing, newspapers, tobacco, curios, and bathroom supplies, along with an unspecified variety of "piece goods, fancy goods, . . . miscellaneous goods, and second-hand goods."[72] The centrality of this kind of trading income to African urban budgets was made clear in the *Mombasa Social Survey* of the late 1950s. Writing about household finances, the survey explained that "it is utterly useless to talk of the earnings of Africans based on wage rates only," as people generated significant income by "providing services outside regular employment."[73] The study also noted that "a wife supplements the income of her husband by cooking for single men, and washing, ironing, mending and so on and, of course, by practicing the world's oldest profession." Despite not having access to wage labor, "the majority of African women living [in Mombasa] earn[ed] some type of income."[74] In Mombasa, African families at the bottom of the income scale spent approximately 50 percent of their household budget on food, and in many homes a considerable portion of this income was earned by women.[75]

Throughout the twentieth century, small grocery stores were a common sight in rural Kenya, but the dried goods they sold played only a marginal role in the provisioning strategies of the still quite agrarian households in these communities. Tea, sugar, and salt, to be sure, were purchased with some regularity, but the core of peoples' diets came from the fields. Buying grain and other essential ingredients from maduka was done circumstantially rather than consistently. Emma Mudanya, for example, who grew up in the Rift Valley during the 1970s and 1980s, remembered that "most of the things we used to usually eat it was just from the farm, unless we would buy something from the duka like flour or rice, maybe for a change. Maybe spaghetti, just for a change. Mostly we grew our *sima* and *githeri*."[76]

In Mombasa, by contrast, maduka were at the center of the food system. Maize meal continued to make up the largest portion of working-class diets during the twentieth century, and living in an urban environment without access to the means of subsistence, people had to purchase their food. In Mombasa, that meant buying maize meal, or on occasion other grains, at one of the approximately 1,250 maduka in operation there by 1970.[77] Often without sufficient income to buy what they needed, people developed strategies to survive. They drew on credit from retailers and friends alike, purchased in the small quantities they could afford, crowded into single rooms to reduce their housing costs, and created bonds of solidarity and support with people in similar circumstances.

PRODUCE AND PROTEIN IN MOMBASA'S MODERN FOOD SYSTEM

Social inequality in Mombasa meant that ugali, rice, and other grains composed a large proportion of the food that working-class communities ate. However, despite their limited resources, people were not willing to fully sacrifice a variety of textures and flavors in their daily meals. A survey conducted in the late 1930s found that, while a Wadigo family of four committed Shs. 35/- to buying grain-derived starches, they also spent Shs. 7/50 per month on vegetables, Shs. 2/40 on coconuts, and another Shs. 2/40 on general fruits, close to 20 percent of their food budget, along with Shs. 15/- on meat and another Shs. 6/- on milk. The same study showed a considerably poorer Wakamba family of three that spent around a third of their food expenditures on rice, while the rest went to meat, beans, coconuts, and vegetables. For a married Luo couple, starches of rice and maize meal constituted their largest single food expense of Shs. 15/-, but they also committed Shs. 4/- per month to fish, re-creating some of the cuisine from their home region of western Kenya.[78] Budgets were tight, but people tried to eat more than the "posho standard" of boiled grain. These ingredients, fresh produce and proteins alike, were not sold at maduka. They were found in open-air markets or were sold by individual hawkers who worked along the city's streets.

Today, much of the fresh produce sold in Mombasa moves through Kongowea Market on the north mainland, just over the bridge that connects it to the island. There, traders can buy fruits and vegetables wholesale and sell them in various retail settings throughout the city. However, during most of the twentieth century, the centralized hub for wholesale produce was located on Mombasa Island, at Mwembe Tayari Market. Now demolished, it was built around 1920 and became the place where fresh fruits and vegetables first arrived in the city, coming from nearby market gardens, coastal farms farther afield, and up-country producers—even as far as Tanzania.[79] Among the main buyers at Mwembe Tayari were retail vendors who then sold these fruits and vegetables at one of the city's municipal markets. For most of the colonial period, the largest was MacKinnon Market, a large open-air structure housing 180 small stalls on the border of Old Town where vendors sold fresh fruits, vegetables, and meat. Additionally, during the early-colonial period, there was an official fish market inside Old Town close to the original harbor, while at Mwembe Tayari there was also a retail section alongside the wholesalers where individual consumers could buy fresh food.[80]

These state-run institutions, though, did not always fit the practical geographies of daily life in the city. During the first decades of the twentieth century, African migrants were concentrated in the Majengo neighborhood on the western side of the island, and many worked in the nearby industrial, port, and railway industries. With Mwembe Tayari, MacKinnon, and the Old Town fish markets on the eastern side of town, a walk from home to work for most did not include passing by a place where the state approved of the sale of fresh food, so small-scale entrepreneurs and their customers created their own commercialized system of provisioning that mapped more effectively onto working-class geographies. As early as 1919, a sanitation officer noted the existence of "fresh foods" that were "sold by Native and Arab vendors" making up a "numerous class of persons" who, rather than operating in city markets, "conduct[ed] their business in busy thoroughfares and highways."[81] By 1929, Mombasa's medical officer of health observed, "Unauthorised markets can be found all over the town, and occur . . . practically in all cases to meet the demands of the people living or working in the area."[82] This included working-class Majengo, where a large unauthorized food market located on Makupa Road had become a focal point where traders sold foodstuffs to employees of nearby businesses, as well as to other residents. It was located "near the Railway boundary, and . . . [was] largely patronized by railway employees," "cater[ing] to the needs of people who travel[ed] up and down the Kilindini Road to and from the Port."[83]

City officials, with these markets and the urban African population continuing to grow, became concerned about such forms of economic activity happening outside their control. As Majengo expanded, the state came to see building an official market in that neighborhood as a necessity, with the town clerk arguing that it was "very urgently required for the convenience of the population . . . extending through the growing 'African villages' north and east of the Makupa Road."[84] Traders, as we have seen, already sold produce there, but they were not formally administered by the colonial government, and by 1931 officials had completed a plan to remake the map of fresh-food businesses in the city. The retail section of Mwembe Tayari Market was closed on 31 December 1931, and its stall holders were ordered to move to either MacKinnon near Old Town or to the newly constructed and state-run Makupa Market in Majengo.[85] Despite much of Makupa Market filling with fee-paying vendors, the limits of these kinds of municipal institutions were becoming apparent. In April 1932, a report from the city government admitted that "the present position [was] that Hawkers and Street Traders [were] spread over the town, paying neither Government dues of 10/- a month where they [were] liable, nor the Municipal fee of 5/-." Some of these traders sat "singly or in groups," while others more ambitiously operated in "small, unauthorised markets."[86] Unlicensed food traders remained widespread across the city, including near city markets like Majengo where non-sanctioned vendors operated every day. Around Old Town, there were also reports of traders who left MacKinnon to join "the hawkers on the street."[87]

The reluctance of these traders to work in municipal-run markets was not because space was limited, as stalls remained open. At first, the objection may have been to the fees of four to five shillings per month charged for produce stalls in Makupa, but the city government, realizing that this might disincentivize vendors, canceled fees for low-income traders to convince them to work in the official market. Nonetheless, stalls remained unfilled with hawkers and vendors continuing to operate on the streets.[88] In 1933, approximately 30 of 181 stalls at MacKinnon Market were reported to be empty each day, while 40 of 132 at Makupa were unoccupied.[89] These markets did not fill during the 1930s because working outside them remained an attractive and viable choice. Even though operating in them was free, working there also meant doing business close to a large number of competitors. Many found other locations preferable, and the state had only minimal ability to stop them. As elsewhere in urban East Africa, the British colonial state in Mombasa lacked the capacity to enforce many of its trading bylaws.[90] Indeed, many officials frankly admitted that they could not effectively implement their own laws, as when the superintendent of police told his municipal colleagues in 1932 that the present "police force in Mombasa [was] inadequate for . . . [this] purpose."[91] The next year, city authorities observed that "small private markets" were "entirely uncontrolled" on Mombasa Island, while they had no effective authority over commerce in mainland areas. "It was agreed in committee," wrote the town clerk in 1933, "that we shall have to shut our eyes to main land conditions."[92]

The number of these vendors as well as the scale of the government's official market infrastructure continued to grow along with the city in the following decades. As Mombasa Island became more densely populated by midcentury, the municipality expanded its markets. Though Makupa had struggled to fill during the 1930s, over time it developed into the largest market in Mombasa, growing from 132 stalls in 1933 to 244 by 1970. By then, around 15,000 people each day went to its location on the northwestern part of the island looking for fruits, vegetables, or the other innumerable "sundries" available there, spending a daily total of between $3,500 and $5,000.

FIGURE 2.2. Unidentified women selling dried fish in Mombasa during the early 1900s. From Oxford, Bodleian Libraries, MSS. Afr. S. 1607/1.

MacKinnon, once the largest market, was by 1970 the second biggest in the city with 6,500 daily customers, though its revenue was comparable at $3,000–4,000, driven by higher prices. These two markets together dominated fresh-food retailing, accounting for 85 percent of all such commerce on Mombasa Island. Beyond MacKinnon and Makupa, people also had the option to shop at the retail side of Mwembe Tayari, which had by then reopened, or in Tudor Market on the northern side of the island, newly built in 1966. On the mainland, with its fast-growing working-class suburbs, three new city markets also opened during the 1960s: Changamwe Market (1960) and Magongo Market (1968) on the west mainland and Likoni Market (1968) on the south mainland.[93] In these municipal institutions as well as on the streets, working-class consumers had considerable access to fresh fruits and vegetables in Mombasa, in centralized locations and from vendors spread out across the geography of the city.

The commercializing economy in Kenya's port town also made meat available in vastly greater quantities there than in the rural communities that migrants had left. Except for the consumption of fish in western Kenya, rural diets were mostly vegetarian around the turn of the twentieth century, as discussed in chapter 1. By the late-colonial era, the consumption of meat seems to have declined even further, especially in the Highlands. This was because of both state seizures of cattle and the ways that colonial land policy and population growth reduced the amount of grazing land available in Central Kenya for livestock.[94] Summarizing the dietary patterns of the Kikuyu, C. R. Philip observed in a 1943 nutrition survey that "meat is so infrequently eaten by the masses that the intake is considered negligible."[95] In the city, though, even the poorest consumers ate meat on a comparatively regular basis. During the late 1930s, in a survey of seven working-class household food budgets, from the lowest to the highest, all included meat as a significant monthly expenditure.[96] Indeed, in 1945, a labor inquiry observed that, among working-class Africans, there was "a great demand for meat" and that "the majority of African workers [were] mainly dependent on it for the protein content of their diet."[97] In Mombasa, it was available at stalls in city markets or from stand-alone butchers; depending on tastes and resources, this meant either beef or goat, with the latter less expensive. Cheapest of all, offal (organs) was also widely available. Geography could also affect cost, as meat tended to be most expensive in island markets like MacKinnon, while buying it at wholesale butchers on the mainland where individual consumers shopped too was considerably cheaper.[98]

For migrants, this kind of access to meat had no parallel in their rural communities. Working-class consumers in Mombasa operated under all kinds of financial constraints as they tried to find nourishing and enjoyable food, but life in the city also meant that meat became a much more consistent part of the daily meal.

WOOD, WATER, AND THE COMMODIFICATION OF NATURE

Drawing water out of grain has been among the most successful and enduring of all human technologies. Drying fresh seeds preserved these carbohydrate-rich foods for long periods of time, allowing grains to sit in storage in rural areas to feed the local community long after the harvest had ended. As markets and transportation infrastructures expanded, these dried cereals could also become commodities able to travel considerable distances and be stored until they found a buyer, whether in a Chicago-area grain elevator or a maduka shop in Kenya's port city.[99] However, the very process that preserves grain also renders what had once been fresh and chewy seeds into a hard and nearly inedible substance. To convert these stored calories back into consumable food, they have to be rehydrated, and so people need ready access to fuel and water. In Mombasa, this meant boiling and simmering maize meal or rice, or using water to create a dough from wheat flour, which would then be fried on a pan or in oil. In rural communities, children had the daily chore of gathering firewood and water for cooking from the surrounding environment, effectively drawing these resources from common land.[100] In the city—as with grain, vegetables, fruit, meat, and other pantry items—water could only be acquired with cash. The possibility of gathering wood lasted longer, but quickly fuel too became an item that most urban people had to purchase.

In Mombasa, the commodification of cooking fuel was an uneven process. During the first half of the twentieth century, large portions of the island and surrounding mainland remained covered in vegetation, and people could find firewood there. Nonetheless, the busy schedule of wage labor prevented many from collecting fuel, so by no later than the 1930s, working people regularly had to buy it, and it became a significant expense. Muriuki Kathungu, who did road construction work for the municipality in 1939 and made Shs. 21/- per month, spent around 40 percent of his income on food and an additional 10 percent on the firewood to cook it.[101] During the 1940s, the "great majority" of Africans purchased their fuel, the "split mangrove firewood of the kind commonly offered for sale in the native locations."[102] That same decade, wartime pressures made firewood increasingly expensive, and its price rose by as much as 300 percent. Even with wage increases, people at the bottom of the pay scale spent more than 20 percent of their income on it.[103] However, city residents able to collect firewood in those areas of the city not yet built over could mitigate these costs; this labor tended to be done by women. For example, in Mbaraki on the southern part of the island, residents were able to "supply their needs . . . from an adjoining mangrove swamp which [was] . . . being cleared . . . by a worker's wife." Another option was to gather wood on the more rural mainland, but this involved additional time, as for one woman who "spent a large part of the day [there] and returned with a bundle of bushwood."[104]

By the end of the 1950s, the environmental and economic context of the urban cooking fire had changed, as two factors finished the process of commercializing domestic fuel consumption. Expanding urbanism in Mombasa decreased the amount of firewood that individual families could gather at the same time that new fuel supplies began pouring into the city, depressing prices. Charcoal and paraffin oil became more widely available during the 1950s and started to replace wood in African kitchens. As late as 1947, firewood had been reported as the main fuel in working-class households, and "charcoal [was] not much used by Africans in Mombasa." By 1951, though, charcoal use was increasing, with an official noting that numerous charcoal dealers were selling a "large proportion" of their supply to "Africans in open spaces and markets."[105] Around that same time, the district commissioner also observed that "many Africans use[d] oil burning stoves for cooking. Many others use[d] Charcoal by the bag-lot." At the prices offered, he concluded, "Charcoal was not [as] . . . important [a] commodity in the African cost of living as it used to be."[106] Later in the decade, even Africans living in Kongowea on the north mainland, where they would have had more access to gather firewood than on the island, mostly used oil or charcoal for cooking.[107] By 1959, a mass market for charcoal had been established, with 116 charcoal sellers counted by the municipality that year.[108]

Thus, the commodification of cooking fuel was an extended process in colonial Mombasa, one not complete until the end of the 1950s. However, during those decades, water was a daily necessity that always had to be purchased. The question of Mombasa's water supply, as Justin Willis has argued, was an immediate and existential issue for the British as they took control in East Africa at the end of the nineteenth century. Before 1900, the comparatively smaller population of people who lived on the island, varying between 10,000 and 19,000, could consistently rely on water drawn from aquifers in the coral rock beneath the surface. However, with British rule, increased industrial activities from the railway and port placed unsustainable stress on the island's aquifers, and it became evident that any further expansion of commercial shipping in the city required developing a new and larger source for municipal water supplies. Given that Mombasa was meant to be the gateway that connected Britain's protectorates in Kenya and Uganda to the global economy, this raised the stakes of the city's water supply to an imperial concern. In this context, a loan of £90,000 was allocated to build a pipeline to bring water from the nearby Shimba Hills to the island. During the 1910s, local and migrant workers spent years building the fifteen-mile pipeline, and by 1918 a new supply of water began to reach customers in the city.[109]

Therefore, starting in the late 1910s, the island had a state-run system that brought water to fee-paying users. However, it was not piped directly into the homes of working-class Africans. Instead, the municipality created centralized kiosks where individual consumers could purchase water in four-gallon jugs (called *debbies* or *jerrycans*). By 1945, there were thirty-four such water kiosks in the city, which were open every day from 6:30 to 11:00 a.m. and then 2:00 to 5:30 p.m. Such a schedule created obvious challenges, given that the kiosks were open mostly when people had to work, an issue exacerbated by the fact that municipal water attendants often closed them early. Mombasa's working class labored for long hours in physically demanding jobs, and the prospect of squeezing in time to carry two to three four-gallon jugs of water home from the kiosk each day was, understandably, not particularly attractive. In such circumstances, new businesses emerged to mitigate these inconveniences. Water carriers, usually Arab or African men, offered a home delivery service, standing in line at the kiosk and then hauling the daily supply of water to their customers. This convenience came at a cost, though. The municipality charged one cent per *debbie* at the municipal kiosk, and people who arranged daily deliveries, usually on a monthly contract, paid five cents per jug. Despite the premium price charged by water carriers, many people found ways to fit this service into their tight budgets, an indication of how much they valued not having to haul their own water.[110] James Miruka, who lived in Mombasa during the 1950s and 1960s, remembered seeing these vendors walking throughout the town with a wooden pole over their shoulder, balancing a bucket of water on each end.[111] Indeed, paying for water delivery was common enough that if someone had to carry their own it signified a comparative level of poverty. As observed in 1947, "for reasons of prestige it [was] considered more desirable to make use of a carrier," as this was "taken as a sign of social standing to be able to do so."[112]

Water and fuel were not necessary for the consumption of all foods in modern Mombasa. As we have seen, in this tropical city, fresh fruits were widely available for sale, both in city markets and from the hawkers who worked along the streets. These certainly provided welcome snacks, while bananas could even serve as a more filling meal when needed. However, most foods, such as grilled meat and fried fish, needed at least fuel, while the staple grains of maize meal, rice, and wheat flour required both heat and water. In the urban and commodified environment of the city, by the middle of the twentieth century, these resources could not be gathered. They had to be purchased.

* * *

Consumption in a market economy offers seductive possibilities. The potential to have individualized control over how you dress, the home in which you live, the popular culture that entertains you, and the food that you eat presents the opportunity to self-fashion your identity through commodities, a defining feature of modern capitalism.[113] Indeed, migrants in Mombasa were eager to escape the stifling uniformity that rationing imposed on their diets during the first decades of the twentieth century. From maduka and city markets to roadside traders, the city offered a multitude of choices for people with money to spend. Today, consumer possibilities for food have expanded still further in Mombasa. The maduka and vendors are still there, and they have been joined by large supermarkets like Naivas and Carrefour, which are connected to regional and global supply chains that offer unparalleled purchasing options to consumers. In Kenya's port city, there has come to be an extraordinary variety of foods available for people to buy.

But along with providing choice and variety, capitalism also constrains and places limits. Despite having many options available, low-income workers in Kenya's port town still largely ate the "posho standard" as they had during the rationing era, because they could not afford to buy much beyond these dense carbohydrates. The freedom to choose under capitalism, in Mombasa as elsewhere, only went as far as the cash or credit a person could access. The ingenuity of people to create survival strategies in these economic circumstances is admirable. However, such strategies also underline how economically insecure African migrants were in Mombasa's racialized social structure. Credit allowed people to acquire food their wages could not buy, but this also tied them to a single duka through accumulated debt that became nearly impossible to escape at their income level. Taking on roommates lowered rent and freed up money for food, but this also meant that people lived in crowded rooms that reduced personal comfort and made sanitation difficult. Mombasa, already a dynamic port town in 1900, grew into a large city during the twentieth century filled with shops, markets, and eateries that catered to a wide variety of tastes. However, the opportunity to benefit from these resources was determined by one's place within the city's gendered and racial class structure. This chapter has focused on how working people managed to acquire raw ingredients to cook at home in this political economy. The next one considers how urban capitalism created a vast array of eateries where people could buy prepared food, especially when they left their home and went to work.

3 ~ Mealtimes and Modern Urbanism

Kitchen Labor and the Working Day in a Capitalist City

WORK AT the docks started early, by 7 a.m. While temperatures in Mombasa were lower during morning hours, heavy humidity usually awaited people when they arrived at work, adding immediate strain to the hard labor of a busy port. Whatever food they had eaten before arrival, perhaps fried snacks or sliced bread, these calories burned fast as workers loaded and unloaded cargo from docked ships. At noon, five hours in, the lunch break began.[1] During the early 1950s, dock workers did not have to look far for a warm meal. Just beyond the gates to the port stood at least sixty street-food vendors operating small eateries under shady trees.[2] A short distance from there, cargo also circulated through nearby "godown" storage facilities and Mombasa's train station, the terminus of the Uganda Railway, where many other workers also emerged hungry and looking for a meal around midday. While commodity transport dominated the economy and employment, large numbers of people also worked for oil companies, breweries, and small manufacturers located in this fast-growing industrial district on the western side of Mombasa Island. In total, more than half of the city's wage earners worked in the neighborhood, creating the largest consumer market for lunch food in the city.[3] That's why vendors like Musomi Ndonyo, a migrant from Ukambani, chose to set up a business there. Indeed, Ndonyo had found a good spot. Workers from almost any employer in the industrial quarter would be able to fit the short walk to his food cart, centrally located opposite the railway station, into their lunch break or could choose from the "over 30 unlicensed food vendors" nearby who "operate[d] in front of the E.A. Mercantile Co[mpany]." Street eateries like these were concentrated in the industrial area, but many others were "scattered in and around Mombasa." Each day, these small businesses provided the city's tens of thousands of workers their lunch. After eating, their customers returned to work for the rest of the day.[4]

This lunchtime routine was a marked change from how food fit into the working day of Kenya's agrarian societies. In rural areas, people regularly traveled far from home to work in their fields or tend to livestock, which made it impracticable to return to their residence for lunch. Therefore, midday eating was closer to a snack than a meal, as people ate whatever they could carry with them or gather from the surrounding environment. Breakfast and dinner, occurring before and after work, were the main meals. Lunch was rare. In the city, though, the midday meal became part of the regular routine. People in Mombasa also worked far from their residential kitchen, as the spatial growth of the city led to long commutes for many in the working class. However, the economic geography of urban capitalism made regular lunch breaks possible. Neighborhoods like Mombasa Island's industrial district—crowded with dense concentrations of workers handling cargo, servicing trains, brewing beer, and manufacturing other commodities—generated unparalleled demand for prepared food, which meant that people like Ndonyo were strongly incentivized to open street-food businesses there. People working on their rural farms also liked having a filling meal at midday, but they could only do this when their work happened to keep them close to home, which it often did not. By contrast, in Mombasa, the existence of dozens of street-food vendors a short walk from the worksite meant that people could choose to have lunch every day, assuming they had the money to spend. This cemented lunch into the routine of the urban working class.[5] In turn, by bridging morning to afternoon with a filling meal, returning customers to their jobs with their hunger satiated, these vendors also became essential to the reproduction of the long working day of urban capitalism.

Before and after work in Mombasa, though, people were back at home in their residential neighborhoods where they had access to their domestic kitchen. In the rural communities that migrants had left, breakfast and dinner were almost always consumed within the household, and they typically ate food prepared by mothers and wives or occasionally other female relatives. However, in Kenya's port town, these morning and evening meals reflected the structure of migrant communities and the commercial economy of the city. As in the countryside, if women lived in the home, then they prepared breakfast and dinner for their family and often extended kin as well, but the nearby accessibility and cheap prices of street food also meant they could reduce the work they had to do in the kitchen. As with busy working-class communities elsewhere in the world, domestic cooks in Mombasa saved time by purchasing precooked food from vendors, bringing it home to supplement what they were preparing in their own kitchen.[6] Women cooked much of this food inside working-class households, but even though conjugal homes with husbands, wives, and children were increasing in number, many men in Mombasa still lived with only male friends and relatives. As in the early-colonial period, they made "pragmatic adjustments" in the domestic division of labor, temporarily taking on work gendered as female.[7]

When living with men of a similar age and income, male housemates shared the responsibilities of cooking and cleaning. However, economic and generational differences also structured the division of labor in all-male homes, a trend that increased over time. Before the late-colonial era, as Frederick Cooper has shown, African wage rates were low across the spectrum of available employment, and few jobs offered salary scales in which pay increased with seniority. From people new to migrant labor to those with experience, at work and inside their homes, African workers were made poor in relatively equal measure by the wage system of colonial capitalism. Labor stabilization at midcentury, though, created more access for Africans to higher-paid work and introduced salary scales. The people who acquired these jobs, whether at the port, railway, or other government and private employers, earned much higher wages and had benefits, but these positions became harder to get over the decades. In Mombasa as well as Africa more widely, this created what Cooper has called "islands of labor reform," where an increasingly small percentage of urban residents had secure and comparatively well-remunerated jobs, while the larger majority tried to survive off precarious forms of work, both waged and informal.[8] Lisa Lindsay, studying this period of labor history in Nigeria, has shown how these jobs and the households they allowed men to build became part of how new working-class masculinities formed.[9] Indeed, in Mombasa, men with stabilized employment used their steady wages, benefits, and access to planned housing to create larger households in the city. In these homes, whether living with male dependents or their wives, as higher-earning men, they did not have to cook.

For breakfast and dinner, though, many people also just ate out. Commuters on their way to work could pick up hot tea with a freshly fried snack, while on their way home they would likely pass numerous street-food vendors, often offering dishes from both coastal and up-country cuisines on the same menu. Typically, diners at these roadside eateries were men who did not live with women and were willing to pay for the convenience of having someone else cook and clean, while street food also provided access to dishes that many of them could not prepare at home. Single working-class men, therefore, relied on street food as a way to save time in their busy schedules, many balancing not only a long shift but also a considerable commute. Married men sometimes ate street food for these same reasons, but only those whose wives did not live permanently in Mombasa. This was a common experience. In Kenya and Africa more broadly, working-class families were often both urban and rural, with men usually settling more permanently into cities while women moved between town and country. Women tended to spend more time in rural areas, where they worked the family fields and cared for children and other dependent relatives, coming to Mombasa only for periodic visits.[10] When in town, women regularly prepared meals at home, but when they left, their husbands often returned to being regulars at their favorite street-food eateries.

By the middle of the twentieth century, therefore, new patterns in the mealtime routines of Mombasa's working class were emerging. In the rural communities where migrants lived before they came to the city, ideas about gender and the demands of the working day also shaped when and what people ate, as well as how their food was prepared. However, agrarian economies and the spatial dynamics of rural life created rather different mealtime routines. To better understand the changes that migrants experienced in midcentury Mombasa, we will start this chapter by shifting our attention away from the coast and toward the rural areas of up-country Kenya.

MEALTIMES AND CUISINE IN RURAL KENYA AT MIDCENTURY

Hunger is universal, but the daily routine of eating is determined by the contingencies of history. In rural Kenya during the twentieth century, ideas about gender, as well as the geography of agricultural work, created a culture of cooking and eating in which breakfast and dinner were the most important meals. In these communities, women had the first work in the morning, preparing foods rich in carbohydrates and protein for themselves and their households in anticipation of the coming hours of agricultural labor. Breakfast cuisine was rather similar across rural eastern, central, and western Kenya. As discussed in chapter 1, the beverages made from grains (e.g., *usu* and *uchuru,* also commonly called *uji* in Kiswahili and English) still outpaced tea in rural diets, which people consumed in the morning with root vegetables (especially sweet potatoes and cassava) or *githeri,* the common staple made with whole maize kernels and beans.[11] Breakfast needed to be quite filling not only because rural communities faced a day of physical labor but also because of the distance that people had to travel for their work. Women and men went to tend crops in fields, only some of which were close by, and adult men and male children often herded livestock quite far from where they lived. At midday, therefore, many found they had been pulled away from their household kitchens.[12]

A filling breakfast could sustain people for a good portion of the day, but appetites returned before the work was done, and the solution for many was to carry food with them. Being on the move, their cuisine during the working day was shaped by practicality. Chapter 1 discussed how the calabash gourd, if dried, hollowed-out, and cut in half, made an effective serving dish. Kept whole, it was a useful receptacle for carrying liquid. Walking to fields or alongside livestock, people brought the uji that mothers and sisters had prepared at home with them to work, a beverage that was both filling and refreshing at the same time.[13] Joseph Mwangi, who grew up in rural Central Province during the middle of the twentieth century, explained that because uji was both food and beverage he did not even take water with him.[14] Others carried out uncooked vegetables like sweet potatoes, which were portable, hard to damage, and made for a hearty snack. They turned these raw ingredients into something more consumable by roasting them in small, improvised fires when it was time to eat.[15] These farmers and herders could also draw food from the natural environments where they worked. Vitalis Owiti, who grew up in a rural part of Kisumu District at midcentury, gathered fruits and berries, such as sweet and fleshy guavas and tart conkerberries, as he tended cattle. Owiti, though, did not leave his workday snacks entirely to chance, as he also spread seeds along the herding routes to enrich what he could gather in the future.[16]

The geography of a family's fields and grazing lands also determined the extent to which lunch took this mobile form. Some people were able to work closer to home and so could return to household kitchens for a midday meal. People working in nearby fields were able to simply put down their tools and walk back for lunch, but coming home for a meal for those herding livestock was more complicated because cattle and goats grazing outside their pens needed constant supervision. The men, therefore, returned home in rotations, eating lunch and then heading back out to relieve the next group that would go in for some food.[17] Rural lunches were also seasonal, not simply in ingredients but also in the setting. Sampson Kereu, who grew up in Central Province during the 1940s and 1950s, spent his days herding cattle and helping with cultivation on the farm. He explained that when sweet potatoes were ripe in the fields, they would just pull them up and then, as he said, "We roast them. We eat them." However, as harvest season passed, this was no longer possible, and they would instead return home for a lunch prepared by his mother.[18]

Midday meals, therefore, were contingent in form, taking place in homes, fields, or wherever hunger struck while moving livestock across the terrain. There were also no dishes that people considered to be quintessentially "lunch food." Breakfast foods like sweet potatoes and uji were eaten liberally at midday, while people able to return home for lunch often had githeri. In contrast, the evening meal, back at home, was more consistent and formalized in routine, though there also were not hard distinctions between lunch and dinner food. For example, by the mid-twentieth century, *ugali* was firmly established as the key staple of the Luo in rural areas, being eaten at lunch and dinner. Gregory Osollo Omondi, who lived in Siaya during the 1950s and 1960s, simply stated, "The food of the Luo is ugali."[19] Moreover, while in Central Kenya white maize was pushing alternative grains out of the local cuisine, in rural Nyanza Province millet remained a quite common ingredient in the ugali that people regularly ate for lunch and dinner.[20] This point is illustrated by the experience of Joseph Mariko Agwari, whose family was from Bondo in western Kenya but who was born and grew up in Nairobi. "I lived in town, town, town," he emphasized to me. In the city, ugali was so central to his eating routine that he joked, "I can't go two days without [it]." As in Mombasa, it was always prepared with maize. However, when his mother returned to Nairobi from trips to their rural area in Bondo, she would come back to the city with millet, and they would make ugali with it until the supply ran out, after which they would switch back to the regular maize meal.[21]

Therefore, ugali—made from maize, millet, and sometimes both—was served at lunch and dinner in midcentury Nyanza. However, despite its ubiquity in western Kenya and among urban populations generally, this dish continued to be rare in the agrarian foodways of the Kikuyu and Kamba. The contemporary observers who noted how white maize was taking the place of millet in Kikuyu diets were writing about the ingredients of uji, not ugali, as the latter dish was not consumed with any regularity by either community. Joseph Mwangi, who grew up during this period just south of Mount Kenya, told me that before independence "there was no ugali."[22] Indeed, given the prominence of ugali elsewhere, the author of a 1945 survey of South Nyeri in Central Province seemingly expected to find ugali but did not, writing that "it may have [in the past] been a commoner article of diet than today" (though, as discussed in chapter 1, there is no evidence that it ever was). Instead, he found *irio,* the same mainstay staple that had been at the center of Kikuyu cuisine at the start of the century, the "normal" dish made from "a mixture of maize, bananas, beans and leafy vegetables."[23] Though irio remained the primary dinnertime staple, its components were changing as a consequence of land alienation and the extension of commercial agriculture over more of Central Kenya. English potatoes, a cash crop that local people began to eat too, became an alternative to bananas for the mash at the base of irio. Moreover, the greens that women usually mixed into their irio were becoming scarcer over time. These green leaves had been harvested from plants they cultivated, especially black-eyed peas, and were gathered from the forest, often from amaranth plants, both wild and intentionally seeded. By midcentury, though, black-eyed peas were being pushed out of fields to make way for other cash crops, while more-extensive cultivation reduced forest size and thus the opportunity to gather wild greens.[24]

Thus, changes in agriculture and the ownership of land were leading to less nutritious diets in Central Kenya. The Kamba, farther east in a more arid climate with less rich soil, also saw diminishing variety in their rural cuisine.[25] Maize, as the kernels in githeri and the main ingredient in uji, had become the primary crop that sustained Kamba communities. In 1965, Judith Hayer, based on fieldwork in Ukambani, observed that though Kamba cuisine "used to be based on millet, . . . over the last 50 years maize [had] completely superseded this as the preferred basic food." She also noted that "maize . . . form[ed] the bulk of the Kamba diet, with pulses when available too."[26] This suggests that the isio (or githeri) that people ate at breakfast, lunch, and dinner was changing as well, leaning heavily on maize and less reliant on beans.[27] Maize was thus likely becoming a higher proportion of this staple (a mixture of the two crops) that played such a central role in Kamba diets. Therefore, besides the addition of an occasional cup of tea, the broad outlines of Kamba and Kikuyu cuisines had not changed dramatically since the beginning of the twentieth century, but the underlying ingredients had. Maize was replacing millet in uji; irio had more potatoes and fewer greens and bananas; while the beans that balanced out githeri had become less common in Kamba fields.

From the 1930s to the 1970s, people left these communities to migrate to East Africa's cities in unprecedented numbers, leading to a rapid process of urbanization in places like Mombasa. In their rural communities, local agriculture and the geography of the working day shaped their cuisine and the routines of eating. In Mombasa, foodways and mealtimes were also tied to the structure of work and space, but within the rather different political economy of urban capitalism.

MEALTIMES, STREET FOOD, AND THE WORKING DAY

During the early-colonial period, working-class people in Mombasa had little incentive to eat meals outside their homes. Chapter 1 shows how labor migrants during that time received a portion of their wages as a ration of raw foodstuffs, called *posho.* Living on tight margins with limited cash earnings, they would have been reluctant to spend additional money to eat out when they could cook the food they already had. Mombasa was also still a rather compact urban space during the first decades of the twentieth century. People often worked relatively close to their residence, which, whether they received rations or not, meant they could return to their domestic kitchen during the lunch hour to prepare, or be served, a midday meal. For most people, then, having a meal at an eatery was a choice they made, either for convenience or to try food they could not easily prepare at home. Businesses did exist that sold such cooked food to Mombasa's poorer communities during the early part of the century, but not on a large scale.[28] This included, for example, a vendor an official observed in 1919 who "cooked Mahindi [maize], Mohogo [*sic,* cassava], etc. . . . under the Mango trees" in the island neighborhood of Mwembe Tayari.[29] Vending offered a living especially to coastal women who were excluded from most waged jobs other than as domestic workers, while men did not have the same inducement to go into informal trades like street food, as labor scarcity created strong demand for their work in a gendered system of formal employment.[30] These roadside businesses, therefore, provided income for some and quick, cheap food for others, but they had not yet become an essential component in the reproduction of the working day.

The number of street-food eateries, though, steadily increased over the coming decades, especially from the 1930s onward. When posho rationing ended, this not only created demand for raw ingredients at *maduka,* city markets, and from street traders but also meant that working people could spend a larger proportion of their cash at eateries. The size of this new consumer class was growing rapidly. From 1930 to 1962, the number of Africans living in the city increased from 34,000 to 110,000, and most of them were in the laboring classes.[31] Population growth also transformed the city's geography in ways that made eateries more necessary. With tens of thousands of additional people living in Mombasa, the spatial scale of the port town extended outward. New African residential neighborhoods emerged on Mombasa Island farther from the industrial district, and working-class suburbs including Changamwe, Kisauni, and Likoni also grew on the mainland.[32] With longer distances between home and work, Kenya's port town became a city of commuters. Writing about the north mainland suburb of Kisauni in 1958, colonial sociologist G. M. Wilson described it as "one of the major African dormitory areas of Mombasa," whose residents "work[ed] mostly on the Island."[33] These commutes pulled people away from their residential kitchens, which expanded the market for cooked food in the middle of the day. In the dense consumer markets of a city, people were able to turn to a fast-growing new industry of working-class eateries.

This quantitative growth of a new consumer class, as well as the spatial expansion of the city, created demand. Structural transformations in Mombasa's political economy also increased the number of people looking to informal work like street food as a way to make a living. By the 1930s, the scarce labor markets of the early-colonial period were over, and underemployment and unemployment became lasting features of Mombasa's economy. By 1959, a government estimate reported that between 6,000 and 8,000 people were officially "unemployed" in the city.[34] Such statistics also referred mostly to men and did not include the tens of thousands of women who were de facto excluded from most wage-earning work. From the 1930s onward, there was a gap in Mombasa's economy between the number of people looking to earn cash incomes and the availability of "formal" wage-labor jobs. In 1964, A. H. B. Rydon, a municipal public health official, explained how the stagnant labor market pushed people to work in informal industries like street food, with many starting these businesses because of "the acute unemployment situation" in the city, seen in the "ever increasing numbers of unauthorised foodvendors" who were "plying their illegal trade . . . in open spaces or by the roadside."[35] These dynamics driving informalization were also part of Kenya's economy more broadly. Gavin Kitching has shown how wage-sector employment across Kenya in the postwar era fell proportionally (and at times in absolute terms) when compared to population growth. He estimates that between 1948 and 1969 the adult male population increased by 84.5 percent while total formal-sector employment rose by only 39 percent, thus incentivizing people to look toward petty trade to earn income.[36] Indeed, during the 1970s, Nairobi served as one of the key case studies from which development scholars began to theorize the concept of the "informal sector."[37]

Men and women in Kenya's port town responded to this difficult and gendered labor market by opening small businesses officially in city markets and often unofficially on sidewalks, in road reserves off the side of a street, in parks, in alleyways, or in any other viable spot they could claim. Street food was one of these options. Because many of these eateries were run illicitly, quantitative data gathered from government archives capture only a portion of the people who sold prepared food to Mombasa's working-class majority. These sources indicate that between 1948 and 1973, no fewer than 555 different people ran street-food eateries in Mombasa, while a 1965 survey, which did make an effort to count unlicensed vendors, found 185 of these businesses on the island during that year alone.[38] Qualitatively, descriptions throughout the archive and in oral interviews make clear that these eateries had become a key part of the city's working-class food system by the middle of the twentieth century.[39]

This rapid expansion of street-food eateries during this period also changed the demographics of the industry. In the colonial period, people from Arab, Swahili, and Mijikenda communities played a leading role in these businesses.[40] However, as migration to Mombasa from up-country increased steadily during the colonial era and the decades that followed, women and men from Ukambani, Nyanza Province, Central Province, and elsewhere in the interior came to represent a large proportion of the city's street-food vendors.[41] The industry also became a profession of migrants more generally, including from the rural coast. By 1965, 87 percent of the food vendors working on Mombasa Island were recent migrants, with a median time of seven years spent in the city; many of them chose this business quickly upon moving to Mombasa, perhaps as the realities of the wage-labor job market became apparent. Of these migrant operators, 30 percent had started an eatery within one year of coming in the city, while 44 percent had begun operations within two years.[42] Street food became a way for migrants to earn income in the port town's challenging urban economy, as they were unable to find waged employment or the job they had did not pay enough. Indeed, as vendor Nzalu Ngotho told me, he started his business during the 1960s to supplement his income as a painter for the railway, juggling both formal and informal work.[43]

By the middle decades of the twentieth century, then, these street-food eateries provided essential services to Mombasa's working class, as well as income to people who were not finding adequate opportunity in the wage-labor economy. The following three subsections explore the structure of these businesses and how they fit into and shaped the mealtime routines of working people. Household cooks, both women and men, prepared much of the food that people ate in the city, but urban life also meant that, for those willing and able to pay, there were vendors ready to sell them an inexpensive snack or prepared meal, usually only a short walk from home or work.

The street-food industry, therefore, grew in conjunction with a spatially and demographically expanding city. The petty entrepreneurs running these businesses adapted their eateries to the daily routines of people working in this urban capitalist society. As in the countryside, Mombasa residents needed dense and filling calories in the morning to prepare them for a day of manual labor, except rather than walking to fields and grazing lands they commuted to docks, small factories, retail shops, or a site where they planned to trade for the day. As people awoke in crowded rooms in Majengo and other working-class neighborhoods, the nature of their household often shaped whether they ate breakfast at home or purchased it from a vendor on their way to work. As in rural areas, if women were in urban homes, their first work of the day was to prepare breakfast for their families, though often the cooking process was somewhat simpler in the city. Rather than consisting of multiple dishes prepared from scratch, the morning meal in migrant households was often just a milky and sweet tea with sliced bread. For these women, and the men who lived with their wives, breakfast was therefore mostly a meal eaten at home. The men who lived in all-male households, though, had a different calculation, as the work of starting a cooking fire, minding the tea as it boiled, and then washing the dishes was theirs. Many men and women did start their days this way.[44] However, facing a commute and then a long day at work, people could also choose to pay someone else to cook and clean for them.

Buying prepared food in the morning offered not only relief from kitchen labor but also the opportunity to enjoy the novel flavors of a cosmopolitan urban cuisine. Among the essential morning meals of Mombasa's working class, during the colonial period and the decades that followed, was *chai,* a milky and sugary tea, with *mahamri,* a square doughnut of fried dough made from wheat flour, yeast, sugar, coconut milk, and cardamom. Another widely available breakfast snack was the considerably sweeter *kaimati,* a similarly prepared dough that was formed into a smaller ball, fried, and then saturated with syrup. Those looking for something more savory could order *chapati,* the East African version of the South Asian wheat-flour flat bread, or they could have slices of packaged bread. In rural homes, morning meals were dominated by milled maize or millet in the form of uji, sometimes complemented by sweet potatoes or githeri.[45] In Mombasa, wheat flour prepared into sliced, flat, and deep-fried breads became the main form of breakfast food, all of which was washed down with sweet and creamy tea.

During the morning, these prepared foods were widely available at stalls in city markets and from vendors on Mombasa's streets, the latter including businesses called *gari ya chai* (tea carts), mostly run by Arab and African men.[46] As the name suggests, these tea vendors worked from hand-pulled wooden carts. Some were minimalist: a basic cart packed with food items and a stove to cook the tea. However, other vendors constructed awnings onto their cart, offering shade from the sun or shelter from Mombasa's frequent rains. Other gari ya chai were attached to maduka, extending a "brick-and-mortar" business out onto the street. Rather than having to renovate and relicense the *duka* into a fully authorized restaurant, a shop could simply add a small cart outside and start selling tea and prepared food, which many did.[47] Some tea vendors dispensed with the cart entirely and ambitiously built more-permanent structures. In 1960, for example, Maganga Kashere operated from a "structure made of canvas . . . supported on poles," while a different tea vendor, Machogo Ogola, had a "tin shed" that he "used as a restaurant."[48] Another tea stand was in a "temporary building" composed of "one room divided by a cardboard partition."[49] From such makeshift structures, city markets, and individual carts or those positioned in front of a duka, Mombasa residents at midcentury could easily find a vendor looking to sell them breakfast during their morning commute. In N. M. Deverell's 1947 survey of working-class communities in the city, she described a typical morning routine: "Men have been observed buying mahamri, mofa [*mkate wa mofa,* a less common flatbread based on the Somali *muufo*] and chapatti on their way to work from hawkers in the Makupa Market and Mwembe Tayari. It seems usual to buy two of each and consume them on the way. Some Africans have been seen asking their friends to spare them a piece of their mofa, &c. and so manage to breakfast free."[50]

The prepared breakfast trade, though, was more than these public-facing street-food eateries, and it was organized in ways that were reflective of gendered cultures both urban and rural. Gari ya chai, as stated above, were mostly run by Arab and African men. Between 1948 and 1972, for example, only 7 of the 340 tea vendors who appear in municipal records were women, approximately 2 percent.[51] However, neither Arab men from the city nor African migrants from up-country came from communities where they learned how to cook. Of the breakfast foods they sold, the only item they consistently prepared themselves was chai, which had a relatively simple preparation that required only mixing, boiling, and straining the basic ingredients. These vendors purchased much of the rest of their menu wholesale from Arab (and likely also Swahili) women who prepared mahamri, kaimati, chapati, and mkate wa mofa inside their home kitchens. These women, therefore, were able to commodify the skills they had learned for domestic cooking, while also balancing income generation with other household work.[52] Deverell's 1947 study of working-class Mombasa described such an Arab family living in a four-room house in Majengo where the women (all unnamed) "work[ed] hard preparing food for sale." The mother cooked mahamri every day, a process that began in the evenings around 8 p.m. when she prepared a batch of dough that would proof overnight. The next morning, she fried the individual mahamri, some of which were consumed by her family while the rest were sold at a duka on commission, the shop keeping 12 percent while she took the rest. Her sister-in-law in the same home specialized in kaimati, prepared at considerable scale. Each day, she went through five pounds of flour to make two batches for a total of approximately three hundred kaimati, likewise sold on commission at a duka. This business allowed these women to combine household and commodified labor, feeding their families and earning significant income. On the latter point, Deverell concluded that these "women contribute[d] largely to the family expenses."[53]

In addition to these fried snacks, another common breakfast item that women prepared inside their homes was *mbaazi,* pigeon peas cooked down in coconut milk, turmeric, and other flavorful ingredients.[54] The women doing this business, mostly Swahili and Mijikenda, could also combine domestic and commodified labor when preparing this dish for sale. For example, in the Bondeni area on the eastern side of the island during the late 1940s, an older Digo woman cooked and sold mbaazi. She also regularly had her grandson who lived in Majengo over to eat, and in the morning he often had a serving of the mbaazi she was preparing for her business.[55] Unlike mahamri and other such items, though, the mbaazi prepared by these women was sold directly to customers, likely because, as a sauce-heavy dish best served hot, it was not as portable or storable as fried bread. Therefore, these women's homes were effectively small eateries, selling food right out of their front door. This was James Miruka's memory of his west mainland neighborhood of Changamwe, where he lived during the 1950s. He explained that people "sold [mbaazi] right in front of their houses, and so you could buy it from them."[56]

Commuters regularly purchased these foods on the way to work, but people also had the option to pick up some mbaazi, mahamri, or other items and take them back to complement a breakfast being prepared at home. Indeed, Margaret Auma Ndolo, who lived in railway housing with her husband during the mid-1960s, cooked breakfast each morning, including chapati, but on occasion she purchased mbaazi from nearby Digo cooks and took it

FIGURE 3.1. From vendor Ali Masha, a selection of breakfast offerings lined up from left to right: a *sufuria* (pot) with beans, another with chapati, and a thermos of chai along with a mug for serving. Photograph by Onesmus Mutua, 2024.

back to the house. She was thus able to create the typical pairing of these pigeon peas stewed in aromatic coconut milk with chapati while saving herself considerable time in the kitchen.[57] Moreover, though sliced bread was an easy way at home to have something filling to dip into the morning tea, mahamri offered more flavor and variety. Thomas Mbeda, who lived on his own in Mombasa during the 1970s for four years before he got married, recalls that he made his own tea each morning in the house but often also took it with a mahamri he had purchased from a vendor. He explained, "I bought the mahamri. I can't cook those."[58]

Breakfast in midcentury Mombasa, therefore, was tied to the households where people woke up each morning. They began the day with the option to make a morning meal in their kitchen or to have it prepared for them. However, often not far from their residence, someone was selling chai, breads of various kinds, or mbaazi. Depending on their family situation, or their mood on a given morning, people could choose to have a morning meal at home, take their breakfast from a vendor, or combine these two together. However, once the morning meal was done, many of Mombasa's urban residents soon arrived at work, often far from their domestic kitchen, where they would remain for much of the rest of the day.

Mombasa's role as a port town shaped its geography of working-class employment. At the turn of the twentieth century, the western side of Mombasa Island became the most important site of commodity transport in all of East Africa, connecting the Uganda Railway and the new, fast-growing Kilindini Port. Over the coming decades, that part of the island transformed from countryside into an industrial quarter. Of all the people this pulled into the neighborhood each day, only some of them could reasonably return home during the lunch hour, while many more were effectively stuck there for the duration of their shift.[59] To stay at work for the entire day, from morning until late afternoon, they needed to pay someone to prepare their food.

By no later than 1929, petty entrepreneurs recognized the consumer market this created for midday meals and began setting up small eateries to cater to these wage earners. As one official noted that year, a "temporary market [was] held nearer the Port, about lunch-hour, where cooked foods [were] sold."[60] Demand for these services in this neighborhood continued to grow over the coming decades, which Abdul Kader bin Mohamed explained to city officials in 1953 when applying for a tea-cart license. He wanted to sell "tea and bread at the Rly [railway]" and elsewhere in the industrial quarter, such as High-Level, "where hundreds of workers, servants, labourers and coolies as well as others[,] . . . men and women[, were] working over there at . . . Coffee (curing)," along with those employed at "stores, godowns and warehouses [who] . . . are continually asking for food."[61] During the early 1950s, there were also many dozens and at times even over a hundred street-food eateries just outside the gate to the port that were selling "cheap and good food."[62] People researching dock workers later in the decade recognized the key role that such street-food vendors played during the working day. The large number of eateries close to the docks, they observed, provided "varying types of meals on the spot for the African workers"; among these vendors, "competition [was] keen, and prices ha[d] not . . . increased for many years. The portions [were] large, and the place [was] obviously popular with many of the men." Their report underlined the importance of these food vendors for mainland commuters unable to "get home and back in an hour" during their break, but, as they could buy food close by, Africans did "not, as a rule, leave the Port area for a midday meal."[63]

Around the same time, three officials from the municipal government—Lance Jones, David Ikumi, and George G. Madumadu—conducted a brief survey of street-food vendors in Mombasa. Focusing on the industrial district beyond the port, including the subneighborhoods of High-Level, the

Station, and Mbaraki, they saw many gari ya chai vendors operating close to major employers like the railway and godowns, along with more than thirty food vendors in High-Level. They noted too how there were street eateries in elsewhere in the city, "in various parts of Mombasa" such as the "well known hawker" who was "stationed under a Baobab tree near the New Lady Grigg Hospital." Jones, Ikumi, and Madumadu also underlined how these businesses both provided income to vendors and kept workers fed in a fast-growing city, writing that "this trade is profitable to the hawkers and is of great service to the customers."[64] Though these three officials were writing in the late 1950s, their observations still corresponded to the experiences of Mohamed Amir Temu, who began living in the city during the 1970s. A migrant from Moshi, Tanzania, who worked in construction, Temu ate street food for lunch every day. When asked why, he answered, "Because it was cheap. Because it was easy." Years later, tiring of construction work, he decided to a make a career change. He opened his own street-food eatery.[65]

After independence, the industrial district continued to hold the largest concentration of street-food vendors during the lunch hour. In 1965, more than half of Mombasa's street eateries were located there.[66] This was

FIGURE 3.2. The port at Kilindini Harbour during the first half of the twentieth century. The port was a major employer, and many workers from there ate at nearby street-food eateries. From the Herskovits Library of African Studies, Northwestern University Libraries, the Humphrey Winterton Collection of East African Photographs: 1860–1960.

partly because the steady growth of working-class neighborhoods on the mainland drove street food in the island's industrial areas, as this solidified Mombasa as a commuter city. Some people in these suburbs could stay in their neighborhoods for work, especially in the comparatively industrialized Changamwe, but these areas were largely residential spaces for people who commuted to the island, with many of them heading for the industrial district. These suburbs grew quickly in the years after independence. Between 1969 and 1974 alone, for example, one study estimated that the population of the north mainland increased from around 30,000 to 43,000 people and that 86 percent of those surveyed there during the early 1970s worked on the island. Indeed, every day a "special bus service [ran] during the rush hours from the . . . [north mainland] to the Islands industrial area."[67] Incentivized by this steady demand, vendors were drawn to open their businesses near the port, railway, and warehouses, as well as on other nearby streets. Jackson Nthuli, who arrived in Mombasa from Ukambani in 1972 and the same year began working for the Kenya Ports Authority (KPA), remembers eating effectively all his lunches from street-food vendors. He explained: "They were all near that KPA. Just come from the office, you get out of the gate. Then you pick, when you go from here to there, you choose whatever you want to eat. You sit down, you eat, and then you go back to work. . . . There were many."[68] Around the same time, David E. L. Angote, who also worked in the industrial district, told the *Daily Nation* newspaper, "I could say along Dar es Salaam Road [in the industrial area] there are about 400 labourers who depend entirely on the kiosks for their meals. . . . They cannot afford hotel [brick-and-mortar restaurants] meals, which range from 5/- for the cheapest."[69]

The street eateries that provisioned these lunchtime meals in midcentury Mombasa came in a variety of forms. As we have seen, gari ya chai vendors continued to operate their businesses during the lucrative lunch hour, but there were also larger establishments, like the ones positioned outside the gates of Kilindini Port, that served a more extensive menu. While many vendors like gari ya chai sold only a few items, these bigger eateries were restaurants, as individual diners chose their meals from a considerably longer list of options.[70] In Kiswahili, the word for "restaurant" is either *hoteli* or *mikahawa,* but those on the street have often been referred to as *vibanda* (*kibanda,* sing.), which means "shed," taking their name from the small, improvised structures where they operated. In a similar linguistic pattern, street eateries were also called *vioski* (*kioski,* sing.), drawn from the English word *kiosk.*[71] During the middle of the twentieth century, these vibanda, with more-diverse and complex menus, were run mostly by women. As with the women who prepared fried breads and mbaazi in their homes, these street vendors were able to draw on their training as household cooks to prepare a variety of dishes, both ones they already knew and in learning new recipes.[72]

Indeed, the food offered to lunchtime diners in these street eateries drew from both coastal and up-country cuisines. Many vibanda opened in the morning and sold similar fare as gari ya chai vendors, then carried these menu items over to lunch. This meant that chapati was a common lunchtime staple, while rice and githeri were added to the midday menu. That githeri was available mostly at lunch signaled a change in how this dish was rendered in relation to time in urban cuisine. Eaten widely during the morning throughout up-country rural areas, in Mombasa, tea, fried snacks, and beans in the form of mbaazi crowded githeri off breakfast tables, both inside households and at street vendors. A flexible dish eaten at any time in the countryside, githeri was becoming lunch (and dinner) food in the city, while chapati became the urban staple that one could find from morning until evening. Lunch-hour vendors also offered numerous relishes to complement chapati, as well as rice (githeri stands on its own). These included fried fish as well as braised meats, such as *matumbo,* a tripe stew. Customers also paired their starches with vegetables, like pan-fried cabbage and *ndengu,* green grams (mung beans) stewed with tomatoes and aromatic spices. However, no vegetable dish became more common in urban Kenya than *sikuma wiki,* which translates to "push" or "stretch the week," cooked-down green leaves that have served as a regular and inexpensive relish. Thus, meat and leafy greens had something in common in Mombasa. The last chapter showed that as meat consumption declined in rural areas, it increased dramatically in the city. Similarly, as it became harder for rural Kikuyu women to find greens to add to irio, those in Mombasa could count on sikuma wiki being on the menu of a kibanda.[73]

As these street-food eateries developed, though, some notable dishes took more time to appear consistently on their menus. For example, *pilau* and *biryani,* two Indian Ocean aromatic rice dishes regularly consumed on the East African coast, seem to have mostly been available only at brick-and-mortar restaurants during the colonial period, but by the final decades of the twentieth century they were regularly on offer at street eateries.[74] Pilau is like githeri and irio in that it stands alone as a starch that does not require an accompanying relish. Everything is combined together as rice is cooked down with meat, potatoes, and spices, including fragrant cardamom and cloves, and is then served with a banana on the plate. Biryani fits more neatly into the starch-and-relish framework theorized by Sidney Mintz, as it consists of meat—goat, beef, or chicken—braised in a spice-infused tomato sauce that is then placed on top of rice.[75] These latter two dishes, filled with meat and spices, and requiring considerable labor and skill to complete, were the most expensive items at street-food eateries. For example, during the 1980s, two chapati cost 60 cents and could be paired with an inexpensive relish, like sikuma wiki, for a cheap meal. Plain white rice was nearly double the cost at 1 shilling (Shs.), but pilau was Shs. 1/50, while biryani with beef or goat was Shs. 2/-. With chicken, the price was Shs. 3/-.[76]

Kenya's most famous dish and the main staple of the migrant working class, ugali, was also not consistently on the menus of street-food vendors during the colonial era. Instead, people ate it at home.[77] A definitive conclusion as to why ugali stayed in domestic kitchens during the colonial period is not possible with the available evidence, but one hypothesis can be suggested. Part of the appeal of ugali over the twentieth century has been the simplicity and speed of its preparation, especially for men at home who were not trained in cooking. There is effectively no prep time for ugali beyond combining the ingredients into a pot, and the small granules of milled maize rehydrate rather quickly in boiling water, coming together as a filling staple in ten to fifteen minutes. Its ease and regularity in domestic kitchens, though, perhaps also made it more mundane, an everyday food. Eating out, instead of repeating the regular fare, presented the opportunity to have something different, like nostalgic staples from home such as githeri for up-country migrants or the opportunity to eat new urban foods like chapati. From the 1970s onward, though, ugali did become a regular item at street eateries. Interviews affirm the dish's increasing frequency on menus during the last three decades of the century, but less clear is why.[78] It was likely the result of the slow accumulation of individual decisions by restaurateurs that this popular, cheap, and easy-to-make staple of the working class should have a place at their roadside eateries, eventually turning it into a consistent offering.

These vibanda, therefore, offered customers the opportunity to eat lunch from a restaurant at midday, selecting from a variety of both up-country and coastal dishes. However, people could also buy food from vendors who specialized in just one item. At midcentury, grilled foods were common on Mombasa's streets, businesses that were mostly run during those years by Arab and African men. The most common grilled options were maize (*mahindi choma*) and meat (*nyama choma* or *mishkaki*). Widely available across the city, nyama choma was seasoned with salt, while mishkaki was prepared with spices. Among the attractions of running these businesses was that they required less capital, as people usually only needed a grill, fuel, and limited ingredients. Street vendors also sold a variety of other snacks throughout the town. These included roasted groundnuts, potato chips, fried cassava, and South Asian snacks like *chevda,* small slices of fried potatoes mixed with spices and groundnuts, and *ganthiya,* long circular strips of fried dough made from chickpea flour.[79] These inexpensive foods could be just a snack between meals, or when budgets were tight, a cob of grilled maize might serve as lunch.

Many of these working-class eateries, big and small, prepared their food on-site, positioned on sidewalks, on road reserves, and in parks and other

FIGURE 3.3. Umazi Mzungu preparing *maharagwe* (beans) at her street-food eatery in Mwembe Tayari on Mombasa Island. Photograph by Onesmus Mutua, 2024.

open spaces, but some vendors cooked out of household kitchens. Unlike women who sold mbaazi to their neighbors in the morning, those operating at lunch faced a different urban geography in the middle of the day. Residential neighborhoods had emptied out by then, with both men and women heading off for a day of wage labor or trading, and so the market for prepared food in these areas was limited. Therefore, many vendors cooked in their homes and carried their food to a higher-traffic area to sell it. As James Miruka explained, during the 1950s, "Wagiriama, even those from Nyanza, Kikuyu, they made the food at home and would come sit with it at a particular place" and then "people could go during lunchtime and buy from them."[80] Similarly, Nzalu Ngotho, who balanced wage labor with running a tea cart, recalled that during the 1960s, women made beans, rice, githeri, and other dishes at home, which they sold on the streets in makeshift structures.[81] Some vendors, though, did live in areas with sufficient people around during lunchtime to sustain what amounted to small restaurants in their home, businesses that were run by Africans from up-country, Swahilis, and Arabs alike.[82] In the late 1960s, municipal authorities observed such household restaurants, which had a "large number of customers coming to eat cooked beans (mbhaazi [*sic*]), cooked cassava (muhugo), porridge (uji) and fried fish," and noted that "these food vendors operated their trade throughout the day," at times making it hard for other families living there to use the communal kitchen and bathroom.[83] This model endured in the city, as more-recent vendors also operated eateries from their residences, like Josephe, who in the late twentieth century ran one on such a scale that, as she put it, "I forgot that it was my home."[84]

In twentieth-century Mombasa, working people spent long days powering the economy of East Africa's most important port town. This labor system was premised on a working day that kept people on the job from early in the morning until late in the afternoon, lasting at least eight hours if not more. Most were afforded a lunch break in the middle of the day to briefly rest and restore some of the calories they had burned during a morning of manual labor, but, far from their home kitchen, they needed someone to prepare them a meal. By the mid-twentieth century, street-food vendors provided this service, nourishing their customers and allowing them to return to work with the energy necessary to finish their shift. Consequently, not only did such businesses provide steady income to those who ran them but also these eateries—operating from carts or makeshift structures, in front of a duka, or inside peoples' homes—were instrumental to the creation of new urban lunchtime routines, and as such, they also became essential to the reproduction of the working day in Kenya's Indian Ocean port city.

Dinner

As afternoon turned into evening, workers commuted back to their residences, and most of them walked by street eateries where people were frying, grilling, and boiling foods for sale. However, back in their neighborhoods, they could choose to eat at home, and many did. At midcentury, men often returned to households that were made up of male friends and relatives; if they wanted to eat there, they had to make "pragmatic adjustments" in the domestic division of labor.[85] In homes with men around the same age, cooking dinner became a shared responsibility, and people began to form new evening routines. As Kabatha wa Washomba explained in 1939, "We cook in turn, one day I, and another day another."[86] Labor researchers collecting data during the 1940s also confirmed such arrangements among migrant men when noting the difficulty of calculating individual cost-of-living budgets because of the practice of "joint cooking by bachelors."[87] This was the kind of household that John Omondi Onyango lived in during the 1950s in Likoni after he migrated to Mombasa from Nyanza Province. Onyango explained that gender norms had to be more flexible while living as a migrant, as when you were "three bachelors, you couldn't cook alone. . . . When you are two guys, you are all men, you are all women. I wash the dishes, he cooks. He washes the dishes, I cook."[88] To cook and to clean in the home, in Onyango's view, was to be a woman, but migration necessitated taking on this labor gendered as feminine.

In households like those of Washomba and Onyango in which men were around the same age, they shared domestic responsibilities. However, many migrants at midcentury began their time in the city living with already established older relatives who had acquired stable employment. Given Mombasa's gendered labor market, this meant they were often men.[89] In these homes, new migrants took on a junior, dependent status, gaining access to shelter and food, and in exchange they did domestic labor. The senior male relative, therefore, bore more expenses but did not have to cook, while younger men in the house, in return for their kitchen labor, were provided security, as well as time to try to find a way to earn income and generally adjust to their new urban life.[90] The existence of these kinds of migrant residences at midcentury was indicated in a 1968 social survey. The study compared households in Tudor Estate, where there was a higher proportion of both up-country migrants and those employed as "skilled workers, clerks, or salesman," with the Majengo neighborhood, where there were larger percentages of multigenerational city residents and people unemployed or working in the informal economy. In Tudor, 50 percent of

FIGURE 3.4. *Biryani,* coastal East Africa's version of an Indian Ocean dish. Photograph by author, 2012.

FIGURE 3.5. *Ugali* prepared on a commercial scale in a *sufuria* (cooking pot). This dish was commonly available at street-food eateries during the second half of the twentieth century. Photograph by Onesmus Mutua, 2024.

households had a relative other than the husband, wife, and children living there, while in Majengo only 38 percent of the homes had such extended kin living with them.[91] This suggests that migrant residences where someone had "stabilized" employment were more likely to house, and probably feed, dependents outside the nuclear family. The strategy of building extended households around more-secure relatives was also clear during the 1970s in government estates, where residents were relatively higher earners and were "allowing their friends or relatives to live with them in their houses."[92]

Interviewees also shared individual life histories that fit within these broader trends. For example, Gregory Osollo Omondi moved from Siaya to Mombasa in 1969 to live with his brother, who was employed by the city police. Omondi was young and focused on his studies, so he depended on his brother financially. Living in police housing in Likoni on the south mainland, his brother purchased groceries for the household, which Omondi then prepared but also ate for free. He recalled decades later that because his brother was "big," Omondi's job was to cook, an arrangement that continued for years. Even after starting a teaching position in the nearby rural town of Kwali, he still lived at his brother's house in Likoni for another five years and would only occasionally "chip in" some money for their food.[93] Barak Olela Abwao, also a migrant from Siaya, who arrived in 1973, similarly joined a household headed by a salaried relative, his brother, who worked for the railway. His brother lived in comparative comfort, having just moved into the newly constructed housing estate in Changamwe that opened that year. In their home, generation took the place of gender, as Abwao took turns with his brother's son cooking the meals they ate at home, dinner as well as breakfast.[94]

The cooking that men did in Mombasa, though, was done circumstantially. Many arrived young and single, and cooking was part of this initial phase of bachelorhood, whether it was labor shared with roommates or done as a junior member of a household. However, if they married, male migrants transferred the job of cooking to their wives. From the colonial period, the little evidence we have on male views of the household division of labor suggests the enduring power of the idea that cooking was the work of women. In 1939, for example, an official from Mombasa's Public Works Department noted that some of the African men who worked for him "refused to cook because they [said] that that [was] the woman's job to cook and not theirs."[95] During Deverell's survey around a decade later, she also noted that "married men would expect their wives to prepare at least one good meal per day."[96] These ideas became practice. In Mombasa, when women lived in the home, they cooked.[97]

However, the ability of migrants to maintain conjugal families in the city often hinged on whether they could afford to do so, and thus men with secure employment were more likely to have their wives cooking for them at home.[98] This was the case in Martina Jera's household in Mombasa. She was born in the city in 1948 after her father and his two wives, including Jera's mother, had moved there so he could take a position at the railway. Very much in one of Mombasa's "islands of labor reform," they lived in railway housing and had steady salaried income, which was supplemented by the street-food business that Jera's mother ran. Living with his two wives in a housing estate close to work, her father was able to eat lunch at home that his second wife prepared, and then in the evening his first wife cooked dinner after she returned from working at her street eatery.[99] Around the same time, Appollo Nyinge Kithakwa, originally from Central Province, was also living in Mombasa. His father started working as a domestic cook for a white family in the city but then took a position in the kitchen at the Coast General Hospital, which Kithakwa described as "a good job, an okay job, slightly high [the pay], and it was permanent. There was no problem of somebody leaving you without a job." Holding long-term employment, Kithakwa's father lived with his whole family in Mombasa and, despite being a professional cook himself, came home every night to eat a meal prepared by his wife.[100]

Moreover, though generation and economic status shaped who cooked in all-male households, gender superseded both distinctions when women were in the home. Many men, as we have seen, followed older male relatives to Mombasa, but established female migrants drew family members to their homes too. For example, Vitalis Owiti first arrived in the city from Nyanza Province with no employment in 1970 at the age of twenty-four and landed in his sister's household in Changamwe. She was a tailor, and her husband worked in customs at the port. However, even though Vitalis was a young dependent in the household, his sister still cooked all the food. Later he moved in with a married male friend who secured him a groundskeeping job; although they bought lunch from street-food vendors while at work, his friend's wife did all the cooking in the household, preparing both men breakfast and dinner.[101] Around this same period, Patrice Omollo Sweta, also from Nyanza, had three wives, and one always stayed with him in Mombasa while the other two remained back in Nyanza Province. In the city, he lived in a compound with extended family where migrating relatives stayed when they first moved to town. The new arrivals there could count on shelter at his home, as well as food prepared by whichever of his wives was living there at the time.[102]

These domestic kitchens, though, also existed in a city with a robust street-food industry. While many of Mombasa's roadside eateries closed after the lunch rush because they focused primarily on breakfast and the midday meal, a considerable variety of street-food vendors remained open during the evening. As at breakfast, some people purchased part of their dinner from vendors to reduce the cooking and cleaning they had to do at home, which became especially important after a long day at work.[103] In 1930, for example, an official observed that "poorer people . . . [bought] semi-cooked food at the Makupa Market and [took it] home for final preparation."[104] Combining street food with household cooking was most often done with fried fish (*samaki wa kukaanga*), which, as reported in the late 1940s, were "sold freely in the evening." Fish were a regular dinner item in working-class homes, especially for the Luo who came from the shores of Lake Victoria and continued to count fish as a major part of their diet in the city.[105] Paying for a precooked fried fish, even more than other dishes, makes sense if considered within the cooking process. Frying is a comparatively wasteful proposition if done at a small scale, as usually at least one inch, if not more, of oil is necessary to cover enough of the fish to achieve the desired texture and taste. When done at commercial scale, though, many fish can be fried in the same oil over and over, making far more efficient use of the cooking fat. Many petty entrepreneurs in Mombasa did just this, setting up a frying station outside their homes and selling cooked fish to customers who walked by after work. A fried fish in hand, these commuters only had to prepare rice or ugali, or nothing if the fish was paired with bread, and they had a quick and easy dinner.[106]

This usually still required a certain level of cooking and cleaning at home, and many people just wanted to eat out for their evening meal. Joshua Kalii, for example, lived in his uncle's house in the north mainland neighborhood of Kongowea during the early-independence period, and they both commuted and worked long hours on the island each day. Even though Kalii was supported by his uncle, unlike others in this situation he did not cook much in their house. Instead, at the end of the working day, he explained that one "could not cook." Upon returning home from the island, he and his uncle would eat dinner at a neighborhood kibanda and then quickly went to sleep.[107] Mohamed Amir Temu felt much the same. He told me that "when the evening arrives" after working, he preferred to eat at vibanda. Instead of taking fried fish home, he stopped at a more full-service place where he could sit and have it there as a meal. Temu told me, "You can go to an eatery and buy fish" where they also prepare a fresh *kachumbari* to go with it, a ubiquitous tomato and onion salad in Kenya that accompanies main dishes. "You can eat it just like that," he continued, "and then go to sleep." Indeed, working physically demanding days at construction sites, the only time Temu cooked at home in the evening was on his days off during the weekend.[108]

Those who ate at these vibanda were often men who resided in households without women, because those who lived with their wives in Mombasa almost always returned to their home for an evening meal. David Muywambu Kivindto, a migrant from Machakos who has been in Mombasa since the 1950s, put it this way: "When you have a wife, you eat at home, she can cook for you, you don't go to the vibanda. Those who go to the vibanda are the casual laborers who don't have a wife. They are the ones who eat in the vibanda."[109]

However, while David's wife, Alice Mutave, has consistently lived with him in the city since the late 1960s and cooked their food, many migrant families in Mombasa and Kenya more widely were often not simply urban or rural. Instead, women often stayed for extended periods in their rural homes, taking care of dependent kin and working in the family fields, while men stayed in the city.[110] When these women visited Mombasa, they cooked in their urban household and so their husbands regularly ate dinner at home. However, when they returned to their rural area, the married men who stayed in the city were just as responsible for their own food as were single men, and they had to decide whether to cook their own meals or buy their food from street vendors. Many chose the latter option.[111] Jacob Muli, who moved to Mombasa during the 1970s and sold curios to tourists, explained these cyclical patterns in his own life in ways that also applied to many others. He recalled, "When my wife was here, I ate at home. I didn't go to the eateries. When she would leave, and I was alone, then I would go back to these restaurants."[112]

Street vendors also became part of the social life of a large port city during the evening hours. People had the option to take grilled meat as well as fried fish home, but they could also find people preparing nyama choma or mishkaki in front of a bar, allowing customers to combine an after-work drink with some inexpensive food. For example, Wambogu Muon sold grilled meat in Mombasa during the late 1960s, operating his business on the veranda next to a bar in the working-class neighborhood of Changamwe on the mainland, a perfect location to find commuters returning home after a day of work.[113] Those looking for sociability without alcohol could go to one of the many hawkers selling *kahawa chungu,* small, strong cups of coffee flavored with cardamom, which were sold during both the morning and the evening. A social beverage generally taken outside the home, kahawa chungu could be easily found on Mombasa's streets, with the sound that hawkers made when they clinked their ceramic cups together. Unlike gari ya chai, though, these vendors generally did not sell food.[114] These were places to go for a hot caffeinated beverage and conversation.

Thus, gender, generation, income, and the dynamics of migrant households shaped how working-class people acquired their evening meal, whether having it at home or out at an eatery. Underlying all these decisions about how and where people ate was the assumption and reality that when women were in the household, they cooked. This gendered division of household labor, the baseline premise that cooking was the work of women, has been among the most durable features of Kenyan societies in the modern era, from rural kitchens in 1900 to urban ones at the end of the century. It operated at the level of "common sense," in the way theorized by Antonio Gramsci.[115] Neither men nor women in interviews challenged the idea that domestic cooking was the work of women; instead this was presented as a self-evident fact. Joseph Mwangi, who lived with his wife in the city, did eat his lunches at vibanda because he worked far from his residence, but breakfast and dinner he ate at home "because [his] wife was there." When asked if he ever cooked, he laughed and said, "*Mimi? Hapana. Bibi yangu, alipika*" (Me? No. My wife, she cooked).[116] The few exceptions that came up in the interviews prove the rule. Margaret Auma Ndolo, for example, moved to Mombasa during the 1960s with her husband, who worked for the railway, and she prepared lunch for him because, living in company housing, he was close enough to walk home during his break. However, in 1968, wanting to earn more money, Ndolo took a job at a coffee factory sorting beans. Tied to regular shifts and working a long distance from her home, Ndolo had her lunch at vibanda, and her husband, still employed close to their residence, had to return to the house during lunch to prepare not only his but also their children's midday meals.[117] Later in the century, Benike Owuir, who earned her income as a taxi driver taking tourists from the airport to their hotels, often picked up passengers with evening arrivals. During those nights, Owuir told me, her husband had to gather ingredients from the refrigerator and prepare them himself.[118] The husbands of these two women cooked regularly, but only because the requirements of income generation in a modern city pulled their wives away from the kitchen during mealtimes.

* * *

As in any political economy, kitchen labor in Kenya's port city drove social reproduction, converting raw ingredients into palatable meals that fed the community. From the 1930s onward, street-food vendors did an increasing amount of this work, especially during the lunch hour. As the city's population grew and the geographical scale of the city extended outward across the island and onto the mainland, more and more workers could not return home for their midday meal. By the middle of the twentieth century, the reproduction of the working day had become dependent on these street-food eateries. Positioned in convenient locations and offering inexpensive food, these vendors linked morning to afternoon, providing the lunchtime nourishment that workers needed to stay on the job until their shift was done. The steady growth of street food, along with other informal businesses, was also generated by a wage-labor market that could not easily absorb Mombasa's fast-growing population. Opening a street-food eatery—like selling fresh produce or used clothes or engaging in other forms of petty trade—became an important way that people earned income in the city as wage labor failed to keep pace.

As these eateries expanded, commercially prepared food became a larger part of people's diets, above all during the lunch hour but also during breakfast and dinner. However, home cooks continued to prepare much of the food that people ate in the midcentury city. In these homes, men also cooked on a scale without parallel in their rural communities but generally only when circumstances required it. If women lived in Mombasa's working-class households, they cooked. This supports the idea developed by Susanne Y. P. Choi and Yinni Peng in the context of modern China that migration, employment, and the spatial realities of urban life led men to take on domestic labor gendered as female but that these were temporary "adjustments." When the circumstances changed, women again took over this household work.[119] In Kenya, the temporary nature of these adjustments is underlined in the life of Gregory Osollo Omondi, who lived with and cooked for his brother in Likoni during the 1970s. After leaving that house, Omondi did not marry, so he continued preparing his own food. Upon returning to his home region near Lake Victoria in 1988, he thus had nearly two decades of experience as a home cook. However, when he got married back in Kisumu, the division of labor in his kitchen changed. Referring to his wife, Omondi explained, "When we are together, she cooks."[120]

4 ~ "Making Food Vendors a Regular and Permanent Feature in the Town"

The Politics of Street Food in Late-Colonial and Decolonizing Mombasa

SAMPSON KEREU sat beside his *kibanda* on Mombasa Island on a gray morning in December 2014. With his restaurant quiet after the breakfast rush, he took some time to discuss his life as a street-food vendor. Kereu talked about how the profession had provided him consistent income over the past four decades. He recalled his customers forming long lines during the lunch hour, with many of them coming to buy his specialty, the Kikuyu dish *mataha* (another word for *irio*), the mash of bananas or potatoes mixed with beans and maize kernels. However, Kereu also emphasized that operating a street eatery like his was risky, as harassment from the municipality was so regular that it became routine. He remembered that often, sometimes even twice in the same day, he had been arrested and had his supplies confiscated. After paying a fine, though, he would be able to retrieve his pots and reopen the business until the next time the authorities came.[1] Indeed, by the time Kereu started his kibanda in the 1970s, such forms of insecurity had become a regular part of working as a street-food vendor.

Historically, the very features that make informal trades like street food appealing to proprietors and customers alike are the same ones that have generated conflict between these petty businesses and city administrations in Mombasa and across the world's urban societies.[2] As discussed in the previous chapter, many of Mombasa's vendors operated illicitly from pushcarts or in self-constructed shelters located on sidewalks, road reserves, and other open areas. This meant they were often unlicensed, asserted officially unrecognized claims to land, worked in structures that violated building codes, and ran eateries with limited access to sanitary infrastructures like running water and toilets. A concern for officials, this business model was integral to the way street-food vendors operated in Mombasa's political economy. Capital start-up costs were minimal, which lowered entry barriers for the poor. Their reduced operating costs kept food prices cheap for the working-class clientele, while their ability to stake claims to open land allowed these eateries to locate themselves close to their customers in places like Mombasa's industrial district. Such informal businesses, though, however practically useful they may have been in the city's economy, did not fit with the way urban planners imagined the future of Kenya's largest coastal town.

Nonetheless, municipal authorities in colonial Mombasa largely allowed street-food eateries to expand and operate for decades, for the authorities lacked the resources to implement their own laws and were reluctant to disrupt the role these vendors played in social reproduction. However, by the late-colonial era, the state became focused on investing in and enforcing a new kind of urban order. As strikes and protests unfolded across late-colonial African cities, the British became concerned not only with "labor stabilization" but also with asserting more control over the perceived "disorder" of informal urban commerce.[3] During the final years of colonial rule in Mombasa, city authorities pursued campaigns to enforce licensing laws and fees, demolish roadside structures, and move vendors into state-constructed facilities where they paid rents and could be more closely inspected. These policies may have brought about a certain kind of order, but by undermining the business model of street food they also precipitated a crisis of social reproduction. This produced a contradiction. The underlying logic of late-colonial labor policy was to create a more stable and predictable workforce, but the full enforcement of the licensing, building, and sanitary laws of modernizing urban planners also made it harder for working people to access food while on the job. Indeed, it quickly became clear that taking away the affordable food that sustained people during the working day was not a particularly effective way to keep labor peace. Positioned at the center of this contradiction, street-food vendors had considerable power in an unequal society, as the need to keep port, railway, and other workers fed in the middle of the day placed clear limits on how far campaigns to remove the roadside eateries could be pushed.[4] In colonial Mombasa, municipal authorities may have wanted to fully implement their version of "urban development," but both government and private employers needed working-class labor power even more.

Independence in 1963 did not easily resolve the contradictory politics of street food. Scholars of decolonization have shown how the meaning of independence in Africa was often translated into economic aspirations, and street-food vendors very much understood liberation from colonial rule as an opportunity to create a legal environment in the postcolonial city in which they could earn a more secure living.[5] The end of British rule made this more possible, as citizenship turned vendors into voters who could and did exert pressure on elected officials. In ways not possible under the racially authoritarian colonial state, people operating working-class eateries found reliable advocates among Mombasa's elected officials who pushed forward both moderate and radical proposals to transform the relationship between street-food vendors and the government. However, other officials continued to dream of a city in which such informal businesses did not exist. Those pushing forward the idea that a modern city was one without informality tended to be appointed civil service officials, like the medical officer of health, who were less subject to popular pressure and had the backing of the national government in Nairobi. Their aim was to "modernize" Mombasa through sanitation and the aesthetics of its urban form, the latter objective connected especially to the city's emerging role in the postcolonial tourism economy.[6] In practice, as occurred during the late-colonial period, this meant removing informal commerce like street food from the urban landscape.

Independence officials were also constrained, as their colonial predecessors had been, by the reality that street-food businesses provided workday food to the laboring classes and income to those who needed it. The solution of the colonial government had been to construct municipal food canteens where vendors could operate their eateries, a policy the postcolonial government adopted in earnest during the first decade of independence. The canteen system, an attempt to create a vast public infrastructure to deliver a social service, fit well into the era of midcentury modernization during which governments pursued large-scale projects that aimed to transform the economy and society.[7] More generally, the postcolonial reinvention of such late-colonial policies, common in decolonizing Africa, carried to independence certain ideas about economic development. In Kenya, this included an underlying assumption about how public programs would be financed that has much in common with the "cost-recovery" framework that has shaped more-recent development policy in neoliberal Africa.[8] That is, as a midcentury modernizing government, the Kenyan state would create new infrastructures and services for everyday people, but there would also be concrete limits to how much the state would subsidize them. To close the budget gap, individual users would bear significant costs, whether for urban mass transit, low-income housing, the redistribution of rural land, or the canteen system.[9] This tendency toward fiscal restraint in social welfare spending existed broadly in decolonizing Kenya, but it was exacerbated for those in the informal economy. This stems, in part, from the reality that urban economic development was conceptualized, above all, as a program to serve wage earners and their families.[10] Especially in the early-independence period, informal vendors were not seen as the proper subject of development. Instead, the way they earned income, in petty trade on the street, was understood as a temporary aberration that would eventually disappear as economic modernization unfolded. Consequently, government funds for the canteen system, as much as the project fit into municipal plans, were slowly dispersed and largely insufficient to the task.

Ultimately, the contradictory politics of street food endured through decolonization. Independence created a novel political terrain, and vendors used their status as *wananchi* (citizens) to achieve some level of reform to state policies. Nonetheless, many government officials still pursued campaigns to drive vendors off Mombasa's streets, including wider projects that sought to rid the city entirely of their trade through mass arrests and the demolition of thousands of roadside structures. Through all these disruptions, though, the underlying political economy that incentivized these kinds of businesses remained. Without a viable alternative to replace the services that street food offered or an economy that provided adequate jobs outside the informal sector, people like Kereu pushed on despite the risks, reopening their businesses after the fines, arrests, and demolitions. During mealtimes, their customers returned too.

SOCIAL REPRODUCTION AND THE LIMITS OF POSTWAR DEVELOPMENT

Mombasa's municipal government first firmly fixed its attention on the city's eateries during the 1930s when it established a normative framework for "restaurants" in its legal codes.[11] In these bylaws, the legality of an eatery became tied to its architecture. If not literally in a brick-and-mortar building, the licensed restaurant was to be housed in structures made from solid and ostensibly permanent materials. The codes stated that "the floor of any room in which food or drink are served" should be made from "cement or wood or some hard, impervious material," while kitchen walls need to be "covered with glazed tiles, cement or other hard material." This sturdy structure also needed access to sanitary infrastructures, in particular "latrine accommodation for the use of customers" and "good and sufficient supply of wholesome water available on the premises."[12] These building requirements effectively made the city's nascent street-food industry illegal, but many in the municipal administration also realized the impracticality of their enforcement in the town's existing economy. A 1936 municipal subcommittee reported that the laws "have not [been] and are still not being strictly enforced on the poor class of natives, Arabs and Indians, as it is clear any attempt at strictly enforcing them would be not only a hardship on the applicants [food businesses], but also on the section of the public served by those applicants."[13] Municipal officials may have wanted to shape the development of eateries in Mombasa, but they could not ignore the caloric needs of the workers whose labor ran the city's economy.

During the 1930s, therefore, the municipality's approach to street food was passive, creating laws that defined what a "restaurant" legally could be without committing resources to enforcing them. After World War II, though, the increasingly developmentalist state began to take a more active role. The city government moved from simply writing laws to creating physical institutions that embodied them. This started with the repurposing of existing space. In the late 1940s, the municipal board began renting out kitchens in liquor canteens to entrepreneurs interested in providing prepared food to the public. Some of the officials involved in this project imagined it as a way to provide "cheap food" to low-income Africans in the city, but in practice this goal was not pursued.[14] Street-food prices were inexpensive because of low overhead, but the city was not willing to subsidize these new canteen kitchens to keep costs and therefore menu prices at a minimum. Instead, as detailed in the African Affairs Department's "Ten Year Development Plan" of 1947, these canteen kitchens "were to be self supporting including payment of staff."[15] At least four of these eateries opened in Mombasa during the late 1940s, in liquor canteens in Mwembe Tayari and Majengo on the island and in Changamwe and Kisauni in mainland neighborhoods, and all four paid rent to the city.[16] The small scale of this project—four eateries in a city of around 100,000 people—ensured that the canteen kitchens would not replace street-food vendors, and the rent they paid also meant their prices would be higher. The most significant aspect of this early experiment in state-run eateries was demonstrating the hesitancy of the government to subsidize food access for the poor, a tendency that proved long-standing.

For the first decade of postwar development, then, municipal investments that aimed to transform working-class eateries were limited. Without an alternative way to feed people while they worked, the government did not attempt to systematically shut down illicitly operating vendors. There was much talk, as in 1947 when officials debated a ban on the sale of street food, and even the more radical idea that all informal trade "be abolished completely," but actual policy was less ambitious.[17] Moreover, alongside those pushing to restrict petty trade were others in the municipal government who continued to advocate for the value it provided the city. No less prominent a figure than the Liwali Mbarak al-Hinawy, the top non-European official on the Kenyan coast, felt that urban revitalization should not be pursued at the expense of ensuring basic needs like the ability to access food, arguing that the municipal board "should not only see to the cleanliness of the town but also to the welfare of its inhabitants."[18] For al-Hinawy, this meant the right of vendors to earn a living, as well for consumers to be able to afford food. Take "the case of the seller of roasted maize," he argued; "to put that person out of business not only deprived that person of his livelihood but deprived a section of the community of a commodity it wished to purchase." At the same meeting, Councilor Jetha was more specific about the class dynamics of eateries in Mombasa, explaining that "the labouring classes cannot afford to go into restaurants," while street vendors provided them "roasted maize at a price within their means."[19]

These views within the municipal board were likely part of what prevented larger campaigns against vendors during the early postwar period. Localized efforts to clear vendors off open land did occur, but even in these instances the approach was constrained by the need to keep workers fed. For example, in 1951, the municipal government shut down a large number of the street-food eateries operating outside the gate to the Kilindini docks, but their customers responded quickly. Mombasa's dock workers—organized, militant, and with the ability to shut down the most important choke point in the region's commodity transport system—convinced the authorities to allow the eateries back and even to build a shed where they could be housed next to the Kilindini Labour Office. Despite this concession, management at the docks wanted to maintain more control over how their land was being used. The shed was built for only 50 of the vendors, but soon thereafter 150 businesses had opened. In response, the port expelled 100 of them, trying to keep with the original design of the complex, despite reports that this led to a "deterioration" in the quality of the food.[20] The inexpensive and convenient calories that vendors provided were crucial to maintaining the port's full working day, but officials were also keen to set limits on the scale of petty commerce on their land. Above all, though, dock authorities found it unthinkable to expel street-food vendors entirely from the area.

This model of accommodation between vendors and dock employers also inspired municipal officials to consider a privatized plan to formalize street food. Instead of relying on state-constructed physical infrastructure to house these eateries, perhaps employers could build canteens inside their compounds where vendors could serve workday meals. This was not such a radical idea for British officials, as similar models abounded in Britain. During the nineteenth century, as noted in chapter 1, most British workers had been atomized consumers, able to acquire only what food their cash wages could buy in the market. However, during World War I and the decades that followed, an increasing emphasis on industrial paternalism precipitated the rise of the workplace canteen in British factories. By midcentury, they were common, with an estimated 30,000 by 1966.[21] In 1952, city officials in Mombasa felt there may have been movement in that direction too, because the port by then provided basic shelter for private street-food vendors, and municipal officials also heard that East African Breweries was considering installing its own canteen, "a fine example," they thought. For the 100 vendors expelled from the docks, city authorities were searching for somewhere for them to work other than illicitly on the streets, and so the Welfare Committee of the Mombasa African Advisory Council sent a circular to "various companies who employ large African labour in the vicinity of the Kilindini Docks" hoping the companies would construct food canteens where the vendors could work.[22] These officials were soon disappointed. Some companies denied the request outright, while others vaguely "referred the matter to their Principals in the United Kingdom." The municipality did not push the idea further, and it quickly faded from policy discussions. Indeed, only in 1961 did officials again query employers about whether they might consider feeding their own workers in a company canteen, to which they received a curt reply. Mombasa's Chamber of Commerce and Agriculture wrote back that "the problem is not one for private enterprise."[23] The city's employers were not interested in creating a new form of industrial paternalism that bound them to feeding their workers. Instead, employers were content to pay laborers cash wages with which they would buy their own food.

THE CONTRADICTORY POLITICS OF STREET FOOD

For a large portion of the postwar era, then, neither the state nor private employers made a sustained effort to build an alternative infrastructure to feed the city's workers. Consequently, there was no resolution to the contradiction between the desire for a city without the informal economy and the reality that street food was essential to social reproduction. Additional localized attempts to curtail street food were made, but most vendors operated with minimal interference for more than a decade after World War II.[24] This changed in 1957. That year, C. D. Rosenwald, Mombasa's medical officer of health, pushed for vigorous enforcement of the city's restaurant bylaws. His specific reason was that vendors might contribute to the spread of typhoid within the town, but Rosenwald was likely also concerned about larger structural transformations.[25] Mombasa's African communities had grown rapidly during the postwar era, and the city's racialized class system meant they were the ones most in need of the services and employment opportunities that street food provided. In 1947, the African population of Mombasa stood at 56,000 people. By 1958, it was nearly 90,000, which means there was likely a similar proportional expansion of the street-food industry.[26] Rosenwald, tasked with maintaining bylaws being ignored on an ever-expanding scale, decided to embark on an unprecedented campaign to rid the city of street-food vendors.[27]

Some municipal councilors, especially the few Africans in the city government, disagreed over this course of action, but their concerns were ignored.[28] During 1957, the council began removing vendors from the areas around Mwembe Tayari, where "the Municipal Inspector had . . . started clearing illicit food hawkers from the market."[29] Authorities then enlarged the operation to the rest of the city, and by August reference was made to the "rigid implementation of Municipal Bye-Laws which prohibits unlicensed food vendors from practicing within the Mombasa Municipality."[30] The following month saw the continuing "imposition" of laws that aimed to end "food vending as hitherto practiced in the town."[31] For decades, city officials had drafted laws aimed at restricting informality in Mombasa, but a recognition of the role these traders played in the city's economy had constrained their ambitions. By the late 1950s, though, a radical attempt was being made to remove working-class eateries and their services from the city's streets.

Predictably, as al-Hinawy and Jetha had anticipated almost a decade before, the expulsion of street-food vendors caused a crisis in social reproduction, affecting the customers who relied on the meals and the vendors who needed the income. As this became clear, officials felt pressure to solve a crisis of their own making.[32] The government could not ignore the problems their policies had created, because the affected African communities would not let them. Using the new openings to state power created by late-colonial political liberalization, residents lodged complaints with Ronald Ngala, the coast's new member of the colony's Legislative Council. Taking up their case, Ngala wrote to Mombasa's city government that "many Africans have been to see [him]" to stress "the need for having some African food at Mwembe Tayari," an area particularly hard hit by the clearances. Ngala had visited the island neighborhood and saw that none of the formal restaurants in the area sold "any African food, e.g., beans, sima [*ugali*], maize, porridge," and the establishments were "too costly for the type of African wishing to have his meals at Mwembe Tayari."[33] They also confidently pressured European officials. F. P. B. Derrick, Mombasa's district commissioner, both read Ngala's letter and "received representations from a number of Africans" on the issue. Sensing the urgency of the situation, Derrick sent a circular to Mombasa's leading municipal authorities, including the town clerk, the chairman of the Municipal Board, the African affairs officer and the medical officer of health. Derrick noted the "very considerable feeling there is among Africans in the town regarding the prohibition . . . on food vendors selling food in the streets and in open spaces." Explicitly concerned about the implications for labor, he urged that "we should go slowly in this matter as otherwise there may well be repercussions. There is little doubt that a very large proportion of the manual laborers employed in this town traditionally obtain their food from itinerant vendors," as they cannot afford restaurants "where the food is much more expensive."[34] Employers were concerned too. The branch manager of the Shell Company of East Africa, located in the northern Shimanzi quarter of the industrial district, requested that the medical officer of health authorize a vendor to sell food to his workforce, someone who could "prepare hot curry stew, japatties [*sic, chapati*], posho, cakes, etc."[35]

Without providing an alternative, Mombasa authorities had disrupted the system that delivered cheap prepared food to low-income workers. In this moment of crisis, the political will materialized to create a state-run infrastructure to provision cooked meals to the city's working poor: a system of food canteens where vendors would operate under the strict surveillance of the state rather than illicitly on the streets. However, this would take time, and in the interim an immediate compromise was needed to mitigate the effects that clearances were having on "both food vendors and the masses of [the] African public."[36] Facing pressure, councilors decided that banning the eateries that fed the city's poor residents without an alternative was untenable. By the end of 1957, there was a "gentleman's agreement" that until sufficient food-vendor canteens existed there would be "no serious enforcement" of the bylaws against illicit eateries.[37] That is, the government decided that the informal economy of street food would be made tacitly legal until a new basis for social reproduction had been established.

As plans for these canteens were debated, the municipality made clear that the first priority was to serve African wage earners. That is, the construction of canteens was intrinsic to the labor question in Mombasa. Consequently, officials were especially concerned that a canteen be put in the industrial district. The attack on working-class eateries had also affected the more-residential neighborhoods of Mwembe Tayari and Majengo, where plenty of people both lived and worked, but the immediate goal was to build a food-vendor canteen in the High-Level area of the industrial quarter, home to the port and the railway.[38] To construct a canteen, the city needed land in an area where the East African Railway and Harbours (EARH) owned most of it. Mombasa-based EARH officials understood the urgency of the situation, but the Nairobi office was less interested in losing control over valuable urban real estate. In their negotiations, Mombasa's government was blunt in stressing the disruptive potential of the situation. Officials urged that "it is most essential in the interest of good labor relations . . . that a Food Vendors Canteen . . . be established in the Kilindini High Ground area with the least possible delay." Many private firms in the area were also anxious that canteens be constructed "to prevent labour troubles or difficulties," concerned enough that they donated £500 to build the canteen.[39] By the end of December, EARH's central authorities had relented, and they provided a space on Mozambique Road right by the railway tracks.[40] With at least one industrial site secured, the council turned toward expanding the network of city-run eateries throughout Mombasa. This included an additional industrial canteen in Shimanzi, just north of High-Level, as well as others in more-residential areas like Mwembe Tayari and Majengo on the island and in the west mainland neighborhood of Changamwe.[41]

However, the transition from policy approval to building and running these canteens was slow. As questions of land, funds, and fees were debated, vendors continued to feed the city's workers, protected by the "gentleman's agreement" that their political organizing had forced upon the administration. Indeed, during February 1958, an official trying to push the process along regretted how, near Makupa Market in Majengo, "a good number of women could still be seen selling food under indifferent conditions under a cashew-nut tree close by."[42] As months turned into more than a year, the limited capacity of the municipality to replace roadside eateries with city-run canteens had become apparent. The issue was not simply the inability to construct sufficient facilities, though that was crucial, but also uneven interest among vendors in relocating themselves to these canteens. Some did see an advantage in taking their businesses off the street and into these spaces where they were less vulnerable to harassment from city officials, but many did not. After a call for applications in January 1958, the city did not receive enough applicants to fill the proposed number of food-vendor stalls.[43] By September, interest had not increased, even as "every possible publicity was made to try to get the right kind of people to apply." Still, municipal officials saw a "very poor response" and were concerned the stalls might remain "empty indefinitely."[44] Like the produce traders examined in chapter 2, many street-food vendors did not see the advantage of moving into a municipal stall. Success in running a street eatery came from keeping prices low and finding a location with a high concentration of customers. These small-scale restaurateurs avoided markets because they required a license fee, adding to overhead, and restricted mobility, tying the vendor to a place surrounded by competitors. Vendors understood the economics of their businesses, and many stayed away. Impatient municipal authorities were beginning to understand this too.

In August 1958, the détente between city officials and illicit eateries came to an end, as the council reinitiated arrests and prosecutions. Vendors again pressured new African representatives in the government to help them. F. J. Khamisi, having recently assumed the Mombasa seat in the Legislative Council, wrote to the municipality and expressed his "dismay and disgust" at these actions, asking for an immediate suspension of the operation. However, Khamisi and his constituents' concerns were quickly dismissed in the name of sanitation, as "the unlicensed food vendors were jeopardizing the health of Africans by not maintaining proper standards of cleanliness." The health committee underlined that because Khamisi was advocating for illicit vendors rather than sanitation standards, he was proving himself a "retrogressive rather than a progressive leader of his people."[45] Sanitation, at least for these officials, superseded the immediate concerns of vendors and their customers. To be a leader in modernizing Mombasa, according to some British officials, was to understand this and enforce the laws.

However, a singular concern for sanitation fails to explain why arrests and prosecutions began again in 1958. Health standards were an equal part of the initial clearances in 1957, but African vendors and their representatives had successfully swayed both the district commissioner and the council to pull back enforcement. What had changed was that officials better understood that simply building canteens was not sufficient to convince vendors to relocate there. As David Harvey has written about such "urban restructuring" in modern cities, "Violence is required to build the new urban world on the wreckage of the old."[46] In Mombasa, the creation of a new spatial and legal order meant that the old political economy of street food had to be destroyed. In the city, the existence of a large number of eateries operating with less overhead and the advantage to locate themselves in places most convenient for their customers siphoned off the consumers that otherwise would have had to frequent the municipality's newly opened canteens. Officials saw this, and so too did those vendors who signed on to work in these city-run institutions. This was made clear two months later, when the council concluded that the further construction of municipal food stalls could be justified only if done alongside the mass prosecutions of those who operated illegally. Vendors working in the canteens also emphasized this when they told the council that "their business was being seriously interfered with by the operations of illicit food vendors" and they could "double their output if the demand were there." The council agreed and "resolved that the licensed traders be protected by taking action to suppress illegal trading."[47]

By the end of the 1950s, health officials and a class of licensed eateries had agreed that the illicit economy had to be destroyed for the new one to take hold. However, people still had to eat, and the municipal canteen system remained too small to adequately feed the tens of thousands of low-income people who were in daily need of prepared food in Mombasa. By 1960, the council relented slightly in its campaign by making it legal to sell bread and *mahamri,* the Swahili doughnut, on the streets.[48] Customers, though, wanted to eat more than bread and doughnuts for lunch, and vendors were willing to provide them with additional options, even if it meant running businesses illegally and risking exposure to arrests and demolitions. These dynamics unfolded in places like Jubilee Square, a park next to the railway station close to working-class customers and among the first places that arriving passengers to Mombasa saw. In 1962, the square had just been renovated, given a "new layout together with a garden" that "had considerably improved the general appearance of the area." The municipality also then started a campaign of arresting and destroying the structures of the *gari ya chai* operating there who were "ruining the appearance."[49] By October, all the small structures had been demolished, but vendors nonetheless remained, continuing to earn their income by selling lunch to workers in the industrial district.[50] Municipal officials pushed forward the campaign against these vendors in Jubilee Square, while they also aimed more broadly to prosecute "unlicensed food selling where possible."[51]

As independence approached, the people running Mombasa's street eateries increasingly found that a profession previously marked by small if steady profits was increasingly defined by insecurity, in which any given day the capital they had invested could be destroyed. However, the role of vendors in the reproduction of the working day gave them power. Employers wanted people to perform hard, manual labor from early in the morning until late in the afternoon, and access to an inexpensive, high-calorie meal was essential to sustaining a content and efficient workforce, the principal goal of late-colonial labor policy. This is the central contradiction of street food specifically, and informality more generally. By midcentury, these businesses had come to serve the needs of working people in the actually existing political economy, but their architectural style, tenuous legal status, and uneven access to sanitary infrastructures rendered them incompatible with the vision of urban modernity held by many in the municipal government. As independence arrived in 1963, street-food vendors and new African officials would have to face the question of whether this contradiction could be resolved.

STREET FOOD AND *UHURU*

Independence created a new political context in Mombasa in which street-food vendors could advocate for a different kind of city than the one that colonial officials had envisioned in the final years of British rule. During the late-colonial period, municipal-level African voting and representation had been introduced on a small scale, but independence opened all seats to mass elections, and Africans, as the majority, became the most important constituency in Mombasa. Like other voting wananchi, street-food vendors gained a new level of access to the levers of urban policy because municipal councilors suddenly relied on their votes. Elected officials wanted to keep voters happy for principled reasons of public service, certainly, but also because these government positions offered rare opportunities to ascend into a growing African elite. Public office provided councilors economic and political power but also bound them to their constituencies, creating ways for poor and working-class people to exert pressure on municipal policy. Unelected career civil service officers in the government also noticed these new political dynamics emerging in the city. Those in the civil service, along with provincial officials and ministers appointed by the central government in Nairobi, were not immune to popular pressure, but they ultimately saw their remit as the impersonal implementation of a particular set of urban development policies aiming to modernize the laws, sanitary conditions, and aesthetics of the city.[52] Vendors, therefore, used councilors and other elected officials to push their vision of urban development into high-level policy debates about the future of the city but also faced powerful opposition from more-abstract and distant forms of governance that checked the populism and radicalism of the early-independence era.

This new political context was apparent in the tone the council took toward vendors in the first years of *uhuru* (independence). During this time,

African councilors reduced sanitary requirements for certain food businesses, provided temporary licenses to a small number of *vibanda* in high employment areas, and tried multiple times to persuade the police not to fine or arrest people running illicit eateries.[53] These were piecemeal solutions, though, and vendors and their representatives understood that consistent and lasting security came only if roadside eateries were made explicitly and permanently legal. Later that year, elected officials in the General Purposes Committee, where many of the bylaws on the informal economy were made, tried to push through a radical new departure in urban policy. They ordered the medical officer of health, still C. D. Rosenwald from the late-colonial era, to provide free licenses to all food vendors in Mombasa as long as their facilities were "reasonably clean."[54] After years of prosecutions and demolitions, this presented the possibility that street-food vendors could operate their businesses without fear of being fined, arrested, imprisoned, or having their small built structures demolished.

However, the idea that roadside eateries would suddenly become fully legal and licensed businesses quickly came into conflict with a different view of urban modernity, one with significant institutional power. Following the decision of the council, the city's public health officials mounted an administrative rebellion against the "disastrous consequences" that would come from this new policy. The reaction was led by Rosenwald, who saw the legalization of vendors as a clear challenge to his long-standing project to modernize Mombasa's sanitary infrastructures. In a letter to the council and other top city officials, he argued that this was nothing short of an existential threat to the current system of business licensing and inspection, the mechanisms the municipal government used to control the way food was commercially prepared in the city. He explained that the owners of licensed restaurants and tea stands were already asking him why they should follow sanitary codes and pay fees if free licenses with few restrictions were available. Such a policy, he assured his colleagues, would additionally remove all incentive for people to operate in municipal food canteens. Rosenwald also saw himself as a steward of modernization more broadly and was concerned about what this potential expansion of street trade would do to Mombasa's global image. If food vendors were not restricted to city-run canteens, they would "inevitably build further unsightly unauthorised buildings," structures that were "neither traditional nor picturesque, but only unsightly and insanitary." This informal architecture, he underlined, had "brought adverse comment from tourists." The letter ended by revealing its rebellious nature, indicating that health officials would refuse to issue these licenses. Rosenwald wrote, "The Council should bear the full responsibility for the consequences, and not be in a position to say that the licences were approved by the Health Department."[55]

The threat succeeded. After receipt of the letter, council support for lifting restrictions collapsed in the weeks that followed. The same General Purposes Committee that had approved the policy met again on 21 June 1965, this time recommending that the council strike it down.[56] During the discussion for a vote at the next larger council meeting, one councilor dramatically stood up and voiced his support for the medical officer of health, while the mayor, Msanifu Kombo, said he hoped that "all councilors [would] do likewise." They voted unanimously to cancel the policy of unlimited free licenses, while national voices also condemned the idea of the mass licensing of street-food vendors. In its coverage, the *Daily Nation* concluded that making roadside eateries legal would have "inevitably [resulted] in the lowering of standards in all sorts of other food handling establishments." Indicating that national government pressure was also likely a factor in this quick policy change, Nairobi-based officials in the Ministry of Local Government, responsible for approving the council's budget, also chastised Mombasa's councilors.[57] The ministry was "extremely perturbed" about this "irresponsible and very disappointing" proposal, especially coming "from the second most important municipality in the country." The national government also solidified local health officials' authority on the issue moving forward, emphasizing how the ministry was "pleased to note" that the council "had . . . decided to take the advice of the Medical Officer of Health on the subject of licensing foodvendors."[58]

A radical policy idea had been proposed and was quickly defeated. Out of this process, though, the municipality did create a more limited administrative space where some people could operate roadside eateries legally. As food canteens were under construction and with more planned, the council approved 60 temporary street-food licenses, the same as the number of stalls that would soon become available in the canteens. The plan was to provide a transitional licensing category for those who would fill these city-run stalls once complete, a temporary status not meant to permanently legalize a class of people running restaurants on Mombasa's streets.[59] While the 60 people who became licensed enjoyed a novel status as legal food vendors, this still represented a vision of urban modernization in which most working in the informal industry were excluded from the city's development plans. If one adds these new canteens to those that already existed, on both the island and the mainland, there were still only 91 street-food stalls by the end of the 1960s.[60] This housed significantly less than half of the city's vendors, a fact the municipality knew. A 1965 government survey told the council that nearly 190 people (and probably many more than this) were running unlicensed street-food businesses on the island alone, while in 1966 the medical officer of health, with all 60 new licenses filled, still had 182 applications on his desk, which were "on the increase day by day."[61] Additionally, around this same time, more than 300 people were on the waiting list for a tea license, a status many gari ya chai used to provide at least nominal legality to their small eateries.[62] Committing to only 91 legal canteen stalls, the city was structurally consigning most people to run their businesses illegally.

Financial considerations were at the center of the limited space allocated for legal street-food vending. While thousands of Kenyan pounds were spent building canteens, city authorities were largely not willing to go beyond the capital they had committed by the mid-1960s. For example, at that time, vendors saw the need for a canteen to be built in the fast-growing north mainland, and representatives of the Coast Province branch of the National Traders Association requested that the council construct one there. However, financing from the city would not be forthcoming, as vendors were told "no money was available for such a project."[63] When the issue of a canteen was brought up again in August, councilors questioned whether it would have an adequate consumer market to support it but also conceded that official interest was low because the council did not already own land there, which meant a new canteen would require a real estate purchase in addition to construction costs that could run from anywhere from 650 to 1,400 Kenyan pounds.[64] Such projects were not a priority.

Fiscal restraint placed limits on how many canteens were built. They also constrained the transformative potential of those that existed. There was some government emphasis on subsidizing canteens in the first years after independence, as officials recognized that this might be necessary to make these institutions appeal to poor vendors who operated with few fees when working illicitly on the streets. This included the new medical officer of health in 1966, N. S. Rihal, who was strongly invested in the canteen system, arguing that year that the "rents of Stalls . . . should be reasonable and it would not be unreasonable if they were subsidized."[65] The reduction or elimination of market fees, though, was only one way to make canteens financially appealing to vendors. As discussed in chapter 2, Mombasa's public water system—where people filled jerrycans at centralized, city-run taps—was a fee-based system, and street-food vendors bought considerable amounts of water. They needed water not only for washing hands, pots, dishes, and cutlery but also as an ingredient in many of their dishes, like ugali, tea, and the dough for chapati. This represented a significant expense, one that canteen vendors during the mid-1960s did not have to pay because they had access to free running water. Indeed, from a public policy perspective, connecting food vendors in canteens to a government tap was among the best arguments for these municipal institutions. Foodborne illnesses from illicit street eateries that had uneven access to running water was a genuine concern for planners, and canteens held the potential to socialize the infrastructure necessary to reduce the risk of disease transmission in the city.[66]

Government commitment to this subsidy, though, was brief. By the mid-1960s, audits of canteen finances revealed that water bills were far outpacing revenues, and the municipality decided that individual vendors needed to pay for their water. As a concession, the city slightly lowered rents, but not to the extent that it made up for the large water bills that vendors faced.[67] Moreover, by 1969, the canteens were still seen as a fiscal liability, and rents were raised to their highest levels since independence.[68] At the end of the 1960s, it had become clear that the canteens were not going to be a subsidized institution that socialized solutions to public health issues. Instead, they were a self-supporting service financed by the fees of individual vendors.[69] Sanitation may have been the most common explanation given for why it was preferable for vendors to work in canteens rather than illicitly on the streets, but the government was not willing to underwrite this policy with sustained funding. Thus, despite clean water being the best defense against foodborne illnesses, at places like the Kinyozi Road Food Canteen in 1968, the city began shutting the water off for vendors who did not pay their bill.[70]

The new medical officer of health was committed to the canteen system, whether subsidized or not, and like his predecessor he was willing to use force to incentivize vendors to move into municipal stalls. When Rihal first assumed office, councilors probed to see if he was more open to providing licenses to street-food vendors, but he quickly rejected the idea because, by definition, "ALL foodvendors are dirty and therefore potentially dangerous when they lack the elementary essentials of hygiene."[71] Like Rosenwald, Rihal disliked street vendors for aesthetic reasons too. Adding visual concerns to sanitary ones, he underlined that Mombasa needed "a consistent and forceful policy so that the unsightly aspect of the Foodvendors' trade be removed from the roadsides in view of the increasing tourist Trade" and that "it becomes incumbent on all of us to present a good image of this country." Rihal also argued that crackdowns on vendors were necessary to support the canteen system, in much the same way that officials had done less than a decade before, during the last years of colonial rule. He wrote that "there must be a forceful policy . . . [to] encourage that Stalls in these Canteens remain occupied." This could "only be achieved by . . . strict control of any Foodvendors operating from the roadside; in fact total removal of all unauthorised and unlicensed Foodvendors from the roadside." This should be pursued, he recommended, with "vigorous action by the Police by way of prosecutions"; additionally, "fines plus occasional jail sentences would act as useful deterrents."[72]

The new medical officer of health wrote with the confidence of someone who wielded power, because he did. Both the national Ministry of Health and Ministry of Local Government backed his authority on the issue. In April, the General Purposes Committee read Rihal's report and on the same day rescinded the previous order that asked for expanded licensing.[73] The permanent secretary of the Ministry of Local Government further solidified Rihal's position, reminding councilors that the medical officer of health had "explained very clearly . . . the health hazards involved in increasing the number of food vendors" in Mombasa. Writing with disappointment, he admonished those who seemed to be advocating a policy that would lead to "making food vendors a regular and permanent feature in the town," a radical move out of step with the national government's approach to the modernization and development of Kenya's cities.[74]

Rihal gained another powerful ally days later when I. M. Mathange, provincial commissioner of Coast Province, toured Mombasa and bluntly concluded that the city "needs a clean-up." The Provincial Administration, a colonial-era governing structure carried through to independence, was a key mechanism for the enforcement of central power in regional localities throughout Kenya. With officials appointed by Jomo Kenyatta, Kenya's new president was, as Paul Ocobock observes, "keenly aware of the localized authority imbued in the provincial administration," and that it provided "a powerful bureaucratic instrument that operated outside the purview of Parliament and answered directly to him."[75] Mathange, as the local representative of Kenyatta and the central government, cut through the protracted conflicts between the city's elected officials and its medical officer of health by ordering "that people who have constructed illegal structures must stop this practice forthwith." Food vendors, he announced, had "two weeks to move into council stalls at Majengo which are lying vacant."[76] After two weeks passed, demolition crews arrived on 25 May 1966 in the industrial district, where many street-food vendors ran their businesses, and began tearing down small eateries. They did not stop until around one hundred were destroyed. From Rihal to Mathange, the point was made. Demolish the "unsightly" structures these vendors had built, push some of those displaced into the canteens, and eliminate the rest of the businesses that remained.[77]

With demolitions unfolding, vendors mobilized themselves politically and took their case to the media. Omar M. Sakarani, president of the Kenya National Traders Association, condemned the action in the nationally circulating *Daily Nation* and asked for support from Ronald Ngala, coastal stalwart and the vice president of the Kenya African National Union (KANU), who had been a strong advocate for Mombasa's vendors.[78] Nicholas Ntinda, the president of the Coast Province branch of the trade association, was quoted in the newspaper weeks later, speaking in stark terms to shame the authorities as he explained that vendors were "suffering from starvation" because of the municipality's actions.[79]

The debates about informality in Mombasa also reflected the way that gender shaped political arguments in early-independence Kenya. Kara Moskowitz has shown how long-standing ideas about widows and motherhood were repurposed in the claims that women made in their efforts to access land in the resettlement schemes during the early-independence period. In this context, not only should widows be accorded land based on their precarity, but mothers also needed economic security so they could raise the next generation of Kenyans who would build the new nation. Such arguments often did not work in rural areas where, despite the reality that women were actively involved in agricultural work, landownership was strongly gendered as male.[80] However, urban informal economies had a different valence, as they were conceptualized as a common form of work for women, and male officials considering licensing laws in Mombasa seemed more pursuable than those examining land cases in the countryside. Indeed, Ntinda additionally explained to the *Daily Nation* that in Mombasa "the majority of hawkers and vendors were elderly widows who had no means of support since their bandas [a shortened term for *vibanda*] were demolished," and he "appealed to councilors to think again as far as issuing licenses were concerned."[81] Over time, such arguments seem to have worked. In 1967, the city created a new food vendors' license geared toward female vendors with stringent limitations. The license authorized women to run small eateries in their homes, though allowing the preparation and sale of only a restricted number of items. Mombasa's chief health inspector, A. A. Omar, explained that his office had approved this licensing category "to help the 'old women' to earn their legitimate living with the minimum risk to public health."[82]

However, vendors still faced harassment, and these gendered forms of protest continued as part of their response. In late March 1970, 150 Muslim women who worked as vendors arrived at the office of Shariff Nassir, descendant of a coastal patrician family and a rising star in KANU. They made "their feelings known over the way municipal inspectors treat[ed] them," protesting also that they "had been refused licenses to sell pre-cooked food." After this confrontation, Nassir explained that most of these women "were widows and need[ed] the money to send their children to school" and that KANU would "be very pleased if the Council will be kind to these ladies by granting them licences if they can comply with the necessary health requirements."[83] Around a week later, ideas about gender, motherhood, and nation were at work in how other officials interpreted the situation, like Juma Ferunzy of the East African Legislative Assembly, who lamented that Mombasa's laws "ha[d] been a nuisance to mothers for quite a long time and should be relaxed" and the laws were "formed during colonial times and they should . . . be changed to keep up with the winds of independence." Additionally, Salim I. Mwaruwa, a member of parliament from the Mombasa area, explained that many Kenyans like himself "were brought up and educated by money earned by [their] mothers through cooking and selling food—which is now being denied them. . . . They have to get money to educate their children otherwise they will be a bother to the council."[84] The balance of power seemed to be shifting, as even national politicians were taking the side of the vendors. Ten days later, despite objections from the medical officer of health, the council pushed through revisions to the new licensing category. The committee raised the quota from 55 to 110 and made it legal for licensees to sell precooked food on the city's streets, as long as the vendors followed sanitary guidelines.[85]

These, though, were easy concessions. They did not cost the government money. The municipality was simply allowing people to operate businesses, displacing the responsibility of sanitation onto individuals in their private homes. The municipal council had not taken on the harder, more radical political task of creating a subsidized canteen system, which required marshalling public capital to buy land, construct canteens, connect piping, and then to pay for maintenance and water bills. Public health is a collective endeavor, and governments can prioritize making sanitary infrastructures available at low or no cost to serve a social purpose. Ready access to clean water was broadly understood to be fundamentally important to preventing foodborne diseases in the city's street-food industry. However, as with much else in the urban economy, it was a service that had to be purchased. The cost of such public policies would soon become apparent.

STREET FOOD AND PANDEMIC POLITICS

The seventh cholera pandemic began when *Vibrio cholera* 01 El Tor, a novel strain of a bacterium long a part of human history, started spreading from Indonesia into other parts of Asia during the early to mid-1960s. Moving quickly through populations without built-up immunities, it had reached the Middle East, Europe, and Africa by 1970. This included East Africa. Cholera was not new to the region, as devastating outbreaks had come there during the numerous pandemics of the 1800s, a history inscribed into the vocabularies of local languages.[86] However, by the start of the twentieth century, cholera infections had declined and did not pose a major public health threat in the region for many decades.[87] In Kenya, though, concern about the novel El Tor strain began to increase during 1971 when infections were reported in the Tana River District near the Somalia border. By March, fifty-two people had contracted the bacterium and twenty of them had died.[88] Mombasa, a dynamic city drawing travelers into it each day, was seemingly at risk for an epidemic.

Epidemiologically, cholera spreads through fecal matter. The best preventative measures against it are effective human waste disposal and access to clean water for washing hands and raw foodstuffs.[89] When these sanitation infrastructures are in place, cholera poses minimal danger to human populations, as its spread is easily contained. For these reasons, scholars view cholera, even more than other diseases, as being primarily driven by political and economic rather than biological forces. For example, sudden large-scale movements of people into an area can overwhelm sanitation infrastructures, as when 1.2 million people quickly fled Rwanda into the eastern Congo following the genocide, precipitating the worst cholera epidemic in modern African history.[90] However, scholars have also pointed to more long-term, political-economic processes in Africa's urban history that have created the conditions that allowed cholera to become a lasting public health problem. During the colonial era, the racialized dynamics of urban planning meant that centralized sewage and piped water were largely reserved for white residential and core commercial neighborhoods, while African quarters were not connected to these services. In the postcolonial period, many elite Africans moved into these formally white areas and were able to access running water and sewage, but public capital was not mobilized for working people on the scale needed to extend these services into their neighborhoods. The rapid expansion of African cities during the second half of the twentieth century only compounded the problem. By the 1970s, the political economy of urban inequality had created the conditions for El Tor to spread.[91]

Mombasa followed this broader pattern. Urban Kenyans had better access to piped water compared to those living in some other African cities, but as informal neighborhoods grew in the decades after independence, fewer and fewer residences and businesses had running water.[92] Certain parts of Mombasa Island did have a centralized sewage system designed to serve a small urban population, but many on the island and all those on the mainland did not. Instead, for excrement removal, the wealthier areas had septic tanks that were regularly emptied, but most of the low-income majority relied on pit latrines.[93] By the early 1970s, the latrines that most people depended on were not being emptied with the regularity needed to maintain sanitation. Consequently, many areas had become "sewage sick," and as an official observed, "so much so that disposal by pits [was] becoming more and more difficult."[94] In 1972, Mombasa's new medical officer of health, U. K. Nathwani, pushed the council to "take urgent steps to provide proper sewerage for the Island of Mombasa before there is a catastrophic outbreak of communicable disease." The city's public health officials were clearly arguing that the patchwork of household-level solutions needed to be replaced with a larger treatment and disposal system, the need for which could "not be overemphasized."[95]

However, a deepening austerity was also settling into the city during the 1970s. More than a decade after Nathwani urgently asked her colleagues to invest in an expanded centralized sewage system, the city's medical officer of health in the mid-1980s had to make the same plea to the council.[96] The political economy of austerity would not provide the infrastructural transformation needed to protect Mombasa from cholera. In Simukai Chigudu's study of Harare's 2008–9 cholera epidemic, he observes how a "political impasse" prevented "an enduring structural transformation" to provide the sanitary infrastructure that could dramatically reduce the long-term risks of cholera. Instead, Zimbabwean authorities "focused their attention on its short-term palliation." The political ecology of cholera in Mombasa was much the same. However, neither Chigudu nor other scholars have pushed the analysis further to understand how these policies of "short-term palliation" affected the lives and livelihoods of people who earned their income by handling food that authorities feared might transmit cholera.[97] The foothold that street-food vendors had achieved during nearly a decade of independence had become threatened by the changing disease ecology of the city.

As fear of an epidemic loomed in Mombasa, working-class eateries were quickly identified as a public health liability, and the restriction of these businesses became a central pillar of the new set of policies bundled together as "cholera control." Official concern over street food is understandable. The epidemiological literature has demonstrated that street food can contribute to the spread of cholera, though it does so alongside more-structural factors, such as whether people have access to running water.[98] In Mombasa, as we have seen, the expansion of big and expensive infrastructure to serve the sanitation needs of the poor majority was not on the agenda. More feasible was to pay the daily wages of inspectors and demolition crews to shut down and demolish roadside eateries.[99] "Short-term palliation," rather than "an enduring structural transformation," became Mombasa's cholera control strategy. As a result, street-food vendors were asked, or indeed forced, to make a disproportionate sacrifice in the interest of public health.

This was the approach from the beginning. In March 1971, with cholera in the northern Tana River District, the municipal council put preventative measures in place, banning all street food in Mombasa.[100] This was a familiar experience to those operating illicit eateries, a move in line with previous attempts to shut down their businesses during the 1950s and 1960s. However, this ban also included all licensed vendors on the streets, and many of the municipality's canteens were shuttered too.[101] In the face of this ban, vendors mobilized and offered a collective response. Pressure was initially applied subtly, but as the municipality held firm, vendors became more militant.[102] By early April, hundreds of out-of-work street-food operators began showing up every day at the deputy mayor's office to protest the closures, trying to shame him and other councilors by "bringing with them children, claiming they had nothing to eat." As these protests unfolded, one anonymous city official told the *Daily Nation* that they had intensified to the point that "the 'tension' had been growing day by day and there was fear 'that some hostile people might resort to taking the law into their own hands.'" The pressure campaign worked, and on 14 April 1971 the council ended its ban.[103] Vendors had again used their collective power to shape urban policy, but their success also stemmed from the fact that the feared cholera outbreak never materialized in Mombasa during 1971.[104] Without a clear, immediate danger, the city's drastic preventative measures could be sustained for only so long. However, the way health and other governing authorities would view street-food vendors in future cholera scares had also been firmly established. They were seen as a primary source of the spread of the disease, and control measures would be directed toward them.

That licensed vendors in canteens were included in this 1971 ban underlines how far austerity was compromising public health in Mombasa. Declining social expenditures in the city not only delayed the construction of new canteens but also eroded investments in maintaining existing ones. As shown in the previous section, a principal argument for canteens was that they could help prevent the spread of foodborne illness, but in 1971 the medical officer of health had observed that some of these institutions "lacked sanitary accommodation and general hygienic standard," while the next year Lance Jones Bengo, director of social services and housing, concluded that "it is very hard to maintain hygienic conditions in any of them."[105] Already an issue, cleanliness concerns deepened as state resources were systemically removed. In 1972, Bengo, despite knowing that sanitation was already precarious, worked with the town treasurer to reduce long-running deficits in the food canteens and argued that "expenditure on [them] should be limited." They needed to be run "without much assistance from the Council."[106] Across all city markets, cleaners were reduced from thirty-six in 1972 to twenty-nine in 1973 and down to twenty-seven in 1974, despite the council also opening a new market that year and increasing pressure on the system from a rapidly expanding urban population.[107] By 1977, Salim Omar, a health inspector in the city, felt that "the whole situation . . . seem[ed] to be out of control" and "no or very little action ha[d] been taken" to improve sanitation in these markets despite constant warnings from health officials.[108]

Austerity also made working in a canteen a less desirable option. During the early 1970s, some vendors had run up arrears from their rent, and Bengo initiated a policy of aggressively collecting these debts.[109] Canteen vendors during that period had also been able to briefly make the city pay their water bills again, but Bengo's cost-saving measures shifted this responsibility back to stallholders. Not only did this make operating an eatery inside a canteen more expensive, but it also incentivized vendors to use less water, the basis of what kept them sanitary. In this privatized model of public health, the cost of running water was borne by individuals who felt they could not afford it. The consequences of such an approach could be seen in 1980, as the medical officer of health complained to Social Services and Housing, the latter department being in charge of markets, that food vendors in the canteens were not paying their bills and "as a result water ha[d] been turned off. The hawkers [were] . . . selling food for consumption under very dirty surrounds."[110] The austerity of the 1970s made canteens less sanitary and removed any financial advantages vendors had from working in them. These changes also occurred as cholera closures made clear that operating in a canteen did not guarantee protection from municipal authorities, removing the last major incentive for running an eatery inside a municipal stall.

The same forces that made canteens less attractive for vendors also made operating illicitly on the streets easier. Personnel cuts hit not only market cleaners but also the people monitoring petty commerce. The number of health inspectors in Mombasa declined from sixteen in 1960 to ten in 1978, a period during which the population of the city nearly doubled.[111] The municipality's Department of Social Services and Housing also did not have enough staff to systematically suppress illicit vending in the city near its markets, admitting in 1975 that an effort "to minimise illegal business carried out within less than 100 yards from the market" had "proved beyond their control and it was necessary to seek assistance from other quarters." With enforcement declining, the street-food industry continued to grow in the city, including the "illegal hawking of food . . . near the Council Foodvendors Canteens." Seeing these developments, "a good number of stall-holders at [the] Council's canteens" had left and set up on the streets "to avoid payment of rent."[112] In Mombasa, there were too few canteens to house vendors, and even those that existed were emptying out. Consequently, during the 1970s, only a few street-food eateries had consistent access to the sanitation infrastructures that helped prevent the spread of cholera.

Fortunately, from 1971 to 1977, no outbreaks occurred in Mombasa. However, preventative mass shutdowns of the street-food industry did happen if cholera was present elsewhere in the region, as in 1975 when the bacterium began spreading in communities in Nyanza Province.[113] Such actions had become common enough in urban Kenya that novelist Mwai Mwangi satirized them along with faltering efforts to create a canteen system in his fictionalized portrait of 1970s working-class Nairobi. Describing bustling Haile Selassie Avenue in Nairobi's Central Business District, Mwangi wrote of a crowd of pedestrians gathering "to watch the good health brigade at work. Cholera the Killer is in town. In the interests of public health all the roadside kiosks and other insanitary eating places have to be destroyed. . . . There are rumours rife that the Council will build organized sanitary Food Kiosks but no mention was made of when. Or what the food prices will be like."[114]

In 1977, referencing Mombasa, an anonymous "trader" wrote a letter to the editor of the *Daily Nation* that took a similarly sarcastic tone, noting the nearly impossible list of sanitation specifications demanded for a tea vendor's license; toward the end, the anonymous writer sardonically reflected that the person issuing the licenses "did not mention if the applicant fails to fulfill these regulations, if his or her kiosk will be crushed by their bulldozer."[115] Even with daily enforcement in Mombasa curtailed by personnel cuts, these periodic demolitions built insecurity into vendors' lives. In 1978, though, the sporadic character of these measures became systematic. Early that year, a deadly cholera outbreak in Tanzania spread to Kenya, and by April it was in Mombasa.[116] Fearing an epidemic, city officials turned cholera control measures into a more totalizing project.

As in 1971 and 1975, closures and demolitions started as a preventative measure, aimed at the destruction of businesses where the infection might spread. On 16 March 1978, before any cases were diagnosed in the city, a demolition crew arrived in the industrial district where "several unhygienic food kiosks in the port area [were] pulled down"; the crew then continued on to other parts of the city.[117] After these initial clearances, a relative lull in demolitions lasted until the first positive cases were confirmed in Mombasa in late April. As news spread, the council again did not make distinctions between licit and illicit vendors. Instead, it simply banned all street food in the city, including licensed eateries on the streets and in its canteens.[118] Moreover, whereas political will and resources had been previously unavailable, personnel and policy became concentrated on clearing Mombasa of small-scale eateries. By the end of April, the city had ten teams of police and demolition laborers that worked nearly every day arresting vendors and demolishing kiosks over the coming months.[119] David Angote, who worked in the industrial district during this time, witnessed a demolition there and described it this way: "On that day, precisely at noon, the said askari [police] invaded two *vibandas* opposite Magnum International and next to Express Handling Services Building. The askaris with their labourers moved in and uprooted the kiosks and used very bitter language during the operation."[120] Most days over the coming months, versions of this scene were repeated on Mombasa Island and throughout the mainland suburbs.[121]

Vendors, though, depended on this income, and many chose to continue operating despite the heightened risk. Using evasion tactics, people would work from a spot for as long as they could but then flee when cholera control teams approached. Common were stories like the vendors grilling maize in Likoni who "ran away after seeing the van" and the tea hawkers on the north mainland who fled "when they saw the team." However, even ten demolition teams can only cover so much of the city at one time, and after they left, such "vendors resume[d] their business."[122] In response to strategies like these, the authorities decided that when they had the opportunity, they needed to completely destroy the physical capital that vendors had to keep them from coming back and reopening. In May, a spokesperson for the medical officer of health explained, "We now make sure we destroy whatever they have."[123] This included the destruction of pots (*sufuria*) and kettles (*bikira*) and the confiscation of food.[124] By 6 May 1978, the authorities could confidently claim to have closed down 90 percent of all food vendors in Mombasa.[125] While this was perhaps an exaggeration given the continuing need to intensely police vendors over the coming months, the campaign was making a serious impact on the industry. By June, as the teams surveilled the usual locations for vendors, they often reported not seeing any in operation.[126] In early July, authorities confidently assessed that the citizens "seem[ed] to have heeded the advice."[127]

During the final months of 1978, the cholera threat in Mombasa subsided, and so too did the campaign to totally shut down street food in the city. Given the continuing need that vendors had for the income, and customers for their cheap meals, the industry quickly rebounded. However, cholera, along with cholera control measures, had become endemic in the city. Some municipal authorities, even those who led these campaigns, were not without sympathy for the disproportionate effect that cholera controls had on food vendors. In 1980, as cholera again was spreading in the rural areas outside Mombasa, A. W. Mugenya, the city's medical officer of health, wrote with regret that outbreaks

> of cholera in any place means not only loss of life but also economic disaster for the area. Human movement becomes limited. Petty traders who earn their livelihood through hawking cannot carry on with their businesses, consequently many fail to meet their water bills, school fees and house rents. This means that for the ordinary man life becomes impossible and anti-cholera operations may permanently ruin the life of these people as they use their savings to keep themselves going during the periods they cannot do their business.[128]

That vendors found themselves in this situation was less an act of nature and more the consequences of a political economy of austerity. The way to protect people from cholera and vendors from demolitions was simple, if expensive: the construction and maintenance of large-scale sewage collection and treatment facilities, along with building and subsidizing spaces where vendors had access to sanitary toilets and clean running water, whether in canteens or through some other model to provide collective public services. Instead, councilors and other officials trying to keep the city safe during a pandemic with diminishing budgets looked toward solutions that were cheaper and more immediate, ones that placed the cost of public health onto the city's street-food vendors.

* * *

By the mid-twentieth century, the structural incentives of Mombasa's political economy were pushing people into informal work like street food. This was also the same time that urban authorities nonetheless decided that such forms of economic activity did not belong in a modern city. Municipal officials gave this idea material force through campaigns of fines, arrests, and demolitions. However, street food was also crucial to the reproduction of the working day in Kenya's port city, and so for much of the postwar era the perceived disorder of such informal commerce was acceptable because it kept organized workers well fed and on the job. These kinds of businesses also eased pressure on the labor market, thus staving off an even worse unemployment crisis.

During these midcentury decades, though, government officials still attempted at various moments to use force to push through such contradictions, using both small clear-outs and mass demolition campaigns. However, unable to change the underlying structures of Mombasa's economy, these efforts failed to remove informality from the city. Despite the apparent failures, the effects of these initiatives on vendors were very real, entrenching instability into their working lives. Facing these challenges, vendors used the tools available to them to shift government policy more in their direction, carving out some limited space for their businesses in the administrative architecture of midcentury modernization. The next chapter examines both the business and the politics of street food during the last decades of the twentieth century, as the moment of state-led capitalism transitioned into the neoliberal era, a period during which the incentives driving informality only intensified.

5 ~ Street Food and Urban Life at the End of the Twentieth Century

ONEMUS MUTUA and I looked back at Mombasa Island as the ferry pulled away. I had seen the island from a distance many times before while speeding across one of the mainland bridges and peering up at the high buildings and surrounding residential neighborhoods from a *matatu* minibus or taxi. I had not, though, been on the ferry for years, and riding it unveiled a view of the island difficult to see elsewhere, showing the narrow channel that leads to the vast complex of Kilindini Harbour off in the distance with its docks full of cargo ships, lining the shores of Mombasa's industrial district. At midmorning, it was not yet lunchtime there. Cargo continued to move on and off the shore. Street vendors, however, would already be busy, boiling, frying, and roasting for the coming rush. As the ferry continued, Mutua and I turned our attention from the island toward our destination, the suburb of Likoni on the south mainland that covers an area almost as large as Mombasa Island itself. Mutua, my research assistant, had secured our first interviews in Likoni, and even though we were heading away from the island during off-peak hours, the boat was at maximum capacity. Upon docking, we moved in regimented unison with the crowds through the narrow front exit off the ferry. Everyone with their own destination, people eventually dispersed as they climbed off the vessel and up the incline ramp.

Likoni is a residential suburb, full of dense working-class neighborhoods in the interior that are bordered by elite homes and hotels along the exterior beaches of the south coast. Mutua, though, explained that we were walking only a short distance to the market stalls along the street that led to the docks. We were going to interview John Omondi Onyango (whose observations have appeared numerous times in this book) and quickly arrived at his open-air shoe repair shop, where he provided us with seats and shade under an awning. Onyango spoke with us for more than an hour, while rapidly repairing shoes the entire time, and detailed his life history, which took him from Siaya in western Kenya to Mombasa, where he had been since 1951. During the interview, I had to strain to hear Onyango over the cacophony of cars, motorbikes, and *tuk-tuk* taxis, gears grinding and horns beeping, as well as the innumerable nearby conversations of commuters, traders, and market customers. The frenetic pace and energy that surrounded our interview was made all the starker as Onyango described his memories of Likoni at midcentury. I asked about street food there during the 1950s, and he explained that back then the south mainland was like a big farm, quite literally as he worked on the market gardens that supplied food to Mombasa. During those years, continued Onyango, you had to go to "town" (Mombasa Island) to find street food, as Likoni was only "bush."[1] Over the coming decades, though, farmland turned into residential and commercial space, and peri-urban countryside into a bustling suburb. As Likoni grew, the need for street food increased too, on the south mainland for those now working and living there, as well as in Mombasa town for the people who commuted by ferry to the island.

Likoni was only one neighborhood in a larger city. Like urban areas elsewhere in Africa, Mombasa grew quickly during the last decades of the twentieth century, and nowhere more than on the mainland suburbs to the south, west, and north of the island.[2] In Mombasa, this demographic and spatial growth led to continuity in certain features of how the street-food industry figured into the city's geography, as commuters from the mainland to the island still needed lunch at midday. However, developing industries also spread into the suburbs, decentralizing urban employment and therefore creating new and increasingly fragmented markets for street food. The geography of these working-class eateries was changing, as was the quantitative scale of the industry. Informal economies had already been growing quickly during the early-independence era, and this process accelerated in the last decades of the twentieth century.[3] With so many more people working in the sector, businesses like street food transformed Mombasa's landscapes. The number of informal eateries covering open areas—sidewalks, road reserves, alleyways, parks, and parking lots alike—grew dramatically, in greater density where they already existed and in new concentrations in emerging sites of consumer demand. This included not only the mainland but also considerable expansion into the Central Business District (CBD) for the first time, establishing street food and other informal businesses on and adjacent to major Mombasa roads like Moi Avenue. In earlier decades, these structures had been limited mostly to the industrial area and working-class neighborhoods. By the end of the century, this bottom-up, makeshift architecture had become a central feature of the aesthetics of much of the city.

Changes to the postcolonial geography and economy of Mombasa also created new alternatives to street food. As the city extended its spatial reach, businesses opened in increasingly isolated areas where workers could not so easily rely on these small eateries. Private employers on the island had ignored the requests of municipal officials that they build cafeterias for their workers, but at the edges of the city, those in the exurbs faced more-pressing questions about how their staff would find a meal during the working day. This compelled some peri-urban companies—both large industrial concerns and the oceanfront resorts that came to dominate the coastal beaches of the north and south mainland—to install cafeterias where their workers could eat.[4] In addition to spatial considerations in these isolated resorts, beachfront hotels also fed their employees as part of the larger global workplace culture of the hospitality and restaurant industries in which "staff meals" were common.[5] These beachfront hotels were part of the larger growth of international tourism on the Indian Ocean coast after independence, as the Kenyan government put great emphasis on the sector in its postcolonial economic development plans.[6] The expansion of the tourism economy also generated new consumer markets and businesses in Mombasa, including many brick-and-mortar restaurants on the mainland and island that catered to foreign tourists, as well as the growing Kenyan middle and upper classes. Like those at beachside hotels, the people in service jobs at these restaurants were employed in a culture in which a workplace meal was expected and often provided.

Therefore, pockets of a more paternalist model of wage labor emerged in specific geographies and sectors of Mombasa's postcolonial economy wherein employers again became responsible for the social reproduction of their workforce, at least during certain mealtimes. However, most people continued to eat street food during the day. Customers and vendors alike leaned on the informal sector in a society undergoing a profound transformation in its political economy. The way that people experienced late twentieth-century capitalism in Kenya depended very much on how they earned their income. From the perspective of wage earners, both those with a job and others that aspired to acquire one, this was a period of decline. Real wages were falling, and formal employment could not come close to keeping up with the large number of Kenyans entering the workforce each year. As summed up by Charles Hornsby, "Life for most formal sector workers was far more difficult than for their parents."[7] For those in the informal sector, the political economy of the late twentieth century was more ambiguous. In part, this is because vendors had experienced state-led capitalist development rather differently than the wage earners who had secured upwardly mobile jobs. The first two decades of independence, as seen in chapter 4, did bring the promise of policy reforms that could provide street-food vendors with greater security in their working lives, but development projects to move vendors into municipal canteens also came with arrests, fines, and demolitions for those who still operated on the streets. Moreover, the austerity built into state-led development only deepened the insecurity of vendors during the 1970s as, absent the physical sanitary infrastructure to keep cholera out of Mombasa, government officials made shutting down street-food eateries a central plank of their "cholera control" measures. By the 1980s, though, a considerable change in how the Kenyan state viewed the informal economy was under way.

In scholarly and popular literature, the global history of neoliberalism during the late twentieth century is often explained in top-down terms in which Western governments and international institutions steeped in Austrian and Chicago school economics used moments of crisis—such as military coups, war, and especially government debt—to push countries in the Global South to transition from statist development to a neoliberal political economy.[8] This interpretation is quite useful to understanding the broader economic changes in Kenya at century's end, as the structural adjustment packages to ease the country's debt burden during the 1980s and 1990s had much to do with the state pursuing privatization, trade liberalization, and, indeed, the declining prospects of finding a job with the government.[9] The state also liberalized its laws concerning informal businesses like street food during this period, but the wider context of structural adjustment is at most a partial explanation for this change.[10] More important is that relaxing restrictions on the informal economy helped to ease the unemployment crisis during the 1980s, offering a way for urban Kenyans to earn incomes that the formal sector could not reliably provide. Such a policy shift also certainly fit into the liberalizing tendencies of late twentieth-century economic thought, demonstrated in the government's new position on informality in *Sessional Paper No. 1 of 1986*, explaining that the state should "create a healthy legal and regulatory climate for informal sector activities by eliminating unnecessary constraints, recommending an appropriate scale and licensing fees and charges, and protecting street hawkers and other self-employed people from overzealous policing."[11]

Given this change, in some ways, these final decades of the twentieth century were a period when street-food vendors had unparalleled security in their working lives. However, in other ways, such a utopian liberal economy in which vendors simply pursued economic opportunities freed from government constraint, competing to offer the best services, never materialized, as such ideal types rely on a vision of economics abstracted from the relations of power. Instead, opportunities opened in liberalizing Mombasa that generated new forms of accumulation and inequality simultaneously. The Kenyan government in this new era remained deeply involved in urban commerce, just in new ways. As in other neoliberal societies, instead of investing public capital in social development projects, the state became a still quite powerful instrument in facilitating private accumulation. Much of the literature on this topic in Kenya has focused on elite land-grabbing, but everyday people like street-food vendors also had to develop the right connections in the government to gain access to licenses and land so they could operate their business legally.[12] In Mombasa, the ability to cultivate these relationships became key to success in the street-food industry, and the inequalities that this created determined not only who profited more than others but also the extent to which vendors were exposed to arrests, fines, and even the demolition of their eateries.

SUBURBANIZATION, WORKPLACE CULTURES, AND ALTERNATIVES TO STREET FOOD

During the independence period, suburbanization and Mombasa's changing economy were redrawing the geography of working-class employment in the city. Work, concentrated for so long on the island, was becoming more decentralized, with greater numbers of people finding employment, both formal and informal, on the mainland. These forces also generated alternative models for the workday meal. Certainly, most employers continued as they had since the 1930s, paying a cash wage to their workers, who then purchased their own food. However, the pressures of rapid urban expansion forced some business owners to reconsider their relationship with their staff.

On the more distant mainland, the companies that moved out there for cheaper real estate or to be able to access the resources under the ground also isolated themselves from the established centers of the street-food industry. In the middle of the city, and even in nearby suburbs, employers spent little time thinking about how their workers would find their lunch, but this was a more urgent issue for managers at a place like Associated Vehicle Assemblers (AVA). The company opened its assembly plant during the 1970s in Mritini, a distant suburb straddling the Mombasa-Nairobi Road on the outer edge of the west mainland neighborhood of Changamwe. This was where Thomas Mbeda Jura worked starting in the 1970s, and he explained that the company built an on-site cafeteria where all the workers ate. It kept employees there during the lunch hour, and they were able to easily return to the job after they finished eating. Jura explained, "You were there all day. You ate lunch inside." In a saturated labor market, though, the company did not feel the need to subsidize the food to incentivize people to work there. Jura recalls that the prices were not particularly cheap, and the cost of his food was taken out of his check at the end of each month.[13] Indeed, AVA was setting clear limits to its obligation to feed its workers.

A more ambitious attempt at industrial paternalism was tried in the exurbs of the north mainland, where then-British-owned Bamburi Cement Factory built a large complex to extract lime underground and process it there on-site. By the time Rose Omwanda arrived at Bamburi in 1977, the complex included the health clinic where she worked. Not only, as she recalled, did Bamburi Cement have a company farm where it grew produce for workers, there was also a canteen in which people could buy cheap, subsidized meals. With her higher salary, Omwanda hired a cook to prepare her meals at home, but most other people ate in the canteen. By 1989, though, as the neoliberal turn saw many businesses around the world shedding obligations to their workers, Bamburi Cement was sold to a new French and German ownership group, which cut these programs. As Omwanda put it, "They just wanted to mix cement."[14]

These industrial businesses built large self-contained complexes in the spacious environs of the city's borders where suburbs transitioned into countryside, more-isolated locations that necessitated taking on some responsibility for social reproduction. While geographical necessity generated this form of industrial paternalism, workers in Mombasa's hospitality sector received food while on the job because of the culture of their industry. This included the fast-growing number of restaurants that served tourists and Kenya's postcolonial middle and upper classes.[15] Indeed, there were enough such restaurants that a guide was published in 1980, *Eating Out in Kenya,* with two subsequent editions coming out that decade. By 1987, the guide dedicated seventy-two pages to restaurants in Mombasa alone, reviewing nearly sixty in the city and quite a few more on the nearby north and south coasts.[16]

One of them on Mombasa Island was Singh Restaurant, just off the CBD on Mwembe Tayari Road. After 1980, the restaurant was run by Darshan Singh Wilkhu when he took over for his father. When it first opened, the restaurant initially served a more working-class South Asian clientele, but Wilkhu recalls that Europeans started coming to the restaurant in larger numbers from the 1970s onward.[17] This included *Eating Out in Kenya* author Kathy Eldon, who described the restaurant as "a very attractive place, furnished with matching tables and chairs, Indian prints and calendars" with food that was "very good and plentiful." Diners could choose from a variety of curries with salads and chutneys, and there were unlimited *chapati,* the latter continuing to come to the table "until the waiter [was] told to stop."[18] Julius Nzioka Nzonga, a migrant from Ukambani who began working at the restaurant in 1980, both cooked and served food, starting in the kitchen and then later becoming a waiter. Not only did he work there, but he also ate nearly all his meals in the eatery. This included South Asian cuisine, as well as "traditional African" dishes like *ugali.*[19] Thomas Mbaja Minara, who also worked as a waiter at a middle-income restaurant on Mombasa Island, recalled that during his shift he could eat chips, drink tea, and have some kinds of meat—though chicken, being more expensive, was reserved for customers. Looking back with fondness, he placed the free food at the center of why he liked that job.[20] With both of these eateries located on Mombasa Island, a street-food vendor would have been only a short walk away, but, being employed in a restaurant, these cooks, waiters, and dishwashers ate where they worked.

Staff meals were also part of working life at the many beachfront hotels that grew rapidly during independence on the sandy shores of the north and south mainland. In these resorts, the workplace culture of the hospitality industry and the spatial dynamics of suburban employment converged. These hotels required large staffs including waiters, cooks, wine stewards, room cleaners, security guards, and the many other jobs that were needed to run such vast institutions of leisure, but they were also comparatively isolated. Hezron Mupaghasa worked at the German-owned Silver Beach Hotel from the mid-1970s to the 1990s and explained that "every hotel had their canteen." He worked the early shift, and each morning left his house quickly without eating breakfast, instead taking his *chai* at work before he started. Employed at the hotel restaurant, his job was busiest when other hotel guests were eating, and so lunch was not served to food service workers until 2–3 p.m. He recalled that, while German workers had free food, Africans had to pay for theirs, and were fired if caught eating food they had not purchased. Even though the prices were relatively cheap, Mupaghasa was conscious of his budget, and mostly skipped the canteen to return home to cook some ugali.[21] Other workers, though, regularly ate their meals at these resorts, as Vitalis Owiti did. Before working at Mombasa Beach Hotel, Owiti had been a groundskeeper at private homes and relied mainly on nearby *vibanda* for his meals. However, as a hotel security guard, he had prepared dishes of meat with rice and potatoes brought to him at his post.[22] Joseph Mariko Agwari, who worked at Neptune Beach Hotel, remembers that these kinds of meals were available at all the resorts and featured a wide variety of foods. This included Kenyan cuisine like ugali and chapati, alongside "English food."[23]

Beach tourism, though, also relied on informal labor. Curio vendors sold souvenirs like carved statues, bracelets, paintings, and other such items that became a common purchase on a Kenyan vacation, and many of these vendors worked on the beaches that faced the Indian Ocean. This included Jacob Muli, whom I interviewed in 2014 inside his small enclosure that provided shade and a place for his inventory of curios, built on a high point of a north mainland beach. Muli and other vendors worked near the resorts to sell their carvings to tourists and were surrounded by brick-and-mortar restaurants, though all with prices that were much too high. Moreover, as independent hawkers, they did not have access to discounted food in hotel cafeterias like formal employees did.[24] When curio sellers first started operating on the beaches, there were not yet any street-food eateries close by. Patrick Kasau started curio trading on the beach in the mid-1970s and recalled that without access to affordable food, he usually worked the entire day without eating. He explained, "There were no *kibanda* near the area, only hotels [brick-and-mortar restaurants]." Eventually, though, street-food vendors discovered the consumer market for workday meals in this part of town. As street eateries began to open, Kasau happily remembered, "Now I can go to lunch," and from that point "everyone [selling] on the beach [went] there."[25] Other informal tourism workers, like taxi driver Benike Owuir (introduced in chapter 3), could also take their meals at these eateries. Driving to and from these hotels, she was able to save time and gas money by buying her meals from one of the many street-food eateries that lined the roads leading up to these oceanfront hotels.[26] Moreover, even employees of the hotels sometimes ate street food, as the staff meals were not always conveniently timed for all workers. As Agwari explained, at the Neptune Beach Hotel, the company meal was served only for dinner. Consequently, for "lunch you had to go buy outside," at the vibanda.[27]

In postcolonial Mombasa, paternalism returned, in a limited way, to the city's working-class food system. Some industrial employers in more-isolated exurban areas took on the responsibility of providing, and even selling, prepared food to their workers, while hotels and restaurants fed their staff from their commercial kitchens. During the second half of the twentieth century, people assembling cars, producing cement, and catering to the needs of international tourists and the local elite regularly were able to eat a meal without ever leaving work. However, most people in the city continued to have their lunch on the side of the road.

THE BUSINESS OF STREET FOOD AT THE END OF THE TWENTIETH CENTURY

Midcentury urban planners had envisioned Mombasa as a city where informality would, eventually, no longer exist, replaced by formalized businesses housed in sturdy and licensed structures. Over the coming decades, though, the opposite happened. Systematic quantitative data on street-food vendors in Mombasa is scarce, but qualitative descriptions abound about how they and other informal businesses were rapidly expanding across the city. This is best illustrated by the regularity with which municipal authorities referred to the "mushrooming" of unauthorized structures around Mombasa, invoking the idea of spontaneous, uncontrolled, and multiplying growth.[28] As at midcentury, this later phase of informalization was driven by the reality that employment in the formal sector could not keep pace with a fast-growing city. After independence, Kenya's urban areas expanded even more rapidly than the continental average, and Mombasa contributed to these explosive rates, more than tripling in size during the last four decades of the twentieth century, reaching a population of 665,000 by the end of the 1990s.[29] Kenyan-wide data provides a sense of the quantitative scale of informalization. Between 1978 and 1985, for example, these kinds of businesses grew in urban Kenya by an average of 7.4 percent each year; from 1981 to 1985 alone, the number of such small enterprises in the country's cities expanded from 157,300 to 215,900.[30] By 1994, over 1.1 million people worked in the informal economies of urban Kenya.[31]

This economic process transformed Mombasa's physical landscape, as the architecture of informality, nascent at midcentury, became a defining feature of the city. Street-food vendors staked claims to an ever-greater amount of the town's open spaces, especially on plots the government kept intentionally vacant for functional and aesthetic purposes, like road reserves and sanitary lanes. In 1987, Town Clerk M. K. Mumba observed that these kinds of areas had "almost all been taken up by kiosk owners."[32] This was true not only in places like the industrial district and working-class neighborhoods, mostly removed from the view of tourists and other international visitors, but also in the highly trafficked downtown, the CBD. In 1988, the mayor of Mombasa observed in a meeting that hawkers, including those selling "tea, maize, [and] roasted meat," had "moved to the main roads such as Digo Road, Jomo Kenyatta Avenue and Moi Avenue."[33] Nearby, the same year, in the sanitary lane that created a wide alley between the famed Blue Room restaurant in Mombasa's CBD and its neighboring building, there was a "huge" kibanda, serving food to the laboring classes who worked in the heart of the city.[34]

Such larger street-food eateries were constructed from a variety of materials ranging from the natural to the heavily processed. They were often held up by *boriti,* mangrove poles that were a long-standing building material on the coast, while another option was to assemble walls with blocks of chipped coral. For roofing, people regularly placed *makuti,* thatched palm leaves, on top of their structure, though corrugated iron (*mabati*) was also in use. If the structure had walls, materials from plywood to cardboard offered protection from the elements and the noise of a bustling city.[35] The size of these kiosks varied greatly, depending on the scale and scope of the business as well as how much land a person controlled. For example, Joseph Ngotho operated his whole business from a slim 20' by 10' structure made of "mangrove poles, cardboxes and makuti thatch," situated in a sanitary lane just off Jomo Kenyatta Avenue in the island's CBD. Others, like Mbwana Mohamed Musio's eatery at the edge of the Mwembe Tayari neighborhood on the island, had more space. There, customers ate in a 25' by 16' building made of a wooden frame sealed by "hard plain board" walls and a corrugated iron roof, with a 10' by 16' kitchen attached.[36] Using both new building materials and others with a deep history on the coast, the architectural aesthetic of these structures became an increasingly prominent part of Mombasa's urban form.

Street food also spread well beyond the industrial district and the CBD, into areas near the mainland beaches, as noted in the previous section, and in many other places with dense concentrations of potential customers. This included the west mainland, and especially in Changamwe, the location of Mombasa's main airport as well as considerable industrial and commercial activity. In that neighborhood, street-food vendors set up in places like the unofficial market adjacent to Magongo Road, which led to the airport. In 1976, city officials described how, "apart from 3 orderly built buildings, the entire plot [was] covered up with kiosks, stalls and unauthorised shanties, all of which [were] used for business purposes," including "Tea and Bread Hawkers" that also sold "ugali, maharagwe [beans], chapati and other food stuffs for consumption."[37] On the south mainland in Likoni, street-food vendors also marketed to the commuters who were going to and from Mombasa, as the ferry docks acted as a choke point that concentrated large groups of people. In 1987, officials observed that on both sides of the road leading to the docks there were "all types of trade being conducted including 'restaurants,' food vendors, tea[,] bread and mahamri," as well as "cassava roasters" and "peanut sellers." Referring to these vendors, they noted that the "rate of expansion . . . [was] very high."[38]

All these new street-food vendors were, as always, feeding the city's wage earners, but the expansion of petty trade in the city meant that more of their customers earned income in the informal economy. For example, they sold not only to curio traders like Patrick Kasau on mainland beaches but also to those working on the island near places with large numbers of tourists. This was how Mary Nambui Chege made a living, commuting each day from her home on the mainland to sell curios in front of Castle Royal Hotel located in Mombasa Island's CBD. There, she was able to spend long working days in her roadside shop because of the increased density of street-food eateries in the center of town. However, leaving for lunch required mutual support among curio sellers, as they stored considerable amounts of inventory in their kiosks, and so her neighboring vendors watched her merchandise while she went to lunch, going there and back in a half hour. She then returned the favor when her fellow curio traders had their lunch.[39]

Food vendors also provisioned workday meals to people selling daily essentials on Mombasa's streets. This included customers like Emma Mudanya, who had migrated to the port city from the Rift Valley in 1996 and earned her income by juggling two small businesses. Her work required a lengthy, strenuous, and physically demanding schedule traveling throughout the town, made easier by the wide availability of affordable prepared food. On a typical day, Mudanya arrived at Kongowea Market on the north mainland, which replaced the demolished Mwembe Tayari as the city's wholesale market, as early as 3 a.m. to buy a large crate of potatoes and then spent the morning retailing them. This first phase of work ended around 10 a.m., after which Mudanya would recharge. She recalled, "I would just buy [breakfast] from the vibandas, . . . a cup of white tea for 10 shillings, a mahamri you could buy it at five bob, which is not expensive." After a rest and before embarking on the second part of her working day, she purchased a proper lunch around 1 p.m. from a street vendor and then began her journey over the bridge to the island, where she spent the remainder of the afternoon selling used clothes. She told me, "I'm going to hawk around, and so I need some energy before I come into town."[40]

In addition to cheap prices and convenient locations, working-class customers also found street food appealing because credit was sometimes available at these eateries. Similar to *maduka* with raw ingredients (see chapter 2), this allowed people to acquire cooked meals when their cash ran low. Credit was common but was offered only under specific conditions. Most importantly, customers needed to develop a relationship with a kibanda owner before they could establish a tab at the eatery. They needed, in short, to become a regular. While this partly meant building a bond of trust, there was also more-practical information that vendors wanted to find out before they extended someone credit. In particular, they needed a way to track the person down, whether by knowing one of their relatives or, more commonly, finding out where they worked. As Catherine Muthoni explained, she had people who worked nearby and ate in her kibanda daily, and sometimes they would come to her business and tell her, "Mama, *nina njaa* [Mama, I'm hungry]." She would feed them, but they would pay later when they could.[41] One way that vendors could ensure repayment was to establish formal relationships with their customers' employers. Emma Mudanya, who started an eatery in the early 2000s, had the management of a construction company pay down their workers' tabs with her before they received the remainder of their wages.[42] Even with these mechanisms, though, providing credit entailed risk, as debts were not always repaid. As Monica Mutiso told me in 2014, "Some of [her customers had] not yet paid."[43]

Thus, whether purchasing with cash or on credit, people continued to be reliant on street food for their daily meals during these decades, though such eateries came to exist on a larger scale across the city's increasingly expansive and decentralized urban geography. The industry also became more important as a source of income, providing a living in a city with limited opportunities in the formal economy. Those who chose street food as their profession came into the business through a variety of pathways. Chapter 3 discussed how women who prepared food commercially at midcentury were commodifying the skills they had learned in their household kitchens. This certainly continued in later decades, but many vendors also trained as cooks in professional settings. Some worked as domestic laborers, cleaning and cooking in elite homes, as with Muthoni, who had a job in the household of a doctor when she first arrived in Mombasa. While there, she prepared the family breakfast, often including *chai, chapati, mandazi,* and *uji,* as well as lunch and dinner, featuring up-country dishes like *githeri* but also classic Indian Ocean options like *biryani* and *pilau.* This position provided her training in classic vibanda dishes, only some of which she would have learned during her childhood, and she was able to develop these skills by

FIGURE 5.1. Hamisi Nyoka having a lunch of *ugali* with *matumbo* (tripe stew) in an eatery in Mwembe Tayari on Mombasa Island. Photograph by Onesmus Mutua, 2024.

repetitively preparing food for her job. After becoming married, Muthoni decided to change professions, and she started a kibanda after realizing that she had ideal training to run the business.[44] For others, their culinary education was more formal. Monica Mutiso, who started her kibanda in 1996, had a long-term plan to work in food hospitality, taking culinary classes at Mombasa Technical College, but decided to start a street-food eatery because she could not mobilize the capital to open a brick-and-mortar restaurant.[45] Street food could also be a family business where people learned on the job as they grew up, as was the case for Hadija Ali Gambere, originally from

Kwale on the coast, who worked first in her aunt's kibanda in Mombasa preparing pilau and biryani before starting her own eatery.[46]

During the last decades of the twentieth century, more men also began to open these larger vibanda restaurants with more-complex menus.[47] Those who started these businesses did not always feel like they had been pushed into the informal economy; instead, some found running an eatery to be a more attractive opportunity. For example, Mohamed Amir Temu, the construction worker turned street-food vendor (introduced in chapter 3), ran a more expansive kibanda rather than a small *gari ya chai* and found the business to be quite appealing. Before starting his eatery, Temu worked as a repairman and then stayed in construction for around two decades. However, in 1985, he opened his roadside eatery, which he greatly preferred; he told me, "Construction work is hard, but kibanda work is easy because you go to the market, buy tomatoes and other things" and then "the work is to cook *sima,* to cook chapati." He found the money from street food to be better too. Even as a headman working construction, a rare job indeed in Mombasa's tough labor market, Temu remembered a daily wage of 1,000 Kenyan shillings. However, his kiosk could net him 1,500 on its best days, and he could also eat all his own meals at work instead of buying them from someone else.[48]

More generally, both men and women remembered street food as a good way to make a living. Women especially described their success in the industry through the way it allowed them to provide for their children, particularly in respect to education.[49] Nuru Ibrahim Hajj started her kibanda in 1988 after her husband died; she told me that it enabled her to educate her seven children, from form one up to form four.[50] Similarly, Elizabeth Malleo, who opened a kibanda in 1996, explained that street food paid three times more than her previous business selling used clothes. Closing only on Sundays to attend church, Malleo made 500 Kenyan shillings per day, income that helped put her children through school.[51] While street food offered a livable income for many, some even managed to accumulate capital. Muthoni told me that with her business, "There is big profit, profit *sana* [very]. I make a lot of money." It provided her the capital to buy a home, and not only could she afford to pay for her children's education, but she sent them to a boarding school, and she hoped to university too.[52] Muthoni was newer to the industry, but others were long established in Mombasa and had relied on the income of street food to provide comparative comfort for decades. Sampson Kereu (introduced in the previous chapter) opened his kibanda in 1976 and described the status he gained from this profitable business in a variety of ways, such as the political connections it provided him, both local

FIGURE 5.2. Mohammed Omar at his small food stand near the General Post Office on Mombasa Island where he sells chai, coffee, mahamri, fried potatoes, and mango juice. Photograph by Onesmus Mutua, 2024.

and national, as well as the economic resources to marry three wives, buy rural land in Central Province, and send his children to school.[53] Kereu was also a close friend and mentor of a vendor named Josephe, who since the 1980s has owned a series of successful street-food eateries. After arriving in Mombasa from the Rift Valley in 1980, she learned the trade while working as a server in a brick-and-mortar restaurant, then opened her own kibanda with the help of Kereu. Josephe felt that good money could be made in the informal economy, but not everybody was willing to work on the streets. She told me that people who came "fresh" from school wanted to work indoors:

"They just thought the business that is good is the one that has a building, a structure like this one [the restaurant where we spoke]." However, with a well-run street-food eatery, "at the end of the day it was huge money."[54]

These well-established vendors ran eateries as their primary source of income, starting with few resources and building large businesses over many years. However, members of Mombasa's political and economic elite also saw profits in street-food eateries as a supplementary income stream. For example, in 1982, a municipal councilor used his position to convince his colleagues to approve the construction of a kibanda on an open space of land close to Mwembe Tayari Market that was supposed to be reserved for a decorative flowerbed.[55] Even further up Mombasa's power structure, Deputy Mayor Samuel Ndoro owned a large food kiosk, also located in the Mwembe Tayari neighborhood on the island. Run by employees, it was a fully operating small restaurant, offering chapati, *maharagwe, sikuma wiki,* ugali, and pilau, sweet snacks like mahamri and cake, as well as tea and soda to drink. Ndoro's kiosk violated nearly all the same health regulations that other vendors' eateries did, but the acting medical officer of health, Dr. E. Mpate, approached the deputy mayor delicately with his concerns. Making clear his "due respect," Mpate wrote with the "humble advice" that the deputy mayor "consult [his] Chief Public Health Officer . . . who [was] more than ever ready to give your Worship an expert advice."[56] Most vendors, of course, were not extended such courtesies by the city government.

As indicated with Ndoro's kibanda, many street-food eateries were also large enough that they had employees. Some were more overtly vertical enterprises, like the deputy mayor's; he was removed from the day-to-day operations, and his employees ran the eatery. More typical, though, were places where the complexity of the business reached the point where employees were necessary to expand the scale of operations but the owner continued to work alongside them. As Nuru Ibrahim Hajj explained, she ran her business by herself at first, but as it grew she decided to delegate, hiring two workers to specialize in preparing ugali and chapati.[57] Monica Mutiso hired staff too for her kibanda in the CBD, situated just off Moi Avenue, but still continued to work every day, adding the help of an assistant cook and a waiter. Taking on employees also allowed vibanda owners to diversify their business, particularly by offering delivery services, especially to office workers, as well as security guards who could not leave their posts. Catherine Muthoni, for example, ran her eatery with two employees, both of whom cooked with her starting at 6:30 in the morning, first preparing chai, mahamri, and chapati for breakfast and then moving on to githeri, pilau, and more chapati again for lunch. However, once the lunch rush came, with much of the food already cooked, her workers transitioned to new roles, one as the waiter and the other handling delivery orders.[58]

Many people thus worked in the informal economy not as business owners but as employed workers. Sometimes the division of labor within these eateries came within the structure of a family, as for Hadija Ali Gambere, who worked at her aunt's kibanda, while Sampson Kereu's business relied on the work of family and non-kin alike. Kereu operated the eatery with his first wife, who prepared uji, chapati, and many other dishes and did deliveries around town. After she died, his second wife then took over this role. However, the kibanda, one of the largest in town, also had six employees, which became increasingly important after Kereu began to lose his sight around 1990. His workers continued to run the business, and he was able to still earn income even though he felt he could no longer do most of the daily work of the restaurant.[59] Even in eateries without family labor, these informal workers operated in a more paternalist context than did most people employed in the formal sector. In Elizabeth Malleo's kibanda, for example, she paid her workers a small salary, which was also supplemented with free food and a place to sleep.[60] Hajj's employees were not given accommodation, but they ate breakfast and lunch for free at work and then she packed them food for their dinners at home. From Hajj's perspective, this was not part of their wages but rather a form of generosity, a gift that she gave to her workers.[61] In street-food eateries, the profits produced were far below those of larger companies, but conflicts over the distribution of these surpluses nonetheless occurred. The workers at Josephe's business were frustrated enough that they went on strike, prompting her to develop strategies to stifle their organizing. She explained, "I came to learn that one day, they strike. . . . So I have to learn to do all these things even during their absence, and during their presence. So to me, I have no pressure now from the workers. If you fail to come, I'm fine. If you don't, I'm there."[62]

Thus, by the end of the twentieth century, a tremendous diversity of businesses fell under the category of "street food." Some were just a single person selling one item of food, like grilled maize, roasted meat, or perhaps fried fish, but others ran restaurants with long menus that were staffed with people to cook, clean, and take delivery orders. Many were somewhere in between. In this industry, as in many others, differentiation was also emerging both within and between these businesses. However, all vendors, regardless of their size or rate of profit, operated in a political climate in which they ran the risk of losing their livelihood. As discussed in the previous chapter, this had been the case in the city for some time, but in late twentieth-century Mombasa, new forms of inequality came to shape the extent to which vendors faced this kind of insecurity. That is, some people were more likely than others to be fined, arrested, or have their vibanda destroyed.

THE POLITICS OF STREET FOOD IN THE LATE TWENTIETH CENTURY

Street-food vendor Sylvester Obanda Ogwell was an ambitious young entrepreneur in the late 1980s. He built an ornate kiosk in a centrally located part of Mombasa Island on Mikindani Street that connected the Central Business District with Kizingo, a high-income residential neighborhood. Perhaps realizing the way this rather visible location exposed him, he pursued a variety of strategies to lend legitimacy to his business. Ogwell secured a municipal trading license and connected his kiosk to running water and electricity, rare infrastructure for a roadside vendor. He had not acquired permission from provincial authorities to occupy the land where he built his kibanda, but neither had many other vendors in Mombasa. He also strove to make his eatery a pleasing sight, installing a "wooden floor, glass windows and high roof," then filling this space "with [a] beautiful wall painting . . . round tables, table tennis, birds in cages and an aquarium." To pay for all this, Ogwell had leveraged himself considerably, taking on a loan of 64,000 Kenyan shillings and spending nearly 100,000 in total. On 1 March 1988, though, a district official, conspicuously accompanied by two police officers, approached Ogwell's kiosk. The government agent was blunt. Ogwell's licenses had been canceled, and his kiosk was going to be demolished, later finding out that this was done so a developer could build apartments in this high-value neighborhood. He protested with petitions to the district and provincial authorities but was assured that such efforts would come to nothing. The secretary of the district commissioner told him that the eviction came from an "order from the higher authority so it was no use . . . to complain."[63] Following this, the district commissioner himself, K. P. A. Langat, addressed the case, but only to underline that Ogwell had no rights to the plot. Dismissing Ogwell's trading license and connections to services, Langat emphasized that "the basis of any occupation or development of land is ownership," defined as "freehold, leasehold or temporary occupation license." Putting the matter to rest and emphasizing his office's authority, Langat concluded that "connecting water, electricity and council licences does not give anybody the right to occupy government land illegally."[64]

Ogwell's experience opening a street-food business in a highly visible part of town represents both the possibilities and the perils of running one of these roadside eateries in late twentieth-century Mombasa. By the 1980s, the politics of street food had changed decisively. With so many urban residents having become reliant on the informal economy for their income, the government could not as easily dismiss the sector, given that it was preventing a far worse unemployment crisis in Kenyan cities like Mombasa.

Moreover, the idea that the canteen system would one day replace the services that street food provided no longer animated debates in the municipal council. Following the disinvestment of the 1970s, the city largely stopped building new canteens in the 1980s, while the number of vendors in the city expanded rapidly.[65] Such a small number of canteens obviously could not house the vast number of street-food vendors in the city. In this changing political economy, vendors were able to gain greater access to public space where they could run their businesses. However, to achieve this new level of security, they needed not only licenses but also to find powerful state officials to back their claims. However, access to the government documents and personal connections that could provide a stable working life was not equally available in Mombasa, as people like Ogwell often found out.

The archival records from the 1980s are replete with both oblique and explicit references to these kinds of relationships between vendors and government officials. This emerging dynamic is also indicative of the declining power of public health officials in the city, as they became increasingly unable to enforce sanitary bylaws because they were stalled or stopped entirely by "political" forces. These conflicts illustrate the shifting structures of power within Mombasa's municipal government, from the first decade of independence, when C. D. Rosenwald and N. S. Rihal could reliably draw on the national government's support to curtail populist policies, to the 1980s, when the authority of public health officials had clearly eroded. For example, in 1982, health authorities were concerned about street-food vendors operating close to Magongo Market on the north mainland but did not push the issue further because they "feared local politicians and hence left the hawkers alone for fear of clashing with those politicians."[66] Later in the decade, in a meeting with the mayor in 1988, Mombasa's beleaguered municipal inspector identified the three main obstacles to enforcing bylaws on the informal economy. In addition to an inadequately small staff of inspectors and insufficient support from the police, he also underlined "Interference from Politicians" as a major issue. The mayor, though, seemed little interested in untangling and exposing the relationships his councilors had developed with small-scale vendors in the city. "On the issue of politicians," the mayor told the municipal inspector to "let him handle it. He should go on doing his job and leave the politicians to the politicians."[67]

Moreover, whereas in earlier decades government debates about street food tended to divide elected and appointed government officials, this distinction was less clear by the end of the century. Indeed, civil service officers used their position to create extralegal structures to grant vendors access to land and relief from municipal enforcement. This included major figures in the city administration like D. Mmbanga, the markets supervisor for Mombasa. In his position, Mmbanga controlled Likoni Market on the south mainland, allowing vendors to use it and the surrounding environment in ways that clearly violated the municipal codes he was ostensibly tasked with enforcing. At Likoni, Mmbanga had vendors pay rent for a spot at the market, and then they could construct an eatery within or adjacent to their allocated stall. These eateries, twenty-seven in all, were effectively illegal according to Mombasa's market codes, as some were located in stalls meant for other trades, while other vendors built unofficial add-ons to create more of a restaurant space. Some small eateries were licensed to operate in the market but instead set up on nearby open spaces on state property. Though all these establishments violated at least one law, Mmbanga, the person most directly responsible for the city's markets, created a parallel structure of authority in which these vendors had secure access to government land.

However, M. A. Skanda, Mombasa's senior public health officer, still saw these kinds of eateries in much the same way his predecessors had. Referring to those at Likoni, he viewed them as "substandard" restaurants operating in "unauthorised structures" that were "overcrowded" with "insufficient water supply and drainage," while also lacking "sanitary facilities of their own." Among these vibanda, Skanda's officers visited Jackson Kimani's frequently, perhaps because he ran the largest of the twenty-seven restaurants that Mmbanga had authorized in the area. In 1986, Kimani opened his eatery outside the market on nearby land, and public health inspectors immediately tried to make him license it and comply with sanitation laws. These efforts, though, were "dislocated by market authorities." In early 1987, health officials tried to enforce sanitary laws again, issuing violations to the food vendors at Likoni, but "due to external interference this did not succeed." Finally, they arrested Kimani and numerous other vendors and took them to the Likoni Police Station. However, Mmbanga quickly intervened directly with the police and got them released. This caused an uproar in the municipal administration, and a tense meeting was held in the town clerk's office during which Skanda accused Mmbanga of "obstruction." While gathered at the seat of municipal power, the town clerk being among the most influential of city officers, health officials won the day. The meeting ended with a resolution that "fresh notices be served on the restaurants or food kiosks" in Likoni and that this be done "in the presence of the Markets Superintendent."[68] However, off the island and back at the market, Mmbanga's power was sturdier. Months later, Skanda reported that more than twenty small restaurants were still operating in and around Likoni Market, paying rents to secure their spots.[69]

Thus, if vendors were able to develop these kinds of relationships with powerful officials, they could secure durable access to public land to pursue their businesses. However, cultivating these connections also required navigating a complex bureaucratic web of overlapping and competing authority within Mombasa's government. For some state officials, the control of public land was a source of power, a resource that could be provided to supporters ranging from small traders to large-scale real estate developers. These relationships were fraught as Kenya entered the era of "land-grabbing," wherein the question of which government agencies and corresponding personnel controlled which parcels of land in the city was not so much an esoteric debate between bureaucracies as it was a competition over who would be able to distribute these valuable resources. In Mombasa, much of the land was technically not administered by the council, in which elected officials held sway. Instead, departments in the provincial and district administrations, especially the commissioner of lands, controlled much of it, particularly the road reserves where many vendors operated. By the 1980s, traders could legally occupy these kinds of urban spaces if the commissioner of lands issued them a temporary occupation license (TOL). This meant that municipal officials could not on their own provide all the requirements that vendors needed to operate legally, as Ogwell discovered. As one district official lamented in 1987, "The tendency has been for the council to approve plans and issue licences for kiosks without caring much where the kiosks are going to be established."[70] In most instances, a vendor who wanted to be totally legal needed to secure both a trading license from the council and a TOL from the provincial administration. Unable to mobilize all the required licensing, many of the people who ran roadside eateries instead operated within extralegal structures to gain access to urban land.

The archival record of official government documents is, unsurprisingly, silent on the details about these kinds of transactions between officials and vendors. However, Mohamed Amir Temu, the construction worker turned street-food vendor, explained in an interview that during the 1980s the municipal council was "like a business."[71] Such descriptions of the government can also be found in media coverage, providing insights into the practice of urban governance during this period not easily found in archives. For example, *Daily Nation* columnist John Mbaria, writing in 2001 and looking back at the 1990s, observed that councilors in cities "all over the country . . . have been selling to kiosk owners spaces which they know well are road reserves."[72] L. G. Mwacharo, in a letter to the editor in 2002, was more detailed. He explained the process in Mombasa this way: "Roadside kiosks are the creation of local chiefs, councilors and MPs. It is a popular way of rewarding voters after election. . . . The prospective kiosk owner would locate empty space on a road reserve and approach the chief with a bribe, and with the assistance of the MP he is 'allocated' the price of the road reserve. Thereafter, administration policemen are given the responsibility of collecting monthly rent from the kiosk owners on behalf of the chief."[73]

These are analyses from people who likely had incomplete information about a complex process that unfolded over multiple decades in a diverse and changing city, so bribery was not necessarily at the root of all or perhaps even most of these relationships, especially if councilors or MPs were looking for electoral supporters. However, these observations do clearly emphasize that accessing and securing urban land required more than simply filling out the necessary forms and waiting for approval. In Mombasa, public land was distributed through more-personal and idiosyncratic relationships between vendors and government officials.

Those able to successfully navigate these politics and dense bureaucracies could enjoy a considerable amount of security in running their businesses. However, urban space is finite, more so in a fast-growing city like Mombasa. For those unable to locate a patron to provide them land and licenses, the late twentieth-century city was a precarious one. This is well illustrated in the experience of Priscilla Mwanake Murundi. During the mid-1980s, Murundi began the process of legalizing the food truck she wanted to operate on top of the ocean bluffs along Mombasa Island's Mama Ngina Drive. Most vendors made their income selling prepared food to people during the working day, but Murundi saw an opportunity in offering snacks and drinks to people relaxing at this popular vista that looked out at the Indian Ocean. Her business was meant to feature prepackaged items like soda, ice cream, candy, biscuits, and cake, as well as cooked food like kebabs and samosas. In writing to the provincial commissioner, seeking his "assistance to set up a small business," she framed her case just right, pointing out that her eatery would be sanitary, as the truck contained a sink with "hot and cold running water" that was supplied by the storage tank, and she would also be parked near the public bathrooms. Moreover, in a city rife with unemployment, her business would have five to nine workers.[74] However, despite these advantages, her efforts to officially register the business languished. Nearly a year later, after having invested significantly in the project, and following harassment and having her husband almost arrested, she wrote to the municipal council asking why "you have stopped the circulation of my plans." Murundi, who was from up-country, saw her exclusion as caused by "envy, hatred" and "bias," underling Mombasa's racial dynamics by writing that there should be no difference in the city between "Ali Abdalla and John Otieno," stereotypical names meant to represent the Arab and Luo communities. She had been hoping to discuss her case with the town clerk, A. M. M. Nasser, for some time, but he had refused to see her.[75] After Nasser read her letter, he wrote back and vociferously denied the allegation that race had played a factor in what was apparently a denial of her application. He concluded with a threat: "I may be forced to take any such action I may think fit to redeem the tarnished reputation of my Council and its officers."[76] Unable to get an audience and threatened, Murundi concluded, regarding the town clerk's last letter, "[It] almost confirms one of my greatest fears, that there I was dealing with someone who had already made up his mind."[77]

Others trying to follow the rules also struggled to secure their place if they did not have the required connections. James Kubai started a small eatery in Mwembe Tayari in 1978 and tried to get registered in 1981 as licensing laws were being liberalized. However, his application stalled, and he waited three years without resolution while watching others around him receive their licenses. In 1984, the municipality finally told Kubai he needed to apply for a TOL with the provincial administration before he could have a license, despite other vendors in his immediate area who had quickly received theirs without this requirement.[78] As his TOL application moved slowly through the provincial administration, Kubai began to hear rumors that nearby and better-connected vendors were conspiring to seize his land. Plans were apparently under way for his stall to be demolished, after which the neighboring vendor would expand his kiosk onto Kubai's plot. Luckily for him, in the course of his application for a TOL, his case had come to the attention of B. R. Maina, provincial physical planning officer, who was not simply sensitive to Kubai's situation but, perhaps more significantly, also to attempts by the municipal government to control the provincial administration's land. Maina intervened on behalf of Kubai, ordering that the demolition be stopped, and also reasserted provincial authority, instructing the town clerk, "This is government land and the Commissioner will sort out the matter soon."[79] Here, a provincial administrator had intervened to stop a demolition when it served the purpose of buttressing his commission's claim to urban land. Other provincial and district officials, though, were ready to demolish small structures and displace vendors when it suited their interests, as Ogwell had experienced with his kibanda.

Ogwell's case demonstrates the way vendors remained vulnerable when they did not obtain all the necessary licenses as well as how, ultimately, the forms of legality available to people working on the streets offered only a small level of protection. Indeed, even if he had acquired the permission of the provincial administration to go with the trading license he already had, his situation would have largely been the same. Vendors were granted these licenses on an explicitly temporary and contingent basis. The government retained the absolute right to evict a vendor the moment the land became designated for an alternative use, whether for a government purpose or to be sold to a private individual or company. That is, even vendors who had obtained all the legal protections available to them, both municipal trading and provincial occupation licenses, effectively had no rights to the land where they worked. For example, District Officer D. T. A. Owino delivered the good news to J. K. Lulu that he had been awarded a license to occupy the unused part of a parking lot but also informed Lulu that he would "be required to vacate the site on notice from this office."[80] If the government wanted to use the land, vendors holding TOLs had no greater claim to their plots than Ogwell. In such circumstances, straightforwardly legal means of securing urban space offered street-food vendors few enduring protections. Instead, sturdier claims were held by those with a patron who would protect their right to the city when a "higher authority" came for their land.

* * *

By the late twentieth century, many street-food vendors in Mombasa were able run successful businesses for years, especially if they had formed relationships with governing officials. Though vendors like Murundi and Ogwell found themselves on the wrong side of the city's governing class without a powerful ally, others were able to secure support that allowed them to fend off efforts to have them removed. This included the people who constructed seven street-food eateries during 1983–84 outside the front gate of the District Fisheries Office, located on the southern part of Mombasa Island, sandwiched between the ferry docks and Kilindini Port. They managed to not only situate themselves in front of this government building but also to incorporate its physical infrastructure into their businesses. The vendors used the fence that surrounded the fisheries office as their back wall, to which they additionally connected the roofs that covered their eateries. They also managed to gain access to the facility's running water, in effect having the government pay their utility bill.[81] In 1988, fisheries officers launched a sustained campaign to have the vendors expelled, but they quickly ran into "an element of political interference." The municipal councilor for the area, Akoth Olang', came to their defense and advocated for restraint because the "traders [had] families who depend[ed] on them, with children in school."[82] Access to such connections in the government were effective. The fisheries department began its effort to clear these vendors in May 1988. Seven months later, the vendors were still there, as the case bounced around

Mombasa's administrative offices. In the last available documentation on the topic, the district commissioner passed it off to the district officer for Mombasa Island with a touch of desperation, asking that "you get in touch with the Town Clerk to see how best you can save the situation."[83]

With the backing of a municipal councilor, vendors could compete even with government agencies over access to land and services. However, such forms of security remained tenuous. The people working outside the fisheries station may have been successful in this particular instance, but they and others continued to work in a political context in which their businesses were, in the final analysis, still seen as undesirable by many in the city with significant authority. In the early 2000s, this included perhaps the most powerful person in Mombasa, Mvita MP Shariff Nassir, a defender of vendors back in the early 1970s but who had come to see them differently as his political priorities changed. The reality of a figure like Nassir turning against informal traders underlines the vulnerability of people who earned their living on the streets. Given the opaque and extralegal ways that many vendors used to secure their plots, they could easily lose control of the situation if the balance of personal and political forces changed within the government. That is, they had little legal recourse to back their claims to land if their patron was outmaneuvered. By 2001, Nassir had become convinced that the people working in Mombasa's informal economy posed a threat to him and his party, the Kenya African National Union (KANU), in the upcoming elections. In an effort to maintain KANU's control of the government, the Mvita MP decided that nearly every informal structure in the city had to be demolished. The book's concluding chapter discusses how the most radical attempt to clear vendors from Mombasa happened at a time when many had, until that point, achieved unprecedented stability in their economic lives.

Conclusion

Working-Class Food and Informality in the Twenty-First Century

> Woe unto you if you are poor, ugly and, therefore, undesirable. The message is violently clear: Kenya's urban centres are not for you.
>
> —David Kakali, *Daily Nation,* 26 January 2002

> Is beauty more important than livelihood?
>
> —K. K. Wales, *Daily Nation,* 29 January 2002

FOOD VENDORS are hard to beat to their kiosks in the morning. People running these eateries have significant work to do if the *chapati, mahamri,* and *chai* are going to be ready for morning commuters. Some start as early as 4:30 a.m., which means that on 22 December 2001, the people who were working for Shariff Nassir's demolition crews were likely awoken in the middle of the night, preparing to carry out their orders while most of the city still slept.[1] By the time many vendors arrived at their kiosks that morning, the crews had already finished. Emma Mudanya, who was a produce trader at the time, remembered that day vividly more than a decade later. She recalled that the demolitions were "done very early in the morning. People woke up . . . and found their *vibandas* were demolished. . . . There was no notice. There was no rumor, there was nothing."[2] One of these street-food vendors was Catherine Muthoni, whose routine was to arrive at her eatery by 6 a.m.; by then on 22 December, her business had already been destroyed. The shattered remains did not represent merely the physical capital lost, which she had taken on debt to acquire; Muthoni was also concerned about how this threatened the income that she used to pay for her children's expenses, especially their school fees.[3] With handheld tools and the mechanized power of bulldozers, Nassir's crews moved through Mombasa flattening these businesses that so many of the city's poor residents relied on for their livelihoods, and others for their daily meals. The aim was radical: to clear nearly every informal structure from Mombasa, including but not limited to roadside eateries. The operation lasted for more than a month.

Since the mid-twentieth century, the justifications for such "crackdowns" on Mombasa's informal economy have drawn on the depoliticized language of urban development: vendors need to be cleared from the city so that Mombasa can become aesthetically, legally, and sanitarily modern. Jonathan Shapiro Anjaria has pointed out how much of the literature we have on such urban dynamics in the Global South comes from scholars who are temporally and conceptually grounded in the recent past and ethnographic present who see these processes above all as products of the neoliberal era. However, using coercive force to create "world cities" attractive to middle and upper classes, tourists, and foreign dignitaries, as well as for the investment of international capital, is not new.[4] In the case of Mombasa, late-colonial projects to engineer an orderly city where informality did not belong were carried over in a new form at independence. During the first decades following the end of colonial rule, Kenyan officials imagined urban space as a key vehicle for development where a certain kind of architectural and legal order was necessary if the country's major cities were to become connection points to the global economy. As discussed in chapter 4, Mombasa's civil servants during the 1960s pressed to remove vendors from the streets lest they sully the city's image for the tourist trade that had risen near the top of Kenya's economic development plans, and the national government stood firmly behind these efforts. Such ambitions for "world cities" in the era before neoliberalism were even stronger in the capital, Nairobi, which officials in 1969 considered "a well-developed metropolis comparable to other big cities in the world," a "modern and sophisticated city" whose "already important role . . . as host to international conferences and similar functions should be expanded." After opening the new Kenyatta Conference

Center in 1973 in the heart of Nairobi's Central Business District (CBD), created to be a hub that would host conferences for global economic and political elites, then–cabinet minister Mwai Kibaki explained that complexes like these represented "a landmark on the road to our future. A prosperous future."[5] Implicitly and often explicitly, the order of this urban future was imagined in contrast to the perceived disorder of economic informality. Aesthetically and functionally, whether during the time of midcentury modernization or neoliberal urbanism, such world cities could not be dominated by the petty street commerce of the poor.

In Mombasa, the existence of such discourses about Kenyan urbanism are at once indispensable and insufficient for understanding why and when demolitions have occurred in the city. This is because, despite the widespread appeal of these ideas within Mombasa's ruling classes, pursuing them in a sustained fashion has proved impractical in a city that depends so heavily on the informal economy for products, services, and employment. Nonetheless, demolitions still happen regularly, often on the individual or neighborhood scale though also citywide on rarer occasions. If the services that businesses like street food provide have been begrudgingly accepted as necessary, we must then explain the persistence of campaigns to expel them from the city. The answer lies in the reality that, for Mombasa's elites, the informal economy is useful until it is not. Employers rely on labor, and the informal economy ensures the continual reproduction of the city's low-wage system. Moreover, the employment and income that informality provides help to prevent urban crises of protest and more-significant forms of revolt that could disturb the social order that preserves ruling-class power. Whatever the aesthetic dreams of Kenyan elites, history has shown that they value a consistent labor force and stable society even more. However, at specific conjunctures, powerful individuals have at least temporarily found greater advantage in the removal of vendors. Indeed, as Claire Robertson wrote about the repression of foodstuff traders in Kenya's capital city during the late twentieth century, sometimes governing authorities felt that "immediate political considerations outweigh[ed] the necessity not only to provide employment but also to feed Nairobi."[6] In Mombasa, during the 1970s, health officials did not see a present or near future in which there would be adequate sanitary infrastructure to keep the city safe from cholera, but shutting down street vendors and publicly destroying their businesses allowed the government to demonstrate that it was "responding" to the crisis. During the 1980s and 1990s, street-food eateries could occupy urban space in crowded and valuable sections of town, providing cheap meals to nearby workers, but when the land was needed for "permanent development," the onus was on the vendor to find somewhere else to go. These more-recent displacements served specific political and economic ends, benefiting particular individuals and classes, but the language of urban development allowed them to be explained as part of a necessary and ultimately beneficial process. During this same period, people in Kenya's ruling party found another reason to expel street-food and other informal vendors from the country's cities, and these actions too could be justified through the language of urban development.

Political liberalization at the turn of the twentieth century in Kenya was a contradictory process. It opened new spaces to challenge the authoritarian rule of President Daniel arap Moi and his party, the Kenya African National Union (KANU), but in this changing political arena, the president's regime also encouraged and tacitly authorized violent political and ethnic cleansing to ensure electoral victories for KANU candidates and to generally give the impression that multipartyism would destabilize a Kenya that only Moi could control.[7] These methods of politically targeted ethnic cleansing took the form of intense interpersonal and communal violence, exemplified in the killings, assaults, and intimidation in the Rift Valley before the 1992 election and in the Likoni neighborhood of Mombasa in the lead-up to the vote in 1997, but as Jacqueline Klopp has shown, KANU also repurposed the administrative practice of urban demolitions and attacks on the property of the poor as a new strategy to drive opposition supporters out of Kenya's cities.[8] This tactic has been employed by ruling parties in other parts of Africa too. As Deborah Potts observed of Operation Murambatsvina in Zimbabwe in 2005, which aimed to eradicate informality from the country's cities and ultimately displaced approximately 650,000 to 700,000 people, the ruling party, the Zimbabwe African National Union–Popular Front, drew on familiar language to explain its campaign. These mass demolitions were done ostensibly to push "modernist planning and the associated image of a 'modern' city" but also, argues Potts, from "a desire to punish urban areas for their almost universal tendency since 2000 to vote for the opposition MDC."[9] Earlier, around the turn of the twentieth century in Kenya, KANU MP Shariff Nassir had similarly become concerned about the voting preferences of certain urban residents in Mombasa, many of whom were migrants from up-country and worked in the informal economy.

Seen over the duration of his long career in politics, Nassir's view of the informal economy was contextual, the perspective of a politician ready to adapt to changing circumstances. In this book, we first met Nassir, son of a wealthy shipping family from the coast, in chapter 4 in 1970 when he was KANU district chairman and soon to be elected as Mvita MP, the latter a position he held for nearly thirty years. Then a rising politician seeking popular support, he became swept up by the energy of 150 female vendors who protested at his office, convincing him to be their defender against local authorities. During the following decades, Nassir also emerged as the most powerful defender of KANU on the coast, a professional role he prioritized above all others.[10] By the early 1990s, with international and local pressures for multipartyism weakening KANU's authority, Nassir had become less sure of the political loyalties of the city's street vendors. In the months before multipartyism was formally inaugurated, Nassir complained of the "mushrooming of 'political kiosks' in Mombasa" that had "recently invaded the city . . . particularly [his] constituency." They "[would] have to be told," he continued, "that they have no business here." Changamwe MP Kennedy Kiliku, then a member of KANU in single-party Kenya but soon to join Mwai Kibaki's Democratic Party for the 1992 elections, understood the political and racial undertones of Nassir's comments. Kiliku, who was Kamba and represented Changamwe, where many up-country migrants lived, responded, "We cannot be made refugees in our own country."[11] However, by 1996, Nassir was still in power and again became a defender of the informal trader. In June of that year, unlicensed street-food and other vendors organized a protest against police harassment, and the traders validated Nassir's authority by going to the KANU office and asking for his assistance.[12] The Mvita MP's power over the provincial administration, police, and municipal council was well understood in the city, and Nassir urged these officials to allow the poor to earn their living, also announcing that he would personally "engage a lawyer to handle cases involving hawkers and other people indiscriminately arrested by the police."[13] For Nassir, the question of whether informal vendors belonged in Mombasa seemed to have less to do with aesthetic, legal, and sanitary questions, and more with whether they were politically useful or a liability.

By the early 2000s, the ability of KANU to stay in power in the era of multipartyism had become more tenuous. Moi's term limit was expiring in 2002, and a previously divided opposition was moving toward strategic unity, a national mood also present in Mombasa, where Nassir, the embodiment of KANU on the coast, faced a region that was turning against the ruling party.[14] Up-country residents of Mombasa were seen especially to be opposition supporters, and their prominent place in the informal economy provided Nassir an opportunity.[15] Like other KANU leaders, he drew on the by-then-established party tactic of using demolitions to drive opposition supporters from urban areas. As his operation began in December 2001, Nassir faced criticism for the clear political undertones of the mass demolitions he unleashed across the city. He responded by relying on well-tested arguments from Mombasa's urban history. A few days after the demolitions started, Nassir sat in his office in the upscale, ten-story Cannon Towers located on the eastern end of Moi Avenue in the CBD and explained to gathered reporters that "the exercise" would continue "until all structures erected on road reserves were demolished to make the town clean," a necessary action that would "attract more investors and help create more jobs."[16] Days later, he kept pushing the message, telling journalists that the city "must be kept clean . . . to attract more tourists and investors," and he urged, "Those against the move should now go around the town and see the difference."[17] In other public statements, Nassir bristled at the idea that these demolitions had anything to do with the coming election arguing instead that they were simply "intended to clean up the town" and "attempts to read politics into the whole exercise were 'misguided.'"[18] The following month, he continued to try to manage how the operation was perceived, such as after his crews demolished most of the vibanda in the parking lot adjacent to Makadara Gardens, a quite visible public square on the island located on the border between Old Town and the CBD. Awkwardly, the only two kiosks that remained standing were owned by KANU officials, yet Nassir tried to assure the public that his operation was not selective in the way it removed structures. It was apolitical, he emphasized, aiming only to "develop" Mombasa. The newly cleared site by Makadara, he reported, "would be beautified and turned into a recreation resort."[19]

Nassir continually defended his project because criticism was consistent and wide-ranging. People connected the operation not only to the election but also to what Jeremy Prestholdt has called the "politics of the soil," the fraught debates and conflicts over the relationship between identity and territorial claims in East Africa. In this instance, contemporary commentators underlined how the demolitions were putting physical force behind the idea that up-country people did not "belong" on the coast.[20] For example, bringing together the two threads just days after the demolition campaign began, *Daily Nation* columnist John Mbaria asked his readers to "consider this. Next year is an election year. Unlike in the past, Mr Nassir now has a credible opponent in former Mayor Najib Balala, who is said to be very popular with people from upcountry. Mr. Nassir . . . is afraid for his political survival, So, what to do? Chase the upcountry folk away."[21]

Newspaper writers considered these dynamics, and they pervaded everyday interactions as well. Mudanya, a produce trader who witnessed the demolitions, recalled that around this time some "coastal" people started saying, "*Watu wabara, warudi kwao*" (Up-country people, return to your homes).[22] Nassir was a veteran politician who used careful language, consistently maintaining that the campaign was merely done for "urban development" objectives, but as the operation moved on in February to demolishing shack settlements throughout the city, he let slip more explicitly racialized language. Explaining this latest round of destruction, he announced, "Slum dwellers will not be spared. Let them go back to their homes."[23]

Nassir also faced pushback from people he might have expected to be allies. While some in tourism celebrated the move publicly, others were horrified as they observed an operation ostensibly done for them. They were concerned, in particular, by the way it made Mombasa look "like it was in the throes of a civil war."[24] Similarly, a letter to the editor of the *East African Standard* voiced worries about how this would shape the global perception of Kenya, stressing that "television images of lorries reversing into the kiosks, askaris breaking up the structures and the hawkers trying to salvage the little they own will be hard to forget," all of which "reflects very badly on Mombasa as a tourist destination," made worse because "foreign media love to broadcast such chaos."[25] There were others who supported the idea of developing Mombasa into a city largely without informality but lamented how this operation overtly politicized the project, brazenly taking it from the domain of the apolitical and using it as an instrument to maintain public office. *Daily Nation* editorial writer Jaindi Kisero reflected on the demolitions by first stating, "Uncontrolled mushrooming of kiosks is something I do not support," but he was nonetheless disappointed by how "we are handling what is clearly a complex urban problem, . . . allowing politicians to dominate this discussion." He then queried, "Can we, really, expect to get disinterested guidance from politicians on this matter, especially at a time when the elections are around the corner and when their likely disposition is to shamelessly look upon people as vote-banks and not as human beings with needs?"[26]

Thought leaders in Kenya were additionally concerned about how this attempt to bring "order" to urban space might ultimately create a more profound disorder in the country's important port city. Running through elite commentary was an anxiety about what these people whose livelihoods had been destroyed would do in an urban economy with few other viable options. Father John Kamau of the Holy Ghost Cathedral in Mombasa warned that "the biggest fear . . . [was] theft since most people ha[d] been rendered jobless by the demolition team."[27] In line with Father Kamau, the editorial board for the *East African Standard* stressed, "Ironically, what the government does not seem to realize is that by dismantling these small businesses, it is (in)directly encouraging criminal activities, prostitution and related vices."[28] Comments like these reflect the power that vendors still had in the city despite the demolitions, leverage that came from the same forces that had for decades placed limits on how far urban development was pushed. Not only did street traders provision inexpensive goods and services, but they were also crucial for social stability. Nassir's exercise threatened to undercut the very foundation of what sustained working-class life in the city, with a destabilizing potential that clearly concerned those who had secured positions at the top of Kenya's society. Small, targeted demolitions were one thing. The total eradication of the informal economy was a far more radical proposition, one with uncertain consequences.

Elites debated these various elements of Nassir's demolition campaign in the press. Those who faced the actual reality of its destructive force used the tools they had to resist the campaign. Vendors organized public protests and drew on their allies in the government, while some also engaged in direct action. Two days into the demolitions, more than two hundred vendors marched on Mombasa's Town Hall; they were joined by Councilor Luyai Liyali from the opposition Social Democratic Party of Kenya. After an hour of verbal confrontation, with some people even making it inside the building, the city government cleared the protests with fifty paid youth militia members who arrived with *rungu* (clubs) and "stormed the Town Hall, pounced on the unsuspecting hawkers and kiosk owners before flushing them out of the Town Clerk's office corridors," with "a number" of the protesters "seriously injured."[29] Following this violence, Councilor Liyali argued that "the demolition of kiosks in Mombasa was tantamount to a declaration of war against the poor by the government," and he "asked all the kiosk owners and hawkers whose property was either destroyed, looted or set ablaze to arm themselves and fight back."[30]

The next day, whether responding to this call or acting of their own initiative, vendors in Changamwe used their strategic location within Mombasa's geography to apply pressure to the government. They shut down the highway that connected Mombasa to the interior and also blocked tourists traveling between the airport and beachside hotels. As demolition crews moved through the neighborhood, vendors built barricades from scattered debris and tires and set them ablaze. The confrontation escalated quickly. The protesters were joined by their MP, Rhamadhan Kajembe, who dramatically threw "himself in front of the bulldozer" that was coming to flatten kiosks. Elsewhere in the neighborhood on Airport Road, protesters also tried to physically stop the demolition crews, and the police guarding the operation opened fire on them. As the day continued to unfold, vendors sacked licensed shops, attempted to burn down a gasoline station, and immobilized a fire truck sent to extinguish the fires on the barricades. At one point, the protesters found Nassir, who infamously followed demolition crews in a limousine, and he had to be "rescued by police after his convoy was set upon by small-scale traders armed with stones and other weapons." During all this, the roads were shut down and "holiday makers were forced back to their hotels, unable to take their flights," as "a queue of vans carrying tourists and other passengers [formed] on both sides of the flashpoint." By the end of the day, the authorities reported that one person had died, though people from the community claimed more deaths had occurred.[31]

Facing fierce opposition from above and below, Nassir nonetheless pushed on through January and then began his demolitions of shack settlements in February. However, despite likely displacing many opposition voters, the operation overall had a negative impact on his electoral prospects. Nassir had gambled and lost. He had gone too far, outpacing the capacity of his allies to justify the scale of this totalizing violence and destruction. Kenneth Ombongi, in his postelection analysis of the campaign for the Mvita seat in 2002, wrote that the demolitions had alienated Nassir from "even the staunchest of his supporters," and most of Kenya's leaders condemned the demolitions. As his colleagues distanced themselves from the operation, opposition figures made it central to their political platforms.[32] Nassir's main opponent for the Mvita seat, Najib Balala, continually brought up the demolitions during his campaign, while others used it to criticize KANU more broadly. For example, Musikari Kombo, an MP from FORD-Kenya, wrote a letter to the editor of the *Daily Nation* stating that "we, in Ford-Kenya[,] are shocked that a government that is supposedly for the good of the people, is turning against them," targeting "law-abiding Kenyans whose only crime is to try to make an honest living in a hostile economic environment created by a corrupt and inefficient Kanu regime."[33] The Catholic Church also condemned the action and explicitly politicized it. Only days after the operation began, a church representative "threatened to mobilize its congregation to vote against the ruling party and Nassir next year if the on-going demolitions [were] not stopped."[34] As votes were being tallied in late December 2002, it became clear that Nassir was going to lose spectacularly. With the final count, he received only 12 percent of the vote to Balala's 84. Ultimately, the loss was more about bigger structural changes in Kenya's politics that saw KANU largely swept from power that year, but the demolition campaign only deepened a political crisis that the former Mvita MP and his party could not escape.[35]

Nassir's electoral defeat, therefore, was decisive. However, the long-term effects of his demolition campaign have been more ambiguous. By late 2001, decades of expansion of the informal sector had led to an urban landscape fundamentally defined by the small structures of petty commerce. These businesses occupied a significant place not only in the industrial quarter and working-class suburbs but also in the CBD and even on Moi Avenue, the city's main commercial thoroughfare best known for the large sculpture of crisscrossing elephant tusks that frame the road. Before the demolitions, wrote a journalist for the *East African Standard,* Moi Avenue might have had the city's "biggest concentration of kiosks, selling a wide variety of goods ranging from second hand clothes, [to] wood carvings, food and antiques."[36] Indeed, a striking picture printed in the *Daily Nation* in January 2002 showed numerous turned-over kiosks just below "the tusks," displaying the ubiquity of these structures in one of the city's most central locations at the moment of their destruction.[37] No precise surveys were done on the scale of the damage, but estimates at the time suggested that approximately 10,000 of the city's 15,000 informal commercial structures had been destroyed within the first four days of the operation, which then continued thereafter for weeks.[38] Interviewees also used totalizing language to describe the demolitions, indicating that nearly all the informal kiosks in the city were gone by February.[39] This had immediate effects. The city's workers suddenly did not have access to inexpensive prepared food during the day. Agnes Maweu, a migrant from Machakos, sold bananas on the city's streets and had regularly enjoyed warm lunches of *githeri, ugali,* or chapati that she bought from vibanda. After the demolitions, though, she had to bring milk and bread from home to eat during the day.[40] Beachside curio seller Patrick Kasau (introduced in chapter 5) told me that after the demolitions "we stayed without." The working day again came with hunger.[41]

However, while Nassir had destroyed the material form of street-food eateries, his crews smashing, crushing, and burning them to the ground, he did not change the underlying political economy that had incentivized this form of commerce. As after the late-colonial crackdowns, the demolitions during the 1978 cholera campaign, and now again following the Nassir operation, people like Maweu and Kasau still wanted to buy a cheap lunch, and vendors needed the income. In late 2001 and early 2002, newspapers were filled with pictures of turned-over kiosks, fires, black smoke filling the air, and piles of rubble, but the *Daily Nation* also published a contrasting image on 17 January 2002. It featured an unnamed man tying twine to stabilize a frame of *boriti* poles, rebuilding "his structure at Kongowea market barely a day after it was pulled down."[42] As Mohamed Amir Temu explained, "What did you do? You rebuilt again. It's destroyed one day, rebuild it the next morning."[43] Of course, starting again during the demolitions was risky, and some waited longer, but people eventually and steadily ventured back to the streets. Indeed, Kasau told me that although he did have to make do without street food for a while, "After a month, the people built some vibanda."[44] In the industrial district too, vendors returned. Mueni Sammi, still working in the area when I interviewed her in 2014, waited six months but then again began providing lunchtime meals to her customers.[45] Others reopened their businesses, but more cautiously after the devastation of 2001–2. As described above, Catherine Muthoni's kiosk was demolished at the beginning of the operation, but rather than remain exposed on the streets, she moved her business indoors. She cooked food in her home kitchen, and then customers could eat on a bench outside. For this increase in security, though, Muthoni saw her receipts decline by half, which she attributed to no longer having happenstance customers walk by the eatery and buy her food.[46]

The industry also continued to attract new petty entrepreneurs. Produce trader Emma Mudanya had watched the demolitions unfold around her but nonetheless decided to open a street-food eatery on Mombasa Island later in 2002. In explaining why she opened a business that came with such clear instability and risk, Mudanya said it was simply an economic choice. "You know," she told me, "seeking for a job, it makes you so much desperate. So, if you don't find something to do, you decide in your heart, I'll be happy, I'll do it. I see this thing happening [the demolitions], but I'm going to do it." She decided to earn her income by selling prepared food on the city's streets: chai, mahamri, chapati, and *uji* in the mornings and ugali with a variety of relishes at midday.[47]

* * *

In capitalist societies, the spatial dynamics of residential and working life shape the way that goods and services become commodified. Indeed, modern capitalism remade rural and urban Africa, but in different ways that reflected how the surrounding environment and geography opened certain possibilities and closed off others. In rural Kenya, commercial farmers and wage earners alike depended greatly on cash in their lives, but most also maintained kitchen gardens in their fields that kept them tied to the means of subsistence. Cities were different. The construction of commercial, government, and residential buildings quickly covered fields, while the sheer density of human settlement in a comparatively small area foreclosed the possibility that the mass of the population could sustain themselves from the land. Anyway, the open land that remained in urban areas became designated for leisure—parks, golf courses, and sports fields—not agriculture.[48] The people who lived in the rapidly growing city of Mombasa during the twentieth century still relied on their labor to provision their food, but much more indirectly. They had to earn wages loading and unloading cargo, sweeping streets, and constructing buildings or could alternatively engage in trade on the city's streets, thereby acquiring currency to convert into food to feed themselves and their dependents. In this, Mombasa's laboring classes were like other urban proletariats in the modern world who left rural food systems and entered cities where cash and credit mediated access to the necessities that sustain life.

Thus, the creation of a new kind of food system in twentieth-century Mombasa was part of the global process of proletarianization, unfolding within the urban context of one colonial and then decolonizing society. During the twentieth century, the racial paternalism of *posho* rationing in the early-colonial period gave way by the 1930s to a food system in which people became individualized consumers. Urban residents bought what raw ingredients they could afford from street traders and *maduka* and prepared the final meals in their kitchens. Inside their home, the work of cooking remained beyond the commodifying tendencies of urban capitalism, as migrant men prepared food for themselves and their brothers, uncles, fathers, and other male friends, while women made all the food when they were part of a household. However, the way the working day became mapped onto the geography of a fast-growing city commodified kitchen labor too, especially around lunchtime. As the city expanded across the island and onto the mainland, work and home became more spatially distinct. Mombasa turned into a commuter town in which working life required people to travel longer distances away from their residential kitchens and the domestic labor that prepared their food. This created a consumer market for kitchen labor, selling conveniently located meals that allowed commuters to complete the long working days of Mombasa's urban economy. Above all, street-food vendors provided this service in Kenya's port city during the twentieth century.

Even after the 2001–2 demolitions, these roadside eateries have remained central to how working people acquire their food during a day of labor. However, echoes of Nassir's operation remain in both the city's food system and its built form. There are now not nearly as many street-food eateries in Mombasa's CBD as photographs, archival documents, and oral interviewees suggest there were at the turn of the twenty-first century. Sidewalks in the center of town are crowded with people but not small structures save for the occasional "Coca-Cola" kiosk with bottled drinks, packaged snacks, and mobile-phone cards or an occasional grilled meat stand abutting from a brick-and-mortar restaurant. Moreover, parks on Mombasa Island, once a favorite spot for an eatery, are now more exclusively sites of recreation and leisure rather than commerce. The enduring legacy of Nassir's operation, therefore, has been to largely close off parks and sidewalks in the CBD to street food, with the only exception being mobile hawkers who sell snacks. Government elites at the time may have criticized the Mvita MP's operation, but they have since seemed interested in keeping informal traders from returning to at least the most visible parts of the town. However, just a slight remove from these main thoroughfares and public spaces, hungry people can still find more-complete meals at a cheap price. In Mombasa, road reserves, alleys, and parking lots have become the main sites where people can reliably find affordable food in the center of the city. Kiosks no longer sit under "the Tusks" on Moi Avenue, but just a block or so away, vendors are set up on road reserves and offer inexpensive and freshly prepared food. Closer to Old Town, as Moi Avenue turns into Nkrumah Road, a right turn onto Mikindani Street reveals a small collection of eateries. There, customers can find menus containing most street-food classics and eat them in the comfort of chairs and tables under the cover of roofs held up by boriti poles. Greater concentrations of vendors can be found in areas farther from the surveillance of the CBD, in locations where customers abound. This includes, most of all, the industrial quarter that surrounds Kilindini Port and the railway, where the modern street-food industry began and a place in which one still does not have to look far to find an inexpensive eatery at lunch.

Thus, Mombasa's laboring classes continue to rely on local, small-scale entrepreneurs for their daily meals, much as they did throughout the twentieth century. This is the case not only when buying prepared food during the lunch hour but also while purchasing the raw ingredients they will cook at home, from maduka as well as individual traders working on the streets or in city markets. However, some comparatively recent trends in the composition of the grocery and restaurant sectors in Kenya portend potentially significant change in the future. In recent decades, there has been a corporatization of food retailing in Kenya, as well as Africa more broadly, which has been driving supermarket and fast-food "revolutions."[49] Many of the first generation of supermarkets were Kenyan-based corporations; like large grocery stores elsewhere in the world, they offered extensive shopping options in one-stop locations. Kenya's supermarket industry, though, has seen extreme volatility in the past few years. Grocery brands that once defined the sector—Nakumatt, Tuskys, and Uchumi—collapsed and went out of business after becoming overburdened by debt, and they were unable to meet operating costs on vast networks of stores across East Africa. Into this vacuum, local and global chains have moved fast to establish themselves as the new industry leaders, and thus far Naivas and its more than ninety stores have the edge. A local corporation, Naivas is also indicative of how international capital has become increasingly interested in the market. In 2020, Naivas raised funds by selling a 30 percent share of the company to investors, which included the World Bank's International Finance Corporation, Amethis Finance of France, MBC Equity Fund from Mauritius, and the German sovereign wealth fund. Moreover, the French grocery giant Carrefour entered the Kenyan market in 2013 and has grown steadily since, now with nineteen stores across the country (and seven in Uganda).[50] While (mostly) locally based companies still dominate the supermarket sector, global corporations have made greater inroads into fast food. In 2011, KFC became the first American fast-food restaurant to open in Kenya, joining the already established South African chains of Steers and Debonairs. Five years later, there were eleven KFCs in Kenya, and now one can also be found on Nkrumah Road in Mombasa's CBD. Once KFC entered the market, more fast-food chains followed, including Pizza Hut, Dominos, and Subway.[51]

At this point, what this expansion of corporate supermarkets and fast food means for most Kenyans remains unclear. While global fast-food chains have grown rapidly in the country, they remain spaces for those with high incomes. That KFC in 2011 opened its first restaurant at Junction Mall in Nairobi is instructive, for that mall is one of the most elite shopping centers in the country. The prices charged at KFC, Subway, and other such chains are out of proportion to what working-class Kenyans can afford. In Mombasa's CBD, most people needing lunch will walk past KFC and look instead for a street-food vendor just off the main road. Supermarkets also play only a marginal role in the food purchases of low-income communities, but for more complicated reasons. Even though some items, especially nonperishable foods, may be cheaper by weight in supermarkets, the scholarship on these large food retailers in Kenya and Africa more widely underlines how the business model fails to work for the household finances of the urban poor. Like working-class communities in midcentury Mombasa (see chapter 2), low-income consumers continue to manage tight budgets by purchasing groceries in smaller amounts more frequently, which they are able to do with street traders and grocers at maduka who will divide a larger packaged good into multiple units, a service not available at supermarkets. Additionally, while corporate grocery stores require immediate payment at checkout, smaller local retailers often offer customers credit, which has long been crucial to how poor people make their economic lives work in the city.[52]

Therefore, despite the growth of corporate and global food retailing in Kenya, there is no sign at present that these companies will soon overtake the role played by the informal economy. Indeed, as recent survey data has shown, low-income communities in urban Kenya still overwhelmingly buy groceries from vendors and small independent shops.[53] In Nairobi, for example, a sample of residents from the Mathare and Kibra constituencies from 2016 and 2017 indicated that only 21 percent of respondents shopped in supermarkets, and their purchases there accounted for only 3 percent of their overall expenditures on food.[54] Moreover, people have continued to rely greatly on the informal economy for employment, including opening eateries and selling produce, among other businesses. From 2016 to 2019, the informal economy increased each year quantitively and as a share of overall employment, declining only during 2020 because of the strains of the pandemic. By 2020, the informal economy accounted for over 80 percent of employment in Kenya outside small-scale agriculture.[55] However, all the people buying foodstuffs from street traders and lunch from roadside eateries represent potential profits not being realized by corporate grocers and restaurants. This leaves open the possibility that such companies could push forward revolutions in production, distribution, and exchange to drive down prices in pursuit of these new markets. Should this happen, it would represent a radical change in the ownership structure and labor process of food retailing in urban Kenya. For the immediate future, though, most people living in the country's cities will continue to buy nearly all their food from street traders, small shops, and eateries on the side of the road.

Notes

INTRODUCTION

1. Interview: Evans Nduati Gitonga, Mombasa, 28 November 2014.
2. John Burnett, *England Eats Out: A Social History of Eating Out in England from 1830 to the Present* (London: Routledge, 2004); David Harvey, *Paris: Capital of Modernity* (New York: Routledge, 2006), 200–201; Katherine Leonard Turner, *How the Other Half Ate: A History of Working-Class Meals at the Turn of the Century* (Berkeley: University of California Press, 2014), 51–90; Jonathan Shapiro Anjaria, *The Slow Boil: Street Food, Rights, and Public Space in Mumbai* (Palo Alto, CA: Stanford University Press, 2016).
3. World Bank graph, "Urban Population (% of Total Population)," based on United Nations World Urbanization Prospects data, accessed 20 September 2021, https://data.worldbank.org/indicator/SP.URB.TOTL.IN.ZS.
4. For the limits of urban agriculture, see a recent study on small cities in Kenya and Zambia that found that only 33 percent of households practiced urban agriculture and, of those, their farmed produce did not substantially affect their food (in)security. Julia Davies et al., "Barriers to Urban Agriculture in Sub-Saharan Africa," *Food Policy* 103 (2021): 1–14. For similar results in urban areas across Southern Africa, see Bruce Frayne, Cameron McCordie, and Helena Shilomboleni, "The Myth of Urban Agriculture," in *Rapid Urbanisation, Urban Food Deserts, and Food Security in Africa,* ed. Jonathan Crush and Jane Battersby (Basel, Switzerland: Springer, 2016), 19–31.
5. Though focused more on rural history, Ellen Meiksins Wood underlined the centrality of changes to food systems in the transition to capitalism: "The emergence of the market as a determinant of social reproduction presupposed its penetration into the production of life's most basic necessity: food." Wood, *The Origin of Capitalism: A Longer View* (New York: Verso, 2017), 97.
6. For Mombasa, see Frederick Cooper, *On the African Waterfront: Urban Disorder and the Transformation of Work in Colonial Mombasa* (New Haven, CT: Yale University Press, 1987). For an older but still the most comprehensive review of the literature at a time when labor history was a more active topic, see Bill Freund, *The African Worker* (New York: Cambridge University Press, 1988).

7. Barbara Laslett and Johanna Brenner, "Gender and Social Reproduction: Historical Perspectives," *Annual Review of Sociology* 15 (1989): 381–404; Evelyn Nakono Glenn, "From Servitude to Service Work: Historical Continuities in the Racial Division of Paid Reproductive Labor," *Signs* 18, no. 1 (1992): 1–43; Tithi Bhattacharya, ed., *Social Reproduction Theory: Remapping Class, Recentering Oppression* (London: Pluto Press, 2017); Jamie Winders and Barbara Ellen Smith, "Social Reproduction and Capitalist Production: A Genealogy of Dominant Imaginaries," *Progress in Human Geography* 43, no. 5 (2019): 871–89.
8. Social reproduction is studied both as "daily," the focus of this book, and "generational," the latter focused on biological reproduction, the raising of children, and care for the elderly.
9. Jane Guyer, introduction to *Feeding African Cities: Studies in Regional Social History,* edited by Jane Guyer (Bloomington: Indiana University Press, 1987), 1. See also Wood, *Origin of Capitalism,* 97.
10. Interview: Agnes Gome, Mombasa, 18 December 2014.
11. For a schematic and abstract framework of the different components of food systems, see Jack Goody, *Cooking, Cuisine, and Class: A Study in Comparative Sociology* (New York: Cambridge University Press, 1982), 37.
12. Alfred Crosby, *Columbian Exchange: The Biological and Cultural Consequences of 1492* (Westport, CT: Praeger, 2003); Sydney Mintz, *Sweetness and Power: The Place of Sugar in Modern History* (New York: Penguin, 1986); James C. McCann, *Maize and Grace: Africa's Encounter with a New World Crop* (Cambridge, MA: Harvard University Press, 2007); James C. McCann, *Stirring the Pot: A History of African Cuisine* (Athens: Ohio University Press, 2009); Tracey Deutsch, "Labor Histories of Food," in *The Oxford Handbook of Food History,* ed. Jeffery Pilcher (New York: Oxford University Press, 2012), 61–80.
13. On gender in rural African food systems, see Diana Wylie, *Starving on a Full Stomach: Hunger and the Triumph of Cultural Racism in Modern South Africa* (Charlottesville: University of Virginia Press, 2001); Elias C. Mandala, *The End of Chidyerano: A History of Food and Everyday Life in Malawi, 1860–2004* (Portsmouth, NH: Heinemann, 2004), 210–17; and McCann, *Stirring the Pot,* 3, 9–10. For gender and cooking in other parts of the world, see Deutsch, "Labor Histories of Food"; Turner, *How the Other Half Ate* , 16, 52; and Amy B. Trubeck, "Kitchen Work, 1920–Present," in *A Cultural History of Food in the Modern Age,* edited by Amy Bentley (New York: Bloomsbury, 2016), 127–44.
14. Michelle Szabo and Shelly Koch, introduction to *Food, Masculinities, and Home: Interdisciplinary Perspectives,* ed. Michelle Szabo and Shelly Koch (London: Bloomsbury, 2017), 6–8. See also Carole Counihan, "Gendering Food," in *The Oxford Handbook of Food History,* 104–5.
15. For all the insights of Szabo and Koch, they do leave the impression that whatever changes have occurred in the gendered division of domestic

labor, minimal as they are, happened quite recently. See Szabo and Koch, introduction, 15–16.

16. For this pattern in other parts of the world, see Deborah Cohen, "From Peasant to Worker: Migration, Masculinity, and the Making of Mexican Workers in the US," *International Labor and Working-Class History* 69 (2006): 81–103; Alessandro Monsutti, "Migration as a Rite of Passage: Young Afghans Building Masculinity and Adulthood in Iran," *Iranian Studies* 40, no. 2 (2007): 167–185; and Susanne Y. P. Choi and Yinni Peng, *Masculine Compromise: Migration, Family, and Gender in China* (Berkeley: University of California Press, 2016).
17. Teresa Barnes's research on Zimbabwe suggests that women engaged in "marital migrancy" spent significant time in town. Teresa Barnes, *"We Women Worked So Hard": Gender, Urbanization, and Social Reproduction in Colonial Harare, Zimbabwe, 1930–1956* (Portsmouth, NH: Heinemann, 1999), 110–18. In contrast, the evidence for Kenya suggests that, between Mombasa and the countryside, women spent more time in their rural homes, a conclusion aggregated from interviews conducted during 2014 and 2015. Arguments drawn from aggregated evidence in interviews are cited hereafter as "Interviews, 2014–15." On the continuing movement between town and country in twentieth-century Kenya, see Colin Leys, *Underdevelopment in Kenya: The Political Economy of Neocolonialism, 1964–1971* (Berkeley: University of California Press, 1975), 180–81; and Richard E. Stren, *Housing the Urban Poor in Africa: Policy, Politics and Bureaucracy in Mombasa* (Berkeley: University of California Press, 1978), 267–68.
18. Choi and Peng, *Masculine Compromise.*
19. Cohen, "From Peasant to Worker," 94. See also Counihan, "Gendering Food," 104–5.
20. Choi and Peng, *Masculine Compromise,* 152–54.
21. McCann, *Stirring the Pot,* 9.
22. Goody, *Cooking, Cuisine, and Class,* 65; Wylie, *Starving on a Full Stomach,* 44–45; Jeremy Rich, *A Workman Is Worthy of His Meat: Food and Colonialism in the Gabon Estuary* (Lincoln: University of Nebraska Press, 2007), 29; Mandala, *End of Chidyerano;* Laura Ann Twagira, *Embodied Engineering: Gendered Labor, Food Security, and Taste in Twentieth-Century Mali* (Athens: Ohio University Press, 2021); Interviews, 2014–15.
23. McCann, *Stirring the Pot,* 9.
24. E. P. Thompson, *The Making of the English Working Class* (New York: Vintage, 1966). The moral economies and agrarian cultures of preindustrial England are more fully fleshed out in Thompson's series of essays in *Customs in Common: Studies in Traditional Popular Culture* (New York: New Press, 1993); Keletso Atkins, *The Moon Is Dead! Give Us Our Money! The Cultural Origins of an African Work Ethic, Natal, South Africa, 1843–1900* (Portsmouth, NH: Heinemann, 1993).
25. Cooper conceded that such a regional approach was beyond the scope of his study on labor politics in colonial Mombasa, but other historians, such

as Keletso Atkins, have demonstrated how rural moral economies and systems of thought shaped the formation of working-class communities in modern Africa. See Frederick Cooper, *On the African Waterfront,* xii–xiii; Frederick Cooper, "Work, Class, and Empire: An African Historian's Retrospective on E. P. Thompson," *Social History* 20, no. 2 (1995): 235–41; and Atkins, *The Moon Is Dead!*

26. Gerhard Lindblom, *The Akamba in British East Africa: An Ethnological Monograph* (Uppsala, Sweden: Appelbergs, 1920), 513, 515. For the ecologies and domestic economies in Kenya's Highlands during the nineteenth century, see Charles H. Ambler, *Kenyan Communities in the Age of Imperialism: The Central Region in the Late Nineteenth Century* (New Haven, CT: Yale University Press, 1988).
27. R. A. W. Procter, "The Kikuyu Market and Kikuyu Diet," *Kenya Medical Journal* 3, no. 1 (1926): 18–19; Ambler, *Kenyan Communities.*
28. *Sweetness and Power,* 8–14. See Audrey Richards, *Land, Labour and Diet in Northern Rhodesia* (London: Oxford University Press, 1939), 46–49.
29. Burnett, *England Eats Out,* 41–42.
30. Patrick Harries, *Work, Culture and Identity: Migrant Laborers in Mozambique and South Africa, c. 1860–1910* (Portsmouth, NH: Heinemann, 1994), 71–80.
31. Atkins, *Moon Is Dead!,* 120–35; Harries, *Work, Culture and Identity,* 71–80.
32. McCann argues that maize porridges became the main food in mining areas where owners fed their workers the cheapest food available, which was maize. This was similar to the dynamic at work among employers and workers in early-colonial East Africa, though the argument here is not simply that maize became dominant but also that the very idea of eating such milled-grain porridges every day was radically new, even for Luo migrants coming from communities with similar dishes. See McCann, *Stirring the Pot,* 137–44. Godriver Wanga-Odhiambo does note that sugar plantation workers in western Kenya found ration-based diets deficient compared to the "varied and nutritious" food they ate in rural reserves but, focused more on sugar production and labor on the estates, does not take the analysis further. Godriver Wanga-Odhiambo, *The Political Economy of Sugar Production in Colonial Kenya: The Asian Initiative in Central Nyanza* (Lanham, MD: Lexington Books, 2016), 187.
33. For the way industrial capitalism and modern urbanism turned rural seasonality into the flat linear time of uninterrupted supply chains, see William Cronon, *Nature's Metropolis: Chicago and the Great West* (New York: Norton, 1991). For time and seasonality in rural African foodways, see Mandala, *End of Chidyerano.*
34. Wylie, *Starving on a Full Stomach,* 47.
35. McCann, *Stirring the Pot,* 33.
36. Richards, *Land, Labour and Diet,* 46–49.
37. Ole Mouritsen Klavs Styrbæk, *Mouthfeel: How Texture Makes Taste* (New York: Columbia University Press, 2017), 16–17. Broader conclusions about mouthfeel and taste are developed especially on ix–xi and 1–30.

38. Twagira, *Embodied Engineering*, 20–21, 30–31, 46–47, 72, 91, 130.
39. For similar reactions of migrants to rations elsewhere in Kenya, see Wanga-Odhiambo, *Sugar Production*, 187.
40. East Africa Protectorate, *Native Labour Commission: Evidence and Report, 1912–1913* (Nairobi: Government Printer, ca. 1913), 322.
41. The classic study on how new commercial supply chains transformed working-class diets, with particular reference to sugar and tea, is Mintz, *Sweetness and Power*.
42. For the changing dynamics of kitchen labor in recent centuries, see Deutsch, "Labor Histories of Food"; Turner, *How the Other Half Ate*, 16, 52; and Trubeck, "Kitchen Work."
43. For premodern eateries, see Melissa Calaresu and Danielle van den Heuvel, eds., *Food Hawkers: Selling in the Streets from Antiquity to the Present* (London: Routledge, 2016); and Katie Rawson and Elliott Shore, *Dining Out: A Global History of Restaurants* (London: Reaktion Books, 2019), 14, 16. In the modern era, see Irene Tinker, *Street Foods: Urban Food and Employment in Developing Countries* (New York: Oxford University Press, 1997); Perry R. Duis, *Challenging Chicago: Coping with Everyday Life, 1837–1920* (Urbana: University of Illinois Press, 1998), 158–60; Burnett, *England Eats Out*, 33–48; Donna R. Gabaccia and Jeffrey Pilcher, "'Chile Queens' and Checkered Tablecloths: Public Dining Cultures of Italians in New York City and Mexicans in San Antonio, Texas, 1870s–1940s," *Radical History Review* 110 (2011): 109–26; Turner, *How the Other Half Ate*, 60–61; Anjaria, *Slow Boil*; and Sandra C. Mediola García, *Street Democracy: Vendors, Violence and Public Space in Late Twentieth-Century Mexico* (Lincoln: University of Nebraska Press, 2017).
44. Richard Pillsbury, *From Boarding House to Bistro: The American Restaurant Then and Now* (Boston: Unwin Hyman, 1990), 24–25, 31; Peter Scholliers, "Workers' Time for Cooking and Eating in Nineteenth- and Twentieth-Century Western Europe," *Food and Foodways: Explorations in the History and Culture of Human Nourishment* 6, no. 3–4 (1996): 244–46; Duis, *Challenging Chicago*, 152–53; Peter Scholliers, "Eating Out," in *A Cultural History of Food in the Age of Empire*, edited by Martin Bruegel (New York: Bloomsbury, 2016), 108–9; Anne Luissier, "Eating Out during the Workday: Consumption and Working Habits among Urban Laborers in France in the Second Half of the Nineteenth Century," in *Eating Out in Europe: Picnics, Gourmet Dining and Snacks since the Late-Eighteenth Century*, edited by Marc Jacobs and Peter Scholliers (New York: Berg, 2003), 337–50; Ulrike Thoms, "Industrial Canteens in Germany, 1850–1950," in *Eating Out in Europe*, 354–55; Abigail Carroll, *Three Squares: The Invention of the American Meal* (New York: Basic Books, 2013), 110–11.
45. Karim Janmohamed, "A History of Mombasa, c. 1895–1939: Some Aspects of Economic and Social Life in an East African Port Town during Colonial Rule" (PhD diss., Northwestern University, 1978), 249; *1999 Population and Housing Census: Counting Our People for Development* (Nairobi: Government Printer, 2001), xxxiii.

46. For the spatial history of Mombasa from the turn of the century up to World War II, see Justin Willis, *Mombasa, The Swahili, and the Making of the Mijikenda* (Oxford, UK: Clarendon, 1993), 75; and Janmohamed, "History of Mombasa," 268–75.

47. Classic studies of informal economies include International Labour Office, *Employment, Incomes and Equality: A Strategy for Increasing Productive Employment in Kenya* (Geneva, Switzerland, 1972); Keith Hart, "Informal Income Opportunities and Urban Employment in Ghana," *Journal of Modern African Studies* 11, no. 1 (1973): 61–89; and Gavin Kitching, *Class and Economic Change in Kenya: The Making of an African Petite-Bourgeoisie, 1905–1970* (New Haven, CT: Yale University Press, 1980), 375–410. For a more recent study of the informal economy in contemporary urban Kenya, focused on Nairobi, see Mary Mjeri Kinyanjui, *Women and the Informal Economy in Urban Africa: From the Margins to the Centre* (London: Zed Books, 2014).

48. For scholars addressing the informal sector and petty trade outside Africa, see Daniel M. Bluestone, "'The Pushcart Evil': Peddlers, Merchants and New York City Streets, 1890–1940," *Journal of Urban History* 18, no 1 (1991): 68–92; Robert Boyd, "Urbanization, Disadvantage and Petty Entrepreneurship: Street Peddling among African American Men in Southern and Northern Cities during the Early Twentieth Century," *Sociological Inquiry* 69, no. 2 (1999): 216–35; Anjaria, *Slow Boil;* García, *Street Democracy;* and Victoria Kelley, *Cheap Street: London's Street Markets and the Cultures of Informality, c. 1850–1939* (Manchester: Manchester University Press, 2019).

49. Income through rents was a major strategy of capital accumulation in urban Africa, as argued in the context of Dar es Salaam by James R. Brennan in *Taifa: Making Nation and Race in Urban Tanzania* (Athens: Ohio University Press, 2012), 9–10.

50. Cooper, *On the African Waterfront;* Frederick Cooper, *Decolonization and African Society: The Labor Question in British and French Africa* (New York, 1996). See also Lisa A. Lindsay, *Working with Gender: Wage Labor and Social Change in Southwestern Nigeria* (Portsmouth, NH: Heinemann, 2003). For similar labor policies starting slightly earlier, see George Chauncy Jr., "The Locus of Reproduction: Women's Labour in the Zambian Copperbelt, 1927–1953," *Journal of Southern African Studies* 7, no. 2 (1981): 135–53.

51. Many sex workers did operate outside residential space, but they tended to only offer sex and not other services like food preparation. Luise White, *Comforts of Home: Prostitution in Colonial Nairobi* (Chicago: University of Chicago Press, 1990). See also Margaret Strobel, *Muslim Women in Mombasa, 1890–1975* (New Haven, CT: Yale University Press, 1979), 138–147; Chauncy, "Locus of Reproduction," 148; and Willis, *Mombasa,* 96.

52. For a classic study on food traders in Kenya, see Claire C. Robertson, *Trouble Showed the Way: Women, Men, and Trade in the Nairobi Area, 1890–1990* (Bloomington: Indiana University Press, 1997). In their respective

monographs on Mombasa, both Strobel and Willis point to the key role of informal food vendors in social reproduction, including those preparing meals, but neither examines the role of street food within the spatial dynamics of the working day, nor do they push the analysis past a few passing comments, leaving the social history of street food largely unexamined. Strobel, *Muslim Women,* 135, 138–39; Willis, *Mombasa,* 96–97, 197. Strobel also published an influential essay on social reproduction in Mombasa, but it focuses primarily on the household and examines the topic within the context of the precolonial city and slavery. Margaret Strobel, "Slavery and Reproductive Labor in Mombasa," in *Women and Slavery in Africa,* ed. Claire Robertson and Martin Klein, 111–29 (Portsmouth, NH: Heinemann, 1997).

53. For his classic essay on the topic, see E. P. Thompson, "Time, Work-Discipline, and Industrial Capitalism," *Past and Present* no. 38 (1967): 56–97. For Africanists working on the history of time-discipline, see Frederick Cooper, "Colonizing Time: Work Rhythms and Labor Conflict in Colonial Mombasa," in *Colonialism and Culture,* edited by Nicholas Dirks (Ann Arbor: University of Michigan Press, 1992), 209–245; Cooper, "Work, Class, and Empire"; Atkins, *Moon Is Dead!,* 78–95; Phyllis Martin, *Leisure and Society in Colonial Brazzaville* (New York: Cambridge University Press, 1996), 3, 71–83; and Rich, *Workman Is Worthy,* 88–89.
54. Atkins, *Moon Is Dead!,* 87. For another example of conflict over the place of lunch during the working day, see Martin, *Leisure and Society,* 81–82.
55. Rich, *Workman Is Worthy,* 88–89.
56. Interviews, 2014–15. Twagira observes that women in rural Niger also brought midday meals out to people working the fields, sometimes even traveling a considerable distance to deliver the food. See Twagira, *Embodied Engineering,* 51–52, 84.
57. Phyllis Martin has suggested, in her work on colonial Brazzaville, that some workers pushed to not have a lunch break, preferring instead to finish the working day earlier. There is some evidence that workers at Mombasa's port in the late 1930s may have been similarly motivated, but, equally, employers displayed no desire to impose a lunch break on their employees. See testimony of Shariff Adrus bin Mohamed, serang at African Wharfage Co.; testimony of Captain Belfrage, chairman of African Wharfage Co.; testimony of W.G.D.H. Nicol of Messrs. Smith, MacKenzie and Co.; testimony of Abdulah Cherajdi, president of Unemployment Coast Citizens Association; and testimonies of Saidi bin Awath and Mbarak bin Ali, employees of East African Literage Co.; all from Kenya National Archives, Nairobi (hereafter KNA-Nairobi), AG/8/119. For mealtimes and the working day in colonial Brazzaville, see Martin, *Leisure and Society,* 81–82.
58. Testimony of Alfred William Tulk, representing Texaco Oil Co., 1939, KNA-Nairobi, AG/8/119.
59. For the French context, see Rebecca Spang, *The Invention of the Restaurant: Paris and Modern Gastronomic Culture* (Cambridge, MA: Harvard University

Press, 2001). Though still recognizing the distinctiveness of modern restaurants, more-recent scholarship has challenged the sharpness of the break from early-modern dining cultures, showing there were some antecedents in earlier institutions like inns. See Beat Kümin, "Eating Out before the Restaurant: Dining Culture in Early-Modern Inns," in Jacobs and Scholliers, *Eating Out in Europe,* 71–87.

60. On food-sharing practices in rural Africa, see Mandala, *End of Chidyerano,* 2; Wylie, *Starving on a Full Stomach,* 101; and Jon Holtzman, *Uncertain Tastes: Memory, Ambivalence, and the Politics of Eating in Samburu, Northern Kenya* (Berkeley: University of California Press, 2009), 73. For the continuation of these practices within urban households, see Atkins, *Moon Is Dead!,* 122–29; and Wylie, *Starving on a Full Stomach,* 108–9.
61. Interviews, 2014–15. For a similar intermixing of personal trust and commercial credit between traders and their customers in Mwanza, Tanzania, though about foodstuff rather than street-food vendors, see Karen Coen Flynn, *Food, Culture, and Survival in an African City* (New York: Palgrave Macmillan, 2005), 50.
62. Goody, *Cooking, Cuisine, and Class,* 101. For an example outside Africa in the modern era, see Alan Drouard's work on the distinctly male profession of the professional cook in France during the nineteenth and twentieth centuries in his "'*Escoffier, Bocuse et (surtout) les autres . . .*': Towards a History of Cooks in France in the Nineteenth and Twentieth Centuries," in Jacobs and Scholliers, *Eating Out in Europe,* 215–28.
63. Michael Denning, "Wageless Life," *New Left Review* 66 (2010): 80–81.
64. Lindsay's early research is principally about male Nigerian railway workers, but she incorporates their wives' work in the informal economy into her analysis of household formation and labor politics in the development era. Lindsay, *Working with Gender.* See also Emily Lynn Osborn, "Casting Aluminium Cooking Pots: Labour, Migration and Artisan Production in West Africa's Informal Sector, 1945–2005," *African Identities* 7, no. 3 (2009): 373–86; and Abosede A. George, *Making Modern Girls: A History of Girlhood, Labor and Social Change in Colonial Lagos* (Athens: Ohio University Press, 2014), 10. For a similar move toward integrating labor history and the study of informal economies in Latin America, see García, *Street Democracy,* 12–13.
65. Caroline Skinner, "Contributing yet Excluded? Informal Food Retail in African Cities," in *Urban Food Systems Governance and Poverty in African Cities,* ed. Jane Battersby and Vanessa Watson (London: Routledge, 2018), 104–5.
66. Colin Leys underlined this point nearly 50 years ago when research into informal economies was just beginning. However, while Leys directs our attention to the way the informal economy sustained low wages, he does not account for or explain the fact that governing and private elites, who were also major urban employers and the apparent beneficiaries of these effects, were indifferent and, in the case of the state, often actively hostile to these small-scale traders. The latter dynamics are at the center of the analysis in *Preparing the Modern Meal.* Leys, *Underdevelopment in Kenya,* 267–68.

67. Cooper, *On the African Waterfront;* Bruce Berman and John Lonsdale, *Unhappy Valley: Conflict in Kenya and Africa,* vol. 1, *State and Class* (Athens: Ohio University Press), 77–100.
68. For late-colonial labor stabilization policies in Mombasa, pursued in response to a wave of strikes, see Cooper, *On the African Waterfront.*
69. On the development of policy on sanitation and control over urban food systems in Kenya and Africa more widely, see James Duminy, "Urban Change and the Multi-Scalar Politics of Food Systems in Colonial Africa," in *Routledge Handbook of Urban Food Governance,* ed. Ana Moragues-Faus, Jill K. Clark, Jane Battersby, and Anna Davies (New York: Routledge, 2022), 35–47; and Duminy, "Historical Urban Food Governance in Africa: The Case of Kenya, c. 1900–1950," in Battersby and Watson, *Urban Food Systems Governance,* 86–88.
70. David Harvey, "The Right to the City," *New Left Review* 53 (2008): 23–40.
71. Cooper, *On the African Waterfront;* Cooper, *Decolonization and African Society;* James Ferguson, *Expectations of Modernity: Myths of Meanings of Urban Life on the Zambian Copperbelt* (Berkeley: University of California Press, 1999); Lindsay, *Working with Gender;* Thomas J. Sugrue, *The Origins of the Urban Crisis: Race and Inequality in Postwar Detroit* (Princeton: Princeton University Press, 2014); Charles Hornsby, *Kenya: A History since Independence* (London: I. B. Taurus, 2012), 190–91, 419–24, 567–71.
72. For waged employment and pay in Kenya during the early-independence era, see Hornsby, *Kenya,* 190–91.
73. For this shift in government policy at a national level in Kenya, see Republic of Kenya, *Sessional Paper No. 1 of 1986 on Economic Management for Renewed Growth* (Nairobi: Government Printer, 1986), 54, 58; and Kenneth King, *Jua Kali Kenya: Change and Development in an Informal Economy, 1970–1995* (Athens: Ohio University Press, 1996).
74. For the changing role of state power in neoliberal societies, see David Harvey, *A Brief History of Neoliberalism* (New York: Oxford University Press, 2005), 64–86.
75. Nana Osei-Opare, "'If You Trouble a Hungry Snake, You Will Force It to Bite You': Rethinking Postcolonial African Archival Pessimism, Worker Discontent, and Petition Writing in Ghana, 1957–1966," *Journal of African History* 62, no. 1 (2021): 59–78.
76. The KNA's regional branch for the coast is an essential source for many topics on Mombasa's independence-era history, but it also contains many unique files on the colonial period.
77. During 2014–15, I was fortunate to work in the Mombasa KNA archive alongside first Caleb Edwin Owen and later Zebulon Dingley, who were developing their own projects based on those records.
78. On petition writing and claim-making in independent Africa, see Osei-Opare, "'Trouble a Hungry Snake'"; and Moskowitz, *Seeing Like a Citizen.* For petition writing in colonial Nigeria, see Bright Alozie, "'Sir, We Have the Honour Most Respectfully to Submit Our Humble Petition': Voices in Ink

and the Politics of Petitions in Colonial Igboland" (PhD diss., West Virginia University, 2021).

CHAPTER 1: THE WORK OF THE DAILY MEAL

1. For meals on plantations, see "Native Labour Commission, 1912–13: Report," in *Native Labour Commission: Evidence and Report, 1912–1913* (Nairobi: Government Printer, ca. 1913), 322.
2. Most urban workers in Britain were fully reliant on wages to buy their food, while rural agricultural workers, because of the extent of enclosures by the end of the eighteenth century, could no longer effectively grow adequate food for their needs and purchased nearly all their food too. See John Burnett, *Plenty and Want: A Social History of Diet in England from 1815 to the Present Day* (London: Thomas Nelson, 1989), 21–63, 107–91; and John Burnett, *England Eats Out: A Social History of Eating Out in England from 1830 to the Present* (London: Routledge, 2004), 17–39.
3. Patrick Harries, *Work, Culture and Identity: Migrant Laborers in Mozambique and South Africa, c. 1860–1910* (Portsmouth, NH: Heinemann, 1994), 71–80. For food rations in urban South Africa, see Keletso Atkins, *The Moon Is Dead! Give Us Our Money! The Cultural Origins of an African Work Ethic, Natal, South Africa, 1843–1900* (Portsmouth, NH: Heinemann, 1993), 120–35.
4. Sidney Mintz, *Sweetness and Power: The Place of Sugar in Modern History* (New York: Penguin, 1986), 8–14. Mintz drew on the work of Richards on the Bemba. See Audrey Richards, *Land, Labour and Diet in Northern Rhodesia* (London: Oxford University Press, 1939), 46–49.
5. For grain porridges served with relishes in other parts of rural Africa, see James C. McCann, *Stirring the Pot: A History of African Cuisine* (Athens: Ohio University Press, 2009), 140–43.
6. Indeed, Guyer has noted that in situations where in-kind provisioning becomes part of labor compensation, workers' struggles often get directed toward "the quality of the provisions." See Jane Guyer, introduction to *Feeding African Cities: Studies in Regional Social History,* ed. Jane Guyer (Bloomington: Indiana University Press, 1987), 30.
7. Karim Janmohamed, "A History of Mombasa, c. 1895–1939: Some Aspects of Economic and Social Life in an East African Port Town during Colonial Rule" (PhD diss., Northwestern University, 1978), 342–47; Frederick Cooper, *From Slaves to Squatters: Plantation Labor and Agriculture in Zanzibar and Coastal Kenya, 1890–1925* (New Haven, CT: Yale University Press, 1980).
8. See labor inspection reports in Kenya National Archives, Nairobi (hereafter KNA-Nairobi): PC/Coast 1/9/30, 1/9/31, 1/9/32, 1/9/35, 1/9/38, 1/9/43, and 1/9/53. See also Janmohamed, "History of Mombasa," 358.
9. H. R. Tate, "Notes on the Kikuyu and Kamba Tribes of British East Africa," *Journal of the Anthropological Institute of Great Britain and Ireland* 34 (January–June 1904): 132. See also David William Cohen, "Food Production and Food Exchange in the Precolonial Lakes Plateau Region," in *Imperialism, Colonialism and Hunger: East and Central Africa,* ed. Robert I. Rotberg

(Lexington, MA: Lexington Books, 1983), 1–18; Frederick Cooper, *Plantation Slavery on the East Coast of Africa* (Portsmouth, NH: Heinemann, 1977); Charles Ambler, *Kenyan Communities in the Age of Imperialism: The Central Region in the Late Nineteenth Century* (New Haven, CT: Yale University Press, 1988); and Margaret J. Hay, "Economic Change in Luoland: Kowe, 1890–1945" (PhD diss., University of Wisconsin, Madison, 1972).

10. H. R. Tate, "Further Notes on the Kikuyu Tribe of British East Africa," *Journal of the Royal Anthropological Institute* 34 (1904): 258–59; G. A. S. Northcote, "The Nilotic Kavirondo," *Journal of the Royal Anthropological Institute of Great Britain and Ireland* 37 (1907): 59; Gerhard Lindblom, *The Akamba in British East Africa: An Ethnological Monograph* (Uppsala, Sweden: Appelbergs, 1920), 501, 511 (based on fieldwork in 1911 and 1912).
11. Lindblom, *Akamba,* 511.
12. Carolyn M. Clark, "Land and Food, Women and Power, in Nineteenth Century Kikuyu," *Africa: Journal of the International Africa Institute* 50, no. 4 (1980): 357–70; John Lonsdale, "The Moral Economy of Mau Mau: Poverty, Wealth and Civic Virtue in Kikuyu Political Thought," in Bruce Berman and John Lonsdale, *Unhappy Valley: Conflict in Kenya and Africa, Book 2: Violence and Ethnicity* (Athens: Ohio University Press, 1992), 315–504; B. Dickson, "The Eastern Borderlands of Kikuyu," *Geographical Journal* 21, no. 1 (1903): 37; Richard Crawshay, "Kikuyu: Notes on the Country, People, Fauna and Flora," *Geography Journal* 20, no. 1 (1902): 26; C. W. Hobley, "People, Places and Prospects in British East Africa," *Geographical Journal* 4, no. 2 (1894): 117; Lindblom, *Akamba,* 502.
13. Hobley, "People, Places and Prospects," 117. See also Dickson, "Eastern Borderlands of Kikuyu," 37.
14. Tate, "Notes on the Kikuyu and Kamba," 136; Lindblom, *Akamba,* 502.
15. Crawshay, "Kikuyu," 32; Dickson, "Eastern Borderlands of Kikuyu," 37.
16. Jomo Kenyatta, *Facing Mount Kenya* (New York: Vintage, 1965), 52–67.
17. Based on a reading of mostly secondary sources, Clark comes to a similar conclusion in "Land and Food."
18. Northcote, "Nilotic Kavirondo," 60.
19. Felix Oswald, *Alone in Sleeping Sickness Country* (London: Trübner, 1915), 38. The opposite page also features a photo insert of a man and woman, each working with a hoe in a field.
20. Hay, "Economic Change in Luoland," 93, 117n14.
21. John A. Carman and M. A. W. Roberts, "Social and Health Conditions among the Jaluo, with Special Reference to Maternal and Infant Welfare," *East Africa Medical Journal* 11 (1934): 109.
22. Lindblom, *Akamba,* 465–85; Crawshay, "Kikuyu," 28–29. On the gendered and generational aspects of livestock work in rural Kenya, see Paul Ocobock, *An Uncertain Age: The Politics of Manhood in Kenya* (Athens: Ohio University Press, 2017), 77–78.
23. This was observed of the Kamba, and evidence from other communities does not indicate that hunted game was consumed by the community

at large. Crawshay, "Kikuyu," 38 (this travelogue has information on the Kamba, not just the Kikuyu).

24. Tate, "Notes on the Kikuyu and Kamba," 132; Tate, "Further Notes," 259; Lindblom, *Akamba,* 511; R. A. W. Procter, "The Kikuyu Market and Kikuyu Diet," *Kenya Medical Journal* 3, no. 1 (1926): 19. See also Ambler, *Kenyan Communities.*
25. Crawshay, "Kikuyu," 38; Tate, "Notes on the Kikuyu and Kamba," 132, 135–36; Northcote, "Nilotic Kavirondo," 58.
26. C. W. Hobley, *Eastern Uganda: An Ethnological Survey* (London: Anthropological Institute of Great Britain and Ireland, 1902), 26; Northcote, "The Nilotic Kavirondo," 65; Hay, "Economic Change," 112–15. This conclusion also draws from my research project on the commercialization of Kenya's fisheries during the twentieth century, including those of Lake Victoria.
27. Lindblom, *Akamba,* 512–13; Tate, "Further Notes," 259; Carman and Roberts, "Social and Health Conditions," 109; J. C. J. Callanan, "Notes on the Foodstuffs of the Luo Tribes," *Kenyan Medical Journal* 3 (1926): 59.
28. Lindblom, *Akamba,* 512–13.
29. Tate, "Further Notes," 259; Northcote, "Nilotic Kavirondo," 62; Lindblom, *Akamba,* 511; Callanan, "Notes on the Foodstuffs," 58. On the place of blood in the foodways of the Samburu, a pastoralist community in northern Kenya, see Jon Holtzman, *Uncertain Tastes: Memory, Ambivalence, and the Politics of Eating in Samburu, Northern Kenya* (Berkeley: University of California Press, 2009), 103–6.
30. Hobley, *Eastern Uganda,* 15, 26; Lindblom, *Akamba,* 513–14; Tate, "Further Notes," 260–61. For women's primary role in cooking throughout rural Africa, see McCann, *Stirring the Pot,* 9–10.
31. Hobley, *Eastern Uganda,* 26. See also Crawshay, "Kikuyu," 35; Tate, "Further Notes," 260; Lindblom, *Akamba,* 513, 543–44; Procter, "Kikuyu Market," 15–19; Callanan, "Notes on the Foodstuffs," 59; and W. Scoresby Routledge and Katherine Routledge, *With a Prehistoric People: The Akikuyu of British East Africa* (London: Frank Cass, 1968), 59–60.
32. Lindblom, *Akamba,* 543–44.
33. Kenyatta, *Facing Mount Kenya,* 53.
34. The ethnography of the Kikuyu by the Routledges is the most systematic in its description of kitchens, cooking instruments, and methods of preparation, but the other sources examined for this section provide scattered evidence that add up the conclusion that the cooking process was similar in Kamba and Luo communities during this period. Routledge and Routledge, *With a Prehistoric People,* 59–60.
35. Procter, "Kikuyu Market," 18–19. See also J. B. Orr and J. L. Gilks, *Studies of Nutrition: The Physique and Health of Two African Tribes* (London: His Majesty's Stationary Office, 1931), 26.
36. Lindblom, *Akamba,* 513.
37. Lindblom, *Akamba,* 488, 512, 514–15.

38. Routledge and Routledge, *With a Prehistoric People,* 53–54.
39. Richards, *Land, Labour and Diet,* 46–49; McCann, *Stirring the Pot,* 137–44.
40. Routledge and Routledge, *With a Prehistoric People,* 53. Both the Kikuyu and the Kamba did make some thicker porridges from milled grain, though these dishes were not staples but were instead eaten only occasionally by women and children or, in the case of the Kamba, as part of a ritual. Lindblom, *Akamba,* 513; Procter, "Kikuyu Market," 18–19.
41. Lindblom, *Akamba,* 513.
42. Procter, "Kikuyu Market," 15–16.
43. Callanan, "Notes on the Foodstuffs," 58–59; Carman and Roberts, "Social and Health Conditions," 109.
44. Callanan, "Notes on the Foodstuffs," 58–59.
45. Crawshay, "Kikuyu," 26.
46. Tate, "Notes on the Kikuyu and Kamba," 132; Tate, "Further Notes," 258–59; Hobley, *Eastern Uganda,* 27; and Lindblom, *Akamba,* 505–6.
47. See labor inspection reports in KNA-Nairobi, PC/Coast/1/9; see also Janmohamed, "History of Mombasa," 358. On the often coercive process through which rural Africans entered wage labor, see Opolot Okia, *Communal Labor in Kenya: The Legitimation of Coercion* (New York: Palgrave Macmillan, 2012); Sharon Stichter, *Migrant Labour in Kenya: Capitalism and African Responses, 1895–1975* (London: Longman, 1982); and Janmohamed, "History of Mombasa," 325–83.
48. This history is embedded in the meaning of the Swahili word *posho* during the nineteenth century, as can be seen in Ludwig Krapf, *A Dictionary of the Suahili Language* (London: Trübner, 1882), 308; and A. C. Madan, *Swahili-English Dictionary* (Oxford: Clarendon Press, 1903), 319. See also Cooper, *Plantation Slavery,* 182–90; and Stephen J. Rockel, *Carriers of Culture: Labor on the Road in Nineteenth-Century East Africa* (Portsmouth, NH: Heinemann, 2006), 141–49.
49. Though the publishing date of Ludwig Krapf's Swahili dictionary is 1882, it was completed in manuscript form by 1860. Krapf, *Dictionary of the Suahili Language,* vii–xii, 308.
50. Cooper, *Plantation Slavery,* 182–90; Kaje wa Mwemye Matano, published interview in *Three Swahili Women: Life Histories from Mombasa,* ed. Sarah Mirza and Margaret Strobel (Bloomington: Indiana University Press, 1989), 33–35.
51. C. S. Sacleux, *Dictionnaire Swahili-Français* (Paris: Institut d'Ethnologie, 1939), 759.
52. Cooper, *Plantation Slavery,* 187.
53. Rockel, *Carriers of Culture,* 141–49.
54. Lawrence Tooth, Acting Solicitor General, to Acting Attorney General, 18 November 1918, KNA-Nairobi, PC/Coast/1/9/35; Atkins, *The Moon Is Dead!,* 120.
55. *Administration Report, 1916–17: Railways, East Africa and Uganda* (Nairobi: Uganda Railway Press, 1917), 6–7, Commonwealth and African Collections,

Bodleian Library, University of Oxford (hereafter CAC), 753.14s/5/1916–17; *Administration Report, 1919–20: Railways, Kenya and Uganda* (Nairobi: Uganda Railway Press, 1920), 5, CAC, 753.14s/5/1919–20; *Administration Report, 1920–21: Railways, Kenya and Uganda* (Nairobi: Uganda Railway Press, 1921), 5, CAC, 753.14s/5/1920–21.

56. For food supply in modern African history, see Guyer, *Feeding African Cities;* Jeremy Rich, *A Workman Is Worthy of His Meat: Food and Colonialism in the Gabon Estuary* (Lincoln: University of Nebraska Press, 2007); Elisabeth McMahon, "Developing Workers: Coerced and 'Voluntary' Labor in Zanzibar," *International Labor and Working-Class History* 92 (2017): 114–33. For Kenya, see Stichter, *Migrant Labour in Kenya,* 70–71.
57. W. J. Simpson, *Sanitary Matters in the East African Protectorate, Uganda, and Zanzibar* (London: Colonial Office, 1915), 6, KNA-Library. See also *Native Labour Commission Report,* 322.
58. Procter, "Kikuyu Market," 15.
59. "Inspection of Labour Camps," 17 July 1919, KNA-Nairobi, PC/Coast/1/9/53.
60. Conclusion drawn from labor inspection reports in KNA-Nairobi, PC/Coast/1/9/53; the quotation is from "Inspection of Labour Camps," 17 July 1919.
61. See Principal Sanitation Officer, Mombasa, to Acting Provincial Commissioner, 6 October 1919, KNA-Nairobi, PC/Coast/1/14/97. There is also evidence of documentation on Mombasa's food markets before 1930 in Kenya National Archives, Coast Province, Mombasa Records Centre (hereafter KNA-Coast), UY/30/1 and UY/30/2.
62. *Annual Report: Mombasa District, 1924,* 9, KNA-Nairobi, DC/MSA/1/3.
63. Testimony of Henderson [no first name given], in *Native Labour Commission Report,* 88.
64. For the ubiquity of maize porridges among wage workers elsewhere in colonial Africa, see McCann, *Stirring the Pot,* 140.
65. For scarcity and workers' leverage in Tanzania, see Thaddeus Sunseri, *Vilimani: Labor Migration and Rural Change in Early Colonial Tanzania* (Portsmouth, NH: Heinemann, 2001), xxii, 51–71, 149–50.
66. Testimony of J. J. Lory, in *Native Labour Commission Report,* 97–98.
67. C. W. Hobley, Provincial Commissioner–Coast Province (hereafter PC-CP), Labour Supply for Mararini Syndicate, 22 November 1915, KNA-Nairobi, PC/Coast/1/9/30; Manager, Nyali Estates, to Hobley, PC-CP, 7 July 1916, KNA-Nairobi, PC/Coast/1/9/43; Hobley, PC-CP, to Manager, Nyali Estates, 15 July 1916, KNA-Nairobi, PC/Coast/1/43; testimony of H. J. Stedman, in *Native Labour Commission Report,* 90. Africans in German Tanzania also used rumor networks to pressure employers in a context of scarcity, where Sunseri argues workers succeeded in shaping work rhythms and culture on the plantation. Sunseri, *Vilimani,* 69. For rumor as a broader topic in African history, see Luise White, *Speaking with Vampires: Rumor and History in Colonial Africa* (Berkeley: University of California Press, 2000).

68. Hobley to Manager, Nyali Estates, 15 July 1916.
69. Testimony of K. MacDougall, Registrar of Slaves, in *Native Labour Commission Report,* 95.
70. Inspection Report, Gazi-Gogoni Estates, September 1917, KNA-Nairobi, PC/Coast/1/9/38; DC, Inspection of Labor Camp, East African Estates, 18 April 1916, KNA-Nairobi, PC/Coast/1/9/38. On Mombasa Island, agriculture was common before 1930, but there is no indication that migrants were growing any of these crops. See *A Project for the Drainage and Town-Planning of Mombasa Island* (Nairobi: Government Printer, 1920), 7, CAC, 753.14/s.40/1920(1).
71. Inspection Report, Gazi-Gogoni, September 1917; Inspection of Gazi Rubber and Fibre Estates, 20 March 1918, KNA-Nairobi, PC/Coast/1/9/38.
72. Steven Stoll, "The Captured Garden: The Political Ecology of Subsistence under Capitalism," *International Labor and Working-Class History* 85 (2014): 75–96.
73. George Chauncy Jr., "The Locus of Reproduction: Women's Labour in the Zambian Copperbelt, 1927–1953," *Journal of Southern African Studies* 7, no. 2 (1981): 135–64.
74. Desertion was also a common tactic on Tanzanian plantations. Sunseri, *Vilimani,* 67–71.
75. L. J. Lightbody, DC, to C. W. Hobley, Provincial Commissioner–Coast Province (PC-CP), 5 December 1916; DC Rabai to C. W. Hobley, PC-CP, 17 December 1916; both in KNA-Nairobi, PC/Coast/1/9/51.
76. Assistant District Commissioner, Mombasa (letter, receiver not clear, but likely C. W. Hobley and/or Executive Engineer's Office, Public Works Department, Mombasa), 27 September 1917; Executive Engineer's Office, Public Works Department, Mombasa, to Hobley, PC-CP, 12 October 1917; Hobley, PC-CP, to Executive Engineer, PWD, Mombasa, 25 October 1917; all in KNA-Nairobi, PC/Coast/1/9/51.
77. Marginalia of Hobley, PC-CP, written on DC Rabai to Hobley, PC-CP, 17 December 1916, KNA-Nairobi, PC/Coast/1/9/51.
78. Hobley, PC-CP, to Executive Engineer, PWD, Mombasa, 25 October 1917, KNA-Nairobi, PC/Coast/1/9/51.
79. Inspection of Labour Camp of Sokoke Estate, 20 March 1915, KNA-Nairobi, PC/Coast/1/9/35.
80. Justin Willis argues that wages decreased for dock workers during the 1920s because labor scarcity seemed to be ending, but this was specific to the docks and casual workers. For contract workers, most of whom were upcountry migrants, their wages and rations increased from the 1910s to the 1920s, suggesting that labor scarcity remained present within their sectors. Conclusions drawn from data aggregated from labor inspection reports in KNA-Nairobi, PC/Coast/1/9, especially 1/9/53; the 1912–13 *Native Labour Commission Report;* and annual labor reports in the Native Affairs Department Annual Reports, accessed at the British Library (hereafter BL). This dataset hereafter will be cited as "Coastal Wage and Ration Data." For the

wages of casual dock workers, see Justin Willis, *Mombasa, the Swahili, and the Making of the Mijikenda* (Oxford: Clarendon, 1993), 184–85.

81. Coastal Wage and Ration Data.
82. Coastal Wage and Ration Data. See also Inspection of Labor Camp, 26 July 1919; Inspection of Labor Camp, 21 September 1923; and Inspection of Labor Camp, 7 October 1924; all in KNA-Nairobi, PC/Coast/1/9/53.
83. Coastal Wage and Ration Data.
84. Frederick Cooper, *On the African Waterfront: Urban Disorder and the Transformation of Work in Colonial Mombasa* (New Haven, CT: Yale University Press, 1987), 54.
85. Krapf, *Dictionary of the Suahili Language*, 388, 395.
86. For a classic study on how industrial capitalism replaces seasonality with regularity, see William Cronon, *Nature's Metropolis: Chicago and the Great West* (New York: Norton, 1991).
87. *Report of the Committee upon Quantitative Problems in Human Nutrition: Report on the Nutrition of Miners and Their Families* (London, 1924), National Archives, United Kingdom (hereafter NA), FD/87; K. Neville Moss, "The Food Requirements of Coal Miners," *Iron and Coal Trades Review*, 31 October 1924, p. 556, NA, FD1/4366. The extension of these ideas to South Africa is examined in Diana Wylie, *Starving on a Full Stomach: Hunger and the Triumph of Cultural Racism in Modern South Africa* (Charlottesville: University of Virginia Press, 2001).
88. For colonial nutrition science and rural African food systems, see Cynthia Brantley, "Kikuyu-Maasai Nutrition and Colonial Science: The Orr Gilks Study in the Late 1920s," *International Journal of African Historical Studies* 30, no. 1 (1997): 49–86.
89. *Native Affairs Department Annual Report, 1926* (Nairobi: Government Printer, 1927), 58, BL.
90. Procter, "Kikuyu Market," 19.

CHAPTER 2: COMESTIBLE COMMODITIES

1. Frederick Cooper, *On the African Waterfront: Urban Disorder and the Transformation of Work in Colonial Mombasa* (New Haven, CT: Yale University Press, 1987). Cooper extends his arguments to the rest of British- and French-colonial Africa in *Decolonization and African Society: The Labor Question in French and British Africa* (New York: Cambridge University Press, 1996).
2. Shane Hamilton, *Supermarket USA: Food and Power in the Cold War Farms Race* (New Haven, CT: Yale University Press, 2018).
3. Jane Battersby, "Hungry Cities: A Critical Review of Urban Food Security Research in Sub-Saharan African Cities," *Geography Compass* 7, no. 7 (2013): 452–63; Jane Battersby and Jonathan Crush, "Africa's Urban Food Deserts," *Urban Forum* 25, no. 1 (2014): 143–51; Jane Battersby and Jonathan Crush, eds., *Rapid Urbanisation, Urban Food Deserts and Food Security in Africa*

(Basel, Switzerland: Springer, 2016). For "food deserts" in the United States, see Robert Gottlieb and Anupama Joshi, *Food Justice* (Cambridge, MA: MIT Press, 2010), 39–58. For produce traders in Kenya, see Claire Robertson's classic study on "market women" in Nairobi, *Trouble Showed the Way: Women, Men and Trade in the Nairobi Area, 1890–1990* (Bloomington: Indiana University Press, 1997). The study of urban fruit and vegetable vendors, mostly women, has also been taken up by scholars examining other parts of Africa and the wider Global South. See, for example, Gracia Clark, *Onions Are My Husband: Survival and Accumulation by West African Market Women* (Chicago: University of Chicago Press, 1994); and Florence E. Babb, *Between Field and Cooking Pot: The Political Economy of Marketwomen in Peru* (Austin: University of Texas Press, 1998).

4. Interview: Jackson Nthuli, Mombasa, 12 January 2015.
5. Conclusion aggregated from interviews conducted in Mombasa from October 2014 to January 2015 and in Nyanza Province in February 2015. Citations for conclusions drawn in aggregate from these oral interviews are hereafter cited as "Interviews, 2014–15."
6. Interview: Benike A. Owuir, Nyanza Province, 6 February 2015.
7. For tea consumption in pastoralist communities in Kenya during the twentieth century, see Jon Holtzman, "In a Cup of Tea: Commodities and History among Samburu Pastoralists in Northern Kenya," *American Ethnologist* 30, no. 1 (2003): 136–55.
8. Interviews, 2014–15.
9. This conclusion draws from my research project on the commercialization of Kenya's fisheries during the twentieth century, including those on Lake Victoria.
10. Interview: James Hunnington Ogola, Nyanza Province, 16 February 2015.
11. Interview: Vitalis Owiti, Nyanza Province, 19 February 2015.
12. Gavin Kitching, *Class and Economic Change in Kenya: The Making of an African Petite-Bourgeoisie, 1905–1970* (New Haven, CT: Yale University Press, 1980); Sharon Stichter, *Migrant Labour in Kenya: Capitalism and African Responses, 1895–1975* (London: Longman, 1982).
13. *Annual Report on Native Affairs, 1937* (Nairobi: Government Printer, 1938); *Report of the Committee of Inquiry Appointed to Examine the Labour Conditions in Mombasa* (Nairobi: Government Printer, 1939), 22, Commonwealth and African Collections, Bodleian Library, University of Oxford (hereafter CAC), 753.14s.6.1939(2).
14. The historian of labor in Mombasa must confront what Frederick Cooper points to as the "paucity of official data" on the city's workers before 1940. However, this section and the next draw extensively on a set of documents that neither Cooper nor other historians have much used, the more than 300 pages of testimony gathered for a committee of inquiry report on the 1939 Mombasa general strike, including interviews with managers, officials, and workers. Used carefully, these testimonies offer an unparalleled view into

Mombasa's social and economic history during the late 1930s. Testimony of Mombasa Municipal Engineer, 1939, both in Kenya National Archives, Nairobi (hereafter KNA-Nairobi), AG/8/119; Cooper, *On the African Waterfront,* 42.

15. The labor inspection reports that filled the government files of the Coast Province in the era of labor scarcity during the first decades of the twentieth century disappeared by the 1930s. For the increasing interest of colonial officials in African workers in a different context, that of labor organizing and strikes, see Cooper, *On the African Waterfront.*
16. *Annual Report on Native Affairs, 1935* (Nairobi: Government Printer, 1936), 164.
17. *Native Affairs Department Annual Report, 1926* (Nairobi: Government Printer, 1927), 69.
18. *Report of the Committee of Inquiry* (1939), 5.
19. Testimony of Robbins [no first name given], Public Works Department, 1939, and Municipal Engineer, 1939, KNA-Nairobi, AG/8/119.
20. Testimony of Robbins.
21. Testimony of Abdulla Mohamed, worker at Vacuum Oil Co., 1939; Alfred William Tulk, Texaco Oil Co., 1939; and John Edwards Claridge, Shell Co., 1939; all in KNA-Nairobi, AG/8/119. See *Report of the Committee of Inquiry* (1939), 5.
22. Testimony of Ali bin Namman, Headman, 1939; Dr. M. A. Rana, 1939; and Makhan Singh, General Secretary of Labour Trade Union of East Africa, 1939; all in KNA-Nairobi, AG/8/119. For the lack of rationing of domestic workers by European employers in Kenya, see *Native Affairs Department Annual Report, 1934* (Nairobi: Government Printer, 1935), 165.
23. Testimony of R. K. Desai, Vegetable Growers Association, 1939, KNA-Nairobi, AG/8/119.
24. Anthony Clayton and Donald Savage, *Government and Labour in Kenya, 1895–1963* (London: Cass, 1974), 188.
25. Testimony of Kabatha wa Washomba, agricultural worker, 1939; and Mwashiri Mulea, agricultural worker, 1939; both in KNA-Nairobi, AG/8/119. Mwashiri Mulea, a migrant shamba worker from Central Kenya, likewise indicated that he did not receive a posho ration from his employer.
26. For prices on agricultural foodstuffs, see Stichter, *Migrant Labour in Kenya,* 95–96.
27. Cooper, *On the African Waterfront,* 44–50.
28. Cooper, *On the African Waterfront,* 46.
29. "Mombasa District Annual Report, 1942," 1–2; and "Mombasa District Annual Report, 1943," 1–2; both in KNA-Nairobi, DC/MSA/1/5. More detailed evidence can be found throughout KNA-Nairobi, PC/Coast/2/9/28. Also see John Lonsdale, "The Depression and the Second World War in the Transformation of Kenya," in *Africa and the Second World War,* ed. David Killingray and Richard Rathbone (New York: Saint Martin's Press, 1986), 121; and Reynolds Richter, "Food Rationing, Labor and Citizenship in Kenya during World War II" (MA thesis, Yale University, 2006), 33–34. Scholarship

on wartime rationing has mostly examined the effects or lack thereof on coastal identities. This is because the rationing system was racialized, provisioning different foods to "Europeans," "Asiatics," and "Natives." For this topic in Zanzibar, where it has been more extensively examined, see Laura Fair, *Pastimes and Politics: Culture, Community, and Identity in Post-Abolition Urban Zanzibar, 1890–1945* (Athens: Ohio University Press, 2001), 48–52; and Jonathon Glassman, *War of Words, War of Stones: Racial Thought and Violence in Colonial Zanzibar* (Bloomington: Indiana University Press, 2011), 53, 320n78.

30. In Zanzibar, where Fair and Glassman based their research, access to rice was the central point of contention around which debates concerning identity hinged. However, as Richter shows, in Mombasa, more important than specific ingredients was that in the years of greatest scarcity, 1942 and 1943, those holding "European" and "Asiatic" coupons had more secure access to supplies than did Africans, who were rationed as "Natives." See Richter, "Food Rationing." Moreover, Africans who had lived in Mombasa for more than six years, 58 percent of the population, could be categorized as "rice eating" and thereby gain access to their preferred grain without needing to classify themselves as "Asiatic." H. S. Booker, "Section I: Report on Economic and Social Background of Mombasa Labour Dispute," in Booker and N. M. Deverell, *Report on the Economic and Social Background of Mombasa Labour Disputes* (1947), 2, KNA-Nairobi, ABK/11/6.
31. *Report of the Committee of Inquiry into Labour Unrest at Mombasa, Part II* (Nairobi: Government Printer, 1945), 76 (hereafter *Report of the Committee of Inquiry, Part II*), Library of the Kenya National Archives (hereafter KNA-Library), 331.11 REP; "Mombasa District Annual Report, 1942" and "Mombasa District Annual Report, 1943."
32. S. V. Cooke, writing in 1942, quoted in *Report of the Committee of Inquiry, Part II*, 70.
33. *Report of the Committee of Inquiry, Part II*, 70–71.
34. H. S. Booker, "Report on Economic and Social Background," 7, and N. M. Deverell, "Section II: A Social Investigation in Mombasa," 72, both reports part of the *Report on the Economic and Social Background of Mombasa Labour Disputes* (1947), KNA-Nairobi, ABK/11/6.
35. "Mombasa District Annual Report, 1948," 11; and "Mombasa District Annual Report, 1949," 3; both in KNA-Nairobi, DC/MSA/1/5. The conclusion for the 1950s is based on a close reading of the archival record of the Kenya National Archives on Mombasa covering that decade, along with Labor Department annual reports for the same period.
36. Testimony of Municipal Engineer.
37. Testimony of Giddeon Harrison, 1939, KNA-Nairobi, AG/8/119.
38. P. P. Connolly, Medical Officer of Health, "Cost of Living, Mombasa, with Monthly Budgets Collected from Mombasa Residents," 29 September 1939, Appendix III in *Report of the Committee of Inquiry* (1939).

39. See estimates for the cost of living and wages throughout the testimonies in KNA-Nairobi, AG/8/119. Cooper refers to these periodic debates among Mombasa officials as the "battle of the budgets," initiated as they tried to establish an increased baseline minimum wage as a response to strikes. Cooper, *On the African Waterfront*, 53.
40. See testimonies about wages in KNA-Nairobi, AG/8/119, and in the *Report of the Committee of Inquiry* (1939).
41. "Mombasa District Annual Report, 1930," 13, KNA-Nairobi, DC/MSA/1/4.
42. James R. Brennan, *Taifa: Making Nation and Race in Urban Tanzania* (Athens: Ohio University Press, 2012), 36.
43. Testimony of John Josiah Stevens, Senior Supervisor, Kenya Landing and Shipping Co., 1939, KNA-Nairobi, AG/8/119.
44. Testimony of Abdulla Mohamed, 1939, KNA-Nairobi, AG/8/119. For another example of a migrant worker in debt to a duka, see the testimony of Mwashiri Mulea in Testimony of Mwashiri Mulea and Rastas Kashoki, dairy workers, Mombasa Labour Commission Enquiry, 1939, KNA-Nairobi, AG/8/119.
45. *Labour Department Annual Report, 1953* (Nairobi: Government Printer, 1954), 44. The cost of maize during this period was calculated from data in *Mombasa Social Survey, Part I* (Nairobi: Cyclostyled, 1956), 228, 242, KNA-Library, RW/301/SRE.
46. Nabwera Burudi, "Housing and Family Census: Government, Municipal and Employer Built Houses on Mombasa Island," in *Mombasa Social Survey: 1956–58* (Nairobi: Cyclostyled, 1958), 5–6, CAC, MSS/Afr.s.919.
47. "Family Budget Survey," in *Mombasa Social Survey: 1956–58*, 5–6.
48. "Income and Expenditure," in *Mombasa Social Survey: 1956–58*, 6.
49. Thus, the condition of indebtedness resembles Michael Denning's observation in regard to work, that "under capitalism, the only thing worse than being exploited is not being exploited." That is, once people have lost access to the means of subsistence and become wholly dependent on cash, losing even an exploitative job threatens their very survival. Michael Denning, "Wageless Life," *New Left Review* 66 (2010): 79.
50. *Report of the Committee of Inquiry, Part II*, 72.
51. *Report of the Committee of Inquiry into Labour Unrest at Mombasa, Part I* (Nairobi: Government Printer, 1945), 36 (hereafter *Report of the Committee of Inquiry, Part I*), KNA-Nairobi, UY/14/29.
52. Such cycles of (relative) plenty and want for those on the margins are described in vivid detail in George Orwell's fictionalized account of working-class Paris around the same time. Rather than maize meal, though, the poor in Paris subsisted on bread. George Orwell, *Down and Out in Paris and London* (London: Harvest, 1963).
53. Deverell, "Social Investigation in Mombasa," 65, 66, 72, 94–95.
54. For similar bulk breaking practices in West Africa around the same time, see P. T. Baur and B. S. Yamey, "Economic Progress and Occupational Distribution," *Economic Journal* 61, no. 244 (1951): 746. For the topic in more

recent economic development literature, in Kenya and Africa more broadly, respectively, see Rosina Wanyama et al., "How Important Are Supermarkets for the Diets of the Urban Poor in Africa?," *Food Security* 11 (2019): 1339–53; and Kate Meager, "Cannibalizing the Informal Economy: Frugal Innovation and Economic Inclusion in Africa," *European Journal of Development Research* 30 (2018): 24.

55. Booker, "Report on Economic and Social Background," 59.
56. Deverell, "Social Investigation in Mombasa," 62.
57. Wanyama et al., "How Important Are Supermarkets?"; Meager, "Cannibalizing the Informal Economy," 24.
58. *Report of the Committee of Inquiry, Part II,* 72; Deverell, "Social Investigation in Mombasa," 98–99.
59. Deverell, "Social Investigation in Mombasa," 95.
60. "Mombasa District Annual Report, 1930," 7–12; Cooper, *On the African Waterfront,* 35; Clayton and Savage, *Government and Labour,* 217.
61. "Mombasa District Annual Report, 1930," 9.
62. "Appendix IV: Notes on Labour in Mombasa," in *Report of the Committee of Inquiry, Part II,* 87.
63. Testimony of Rastas Koshoki, 1939, KNA-Nairobi, AG/8/119.
64. Testimony of Washomba.
65. Deverell, "Social Investigation in Mombasa," 96, 101.
66. "Mixed Meal Distribution," 5 October 1943, KNA-Nairobi, PC/Coast/2/9/28; Richter, "Food Rationing," 42–43.
67. Those included for the latter survey worked for several of Mombasa's major employers, including Kenya Uganda Railways and Harbours, Kenya Landing and Shipping Co., Vacuum Oil Co., Mombasa Municipality, East African Power and Lighting, and Kenya Bus Services. Booker, "Report on Economic and Social Background," 40, 47.
68. G. M. Wilson, "African Labour in Mombasa," in *Mombasa Social Survey, Part I,* 219; Republic of Kenya, Economic Surveys, *Kenya Population Census, 1962: Tables,* vol. 2, *Populations of Locations and County Council Wards by Race, Tribe and Sex* (Nairobi: Government Printer, 1965), 76–79.
69. For Africans who had been resident in the city for less than six years, the population was 4:1 male-to-female, but after six years of residence the sex of the population was nearly even between men and women. Booker, "Report on Economic and Social Background," 2.
70. Lisa A. Lindsay, *Working with Gender: Wage Labor and Social Change in Southwestern Nigeria* (Portsmouth, NH: Heinemann, 2003); Cooper, *On the African Waterfront;* Cooper, *Decolonization and African Society.*
71. *Labour Department Annual Report, 1954* (Nairobi: Government Printer, 1955), 42; *Labour Department Annual Report, 1961* (Nairobi: Government Printer, 1963), 35.
72. "Hawkers, 1952," Kenya National Archives, Coast Province, Mombasa Records Centre (hereafter KNA-Coast), UY/28/98.
73. "Family Budget Survey," 3.

74. "Income and Expenditure," 6.
75. "Family Budget Survey," 6.
76. Interview: Emma Mudanya, Mombasa, 16 December 2014.
77. D. R. F. Taylor, "The Markets of Mombasa," *African Urban Notes* 5, no. 2 (1970): 184.
78. "Appendix III: Cost of Living," in *Report of the Commission of Inquiry*, 58.
79. Taylor, "Markets of Mombasa," 175.
80. Municipal Board of Mombasa: Schedule of Rentals, 1933, KNA-Nairobi, UY/5/69; Donald Fraser, Town Clerk, Mombasa, to Hon. Commissioner for Local Government, Land Settlements, Nairobi, 28 May 1930, KNA-Coast, UY/30/2; Town Clerk, Mombasa, to Resident Commission, Mombasa, 31 March 1928, KNA-Coast, UY/30/1.
81. Principal Sanitation Officer, Mombasa, to Acting Provincial Commissioner, 6 October 1919, KNA-Nairobi, PC/1/14/97.
82. Medical Officer of Health, Mombasa, to Acting Town Clerk, Mombasa, 31 August 1929, KNA-Coast, UY/30/1.
83. Acting Town Clerk, Mombasa, to Medical Officer of Health, 27 August 1929; Medical Officer of Health, Mombasa, to Acting Town Clerk, Mombasa, 31 August 1929; both in KNA-Coast, UY/30/1.
84. Town Clerk, Mombasa, to Commissioner of Local Government, Nairobi, 7 July 1931, KNA-Coast, UY/30/1.
85. D. S. Fraser, Town Clerk, Mombasa, "Announcement," in *Daily Mail*, 4 December 1930, KNA-Coast, UY/30/1.
86. Report on Sub-Committee on Street-Trading By-Laws, 25 April 1932, KNA-Coast, UY/5/25.
87. Municipal Accountant, Mombasa, to Town Clerk, Mombasa, 2 March 1933, KNA-Coast, UY/5/78.
88. Report on Sub-Committee on Street-Trading By-Laws; Municipal Accountant to Town Clerk.
89. Memo: Private Markets, 2 March 1933, KNA-Coast, UY/5/78.
90. The British were no more able to control hawking in Dar es Salaam or Nairobi during the 1930s. See Andrew Burton, *African Underclass: Urbanisation, Crime and Colonial Order in Dar es Salaam, 1919–1961* (Athens: Ohio University Press, 2005), 153–63; and Robertson, *Trouble Showed the Way*, 99.
91. Medical Officer of Health, Mombasa, to Town Clerk, Mombasa, 16 June 1932, KNA-Coast, UY/5/96.
92. Town Clerk, Mombasa, to Hon. Commissioner for Local Government, 10 August 1933, KNA-Coast, UY/5/78.
93. Taylor, "Markets of Mombasa."
94. Interviews, 2014–15; Tabatha Kanogo, *Squatters and the Roots of Mau Mau, 1905–1963* (Athens: Ohio University Press, 1987); D. R. F. Taylor, "Changing Food Habits in Kikuyuland," *Canadian Journal of African Studies* 4, no. 3 (1970): 341–42; C. R. Philip, "Nutrition in Kenya: Notes on the State of Nutrition of African Children," *East African Medical Journal* 20, no. 7 (1943): 231; N.

Humphrey, *The Kikuyu Lands: The Relationship of Population to the Land in South Nyeri* (Nairobi: Government Printer, 1945), 35–36.

95. Philip, "Nutrition in Kenya," 231.
96. "Appendix III: Cost of Living," 58.
97. *Report of the Committee of Inquiry, Part I*, 33–34, and *Part II*, 81.
98. Deverell, "Social Investigation in Mombasa," 62.
99. For the commodification of midwestern grain in the United States during the Second Industrial Revolution, see William Cronon, *Nature's Metropolis: Chicago and the Great West* (New York: Norton, 1991), 97–147.
100. Interviews, 2014–15.
101. Notes of a Meeting of the Street Traders Sub-Committee, 18 April 1932, KNA-Coast, UY/5/25; Testimony of Muriuki Kathungu, road builder, to Mombasa Labour Commission Enquiry, 1939, KNA-Nairobi, AG/8/119; Testimony of Mulea and Kashoki.
102. *Report of the Committee of Inquiry, Part I*, 28–29.
103. *Report of the Committee of Inquiry, Part II*, 83.
104. *Report of the Committee of Inquiry, Part I*, 35.
105. Deputy Price Controller, Coast Province, to Controller of Prices, 26 November 1951, KNA-Coast, CP/1/5; Deverell, "Social Investigation," 66–67.
106. Deputy Price Controller, Coast Province, to Controller of Prices, 27 November 1951, KNA-Coast, CP/1/5.
107. G. M. Wilson, "1956—Kongowea—1958: A Case Study of African Built Housing Controlled by Municipal Rules," in *The Mombasa Social Survey, Part II* (Nairobi: Cyclostyled, 1958), 390, KNA-Library, GP.301/WIN.
108. Report on Charcoal Dealers, ca. February 1959; Report on Charcoal Dealers: Supplemental List, ca. February 1959; both in KNA-Nairobi, UY/12/698.
109. Justin Willis, "'Men on the Spot': Labor, and the Colonial State in British East Africa: The Mombasa Water Supply, 1911–1917," *International Journal of African Historical Studies* 28, no. 1 (1995): 31–32, 46.
110. *Report of the Committee of Inquiry, Part II*, 84–85; Deverell, "Social Investigation," 64–65.
111. Interview: James Miruka, Nyanza Province, 18 February 2015.
112. Deverell, "Social Investigation," 65.
113. The literature on this topic in a global context is vast. For one of the pathbreaking studies on commodities and consumption in modern Africa, see Timothy Burke's *Lifebuoy Men, Lux Women: Commodification, Consumption, and Cleanliness in Modern Zimbabwe* (Durham, NC: Duke University Press, 1996). More recently, see Bianca Murillo, *Market Encounters: Consumer Cultures in Twentieth-Century Ghana* (Athens: Ohio University Press, 2017). Within East Africa, work on this topic includes Jeremy Prestholdt's study of consumer cultures during the economic changes of the nineteenth-century Swahili coast, while Andrew Ivaska considered the topic in 1960s Dar es Salaam, especially for music and fashion. Jeremy Prestholdt, *Domesticating the World: African Consumerism and the Genealogies of Globalization*

(Berkeley: University of California Press, 2008); Andrew Ivaska, *Cultured States: Youth, Gender, and Modern Style in 1960s Dar es Salaam* (Durham, NC: Duke University Press, 2011).

CHAPTER 3: MEALTIMES AND MODERN URBANISM

1. "Report of a Board of Inquiry Appointed to Inquire into Employment in the Port of Mombasa, 1959," 10, Kenya National Archives, Coast Province Regional Office, Mombasa (hereafter KNA-Coast), CP/7/12. Known as the "Parkin Report," this document provides details about working hours and also notes the high levels of morning humidity.
2. Minutes of the Welfare Committee, Mombasa African Advisory Council, 19 June 1952, Kenya National Archives, Nairobi (hereafter KNA-Nairobi), UY/12/27.
3. G. M. Wilson, "Demographic Factors and Population," in *Mombasa Social Survey, Part I* (Nairobi: Cyclostyled, 1958), 140, Library of KNA-Nairobi (hereafter KNA-Library), RW/301/SRE.
4. Minutes of Sub-Committee, Trade and Housing, 18 April 1957, KNA-Nairobi, UY/12/53.
5. To date, the scholarship on how capitalism transformed conceptions of time in Africa, including mealtimes, has drawn largely on E. P. Thompson's idea of "time-discipline," but the argument here is that the economic geography of urban consumer markets was far more decisive in the development of lunchtime routines in Mombasa. See Thompson's classic argument in "Time, Work-Discipline, and Industrial Capitalism," *Past and Present* no. 38 (1967): 56–97. For Africanists writing on time-discipline in Africa, see Frederick Cooper, "Colonizing Time: Work Rhythms and Labor Conflict in Colonial Mombasa," in *Colonialism and Culture,* ed. Nicholas Dirks (Ann Arbor: University of Michigan Press, 1992), 209–45; Frederick Cooper, "Work, Class, and Empire: An African Historian's Retrospective on E. P. Thompson," *Social History* 20, no. 2 (1995): 235–41; Keletso Atkins, *The Moon Is Dead! Give Us Our Money! The Cultural Origins of an African Work Ethic, Natal, South Africa, 1843–1900* (Portsmouth, NH: Heinemann, 1993), 78–95; Phyllis Martin, *Leisure and Society in Colonial Brazzaville* (New York: Cambridge University Press, 1996), 3, 71–83; and Jeremy Rich, *A Workman Is Worthy of His Meat: Food and Colonialism in the Gabon Estuary* (Lincoln: University of Nebraska Press, 2009), 88–89.
6. For the ways that working-class families in the industrializing United States incorporated commercially prepared food into their household meals, see Katherine Leonard Turner, *How the Other Half Ate: A History of Working-Class Meals at the Turn of the Century* (Berkeley: University of California Press, 2014), 52–90.
7. Susanne Y. P. Choi and Yinni Peng, *Masculine Compromise: Migration, Family, and Gender in China* (Berkeley: University of California Press, 2016), 152–54.

8. Frederick Cooper, *On the African Waterfront: Urban Disorder and the Transformation of Work in Colonial Mombasa* (New Haven, CT: Yale University Press, 1987).
9. Lisa A. Lindsay, *Working with Gender: Wage Labor and Social Change in Southwestern Nigeria* (Portsmouth, NH: Heinemann, 2003).
10. For an analysis of these rural-urban migrant households in Kenya, see Colin Leys, *Underdevelopment in Kenya: The Political Economy of Neocolonialism, 1964–1971* (Berkeley: University of California Press, 1975), 180–81; for Mombasa, see Richard E. Stren, *Housing the Urban Poor in Africa: Policy, Politics and Bureaucracy in Mombasa* (Berkeley: University of California Press, 1978), 267–68. This is also an important theme in Southern African history. For Zimbabwe, see Teresa Barnes, *"We Women Worked So Hard": Gender, Urbanization, and Social Reproduction in Colonial Harare, 1930–1956* (Portsmouth, NH: Heinemann, 1999). In a South African context, in a theory that greatly influenced labor history in Africa, Harold Wolpe saw these urban-rural families as fundamental to the system that reproduced cheap labor power, with the cost of social reproduction shifted from urban employers to rural African communities. Harold Wolpe, "Capitalism and Cheap Labour-Power in South Africa: From Segregation to Apartheid," *Economy and Society* 1, no. 4 (1972): 425–56. For the influence of this theory on labor history in Africa, see Thaddeus Sunseri, "Labour Migration in Colonial Tanzania and the Hegemony of South African Historiography," *African Affairs* 95, no. 381 (1996): 581–98.
11. Conclusion aggregated from interviews conducted in Mombasa from October 2014 to January 2015 and in Nyanza Province in February 2015. Conclusions drawn in aggregate from these oral interviews are hereafter cited as "Interviews, 2014–15." See also C. R. Philip, "Nutrition in Kenya: Notes on the State of Nutrition of African Children," *East African Medical Journal* 20, no. 7 (1943): 231. Both uji and githeri have many local varieties and names, as detailed in chapter 1, but when referenced as dishes in a multilingual, national, and/or urban context, speaking in English or Kiswahili, these are the terms used to describe them. As I am here largely examining these communities and their cuisines together, I will refer to them as *uji* and *githeri.*
12. Interviews, 2014–15.
13. Interviews, 2014–15.
14. Interview: Joseph Mwangi, Mombasa, 6 December 2014.
15. Interviews, 2014–15.
16. Interview: Vitalis Owiti, Nyanza Province, 19 February 2015.
17. Interviews, 2014–15.
18. Interview: Sampson Kereu, Mombasa, 11 December 2014.
19. Interview: Gregory Osollo Omondi, Nyanza Province, 13 February 2015.
20. Interviews, 2014–15. For Kikuyu agriculture and diets at midcentury and the dominance of white maize, see D. R. F. Taylor, "Changing Food Habits in Kikuyuland," *Canadian Journal of African Studies* 4, no. 3 (1970): 343; Claire C.

Robertson, *Trouble Showed the Way: Women, Men, and Trade in the Nairobi Area, 1890–1990* (Bloomington: Indiana University Press, 1997), 59–61; and Philip, "Nutrition in Kenya," 231–32.

21. Interview: Joseph Mariko Agwari, Nyanza Province, 11 February 2015.
22. Interview: Mwangi.
23. N. Humphrey, *The Kikuyu Lands: The Relationship of Population to the Land in South Nyeri* (Nairobi: Government Printer, 1945), 34.
24. Interview: Kereu; Taylor, "Changing Food Habits," 343, 347.
25. Interviews, 2014–15.
26. Judith Hayer, "Some Problems in the Valuation of Subsistence Output," Center for Economic Research Discussion Paper no. 14 (University College, Nairobi, August 1965), 9–10.
27. The conclusion about the regularity of githeri at breakfast, lunch, and dinner is drawn from Interviews, 2014–15.
28. Margaret Strobel, *Muslim Women in Mombasa, 1890–1975* (New Haven, CT: Yale University Press, 1979), 129; Justin Willis, *Mombasa, the Swahili, and the Making of the Mijikenda* (Oxford, UK: Clarendon, 1993), 96.
29. Acting District Commissioner, Mombasa, to District Commissioner's Office, 9 August 1919, KNA-Nairobi, PC/Coast/1/14/97.
30. See chapter 1 for the tight labor markets on the early-colonial coast.
31. *Kenya Population Census, 1962: Tables,* vol. 2, *Populations of Locations and County Council Wards by Race, Tribe and Sex* (Nairobi: Ministry of Finance and Economic Planning, 1965), 76–79; Karim Janmohamed, "A History of Mombasa, c. 1895–1939: Some Aspects of Economic and Social Life in an East African Port Town during Colonial Rule" (PhD diss., Northwestern University, 1978), 254, 257.
32. A. G. Bush, *A Project for the Drainage and Town-Planning of Mombasa Island* (Nairobi: Government Printer, 1920), 7, Commonwealth and African Collections, Bodleian Library, University of Oxford (hereafter CAC), 753.14/S/40/1920 (1); *Atlas of Kenya* (Nairobi: Survey of Kenya, 1962), 38.
33. Wilson, "Demographic Factors and Population," 145.
34. On unemployment in Mombasa and Kenya more widely, see Cooper, *On the African Waterfront,* 46, 97, 210; A. G. Dalgleish, *Survey of Unemployment* (Colony and Protectorate of Kenya, 1960), 9, CAC/753.14/v.19/1960 (4); and Gavin Kitching, *Class and Economic Change in Kenya: The Making of an African Petite-Bourgeoisie, 1905–1970* (New Haven, CT: Yale University Press, 1980), 378.
35. A. H. B. Rydon, Report: "Unauthorised Food Vendors," presented to the General Purposes Committee, 5 February 1964, KNA-Nairobi, UY/12/339. For street-food vending as a response to unemployment, also see Minutes of General Purposes Committee, 8 February 1965, KNA-Nairobi, UY/12/339.
36. Kitching, *Class and Economic Change,* 378.
37. International Labour Office, *Employment, Incomes and Equality: A Strategy for Increasing Productive Employment in Kenya* (Geneva, Switzerland, 1972).

38. Data on street-food eateries from 1948 to 1973 aggregated from references to named individuals referenced in municipal documentation who ran these types of businesses, especially in board/council minutes. These documents come from files in the KNA-Nairobi, UY/12 series. The larger dataset also includes information on people who ran businesses during the later 1970s and the 1980s, information analyzed in chapter 5. Hereafter, the dataset using the more limited timeline will be referenced as "Street-Food Data, 1948–73." For the 1965 survey on street food, see "Food Vendors: Mombasa Island," presented to the General Purposes Committee, 10 May 1965, KNA-Nairobi, UY/12/339.
39. Interviews, 2014–15; also see throughout the UY files in KNA-Nairobi and KNA-Coast, as well as the labor reports from this period cited throughout this chapter.
40. Conclusions are based on the demographics of gari ya chai vendors, as well as Interviews, 2014–15 and arguments on the early-colonial period in Strobel, *Muslim Women in Mombasa,* 129; and Willis, *Mombasa,* 96.
41. Street-Food Data, 1948–73; Interviews, 2014–15.
42. Conclusions drawn from data analysis of 1965 survey of illicit food vendors on Mombasa Island, "Food Vendors: Mombasa Island."
43. Interview: Nzalu Ngotho, Mombasa, January 2015.
44. Interviews, 2014–15; N. M. Deverell, "A Social Investigation in Mombasa," in *Report on the Economic and Social Background of Mombasa Labour Disputes* (1947), 65, KNA-Nairobi, ABK/11/6.
45. Conclusions about street-food cuisine during breakfast aggregated from close reading of UY files at KNA-Nairobi; Interview: Ngotho; and Deverell, "Social Investigation into Mombasa," 62.
46. Street-Food Data, 1948–73.
47. The best data on these gari ya chai attached to maduka appeared in the archive between 1958 and 1960, a period during which 33 separate such businesses were identified in Mombasa. Street-Food Data, 1948–73. See also "Application for Licenses," 9 January 1959; and Minutes of Health Committee, 6 November 1959; both in KNA-Nairobi, UY/12/698.
48. Minutes of Health Committee, 6 May 1960 and 10 June 1960, KNA-Nairobi, UY/12/698.
49. Minutes of Health Committee, 6 March 1959, KNA-Nairobi, UY/12/698.
50. Deverell, "Social Investigation in Mombasa," 66.
51. Street-Food Data, 1948–73.
52. Deverell, "Social Investigation in Mombasa," 63, 70, 87–88.
53. Deverell, 87–88.
54. Interview: James Miruka, Nyanza Province, 18 February 2015; Deverell, "Social Investigation in Mombasa," 102; Minutes of General Purposes Committee, 11 November 1968, KNA-Nairobi, UY/12/882; Minutes of General Purposes Committee, 13 April 1970, KNA-Nairobi, UY/12/884.
55. Deverell, "Social Investigation in Mombasa," 102.

56. Interview: Miruka.
57. Interview: Margaret Auma Ndolo, Nyanza Province, 6 February 2015.
58. Interview: Thomas Mbeda Jura, Nyanza Province, 9 February 2015.
59. Wilson, "Demographic Factors and Population," 140.
60. Acting District Commissioner, Mombasa, to District Commissioner's Office, 9 August 1919, KNA-Nairobi, PC/Coast/1/14/97; Medical Officer of Health to Acting Town Clerk, 31 August 1929, KNA-Coast, UY/30/1.
61. Abdul Kader bin Mohamed to Town Clerk, Mombasa, 1 January 1953, KNA-Coast, UY/28/98.
62. Minutes of Welfare Committee, 19 June 1952, KNA-Nairobi, UY/12/27.
63. "Report of the Board of Inquiry Appointed to Inquire into Employment in the Port of Mombasa, 1959," 10–12, 34, 49, KNA-Coast, CP/7/12.
64. Minutes of Sub-Committee, Trade and Housing, 18 April 1957.
65. Interview: Mohamed Amir Temu, Mombasa, 5 December 2014.
66. Conclusion based on analysis of street locations of vendors in the 1965 survey "Food Vendors: Mombasa Island."
67. "Mombasa: Mainland North—An Urban Study, Project Report 3" (Nairobi: University of Nairobi, 1973), 18, 40, 49, KNA-Nairobi, UY/14/27.
68. Interview: Jackson Nthuli, Mombasa, 12 January 2015.
69. "Why Not Occupy These People More Usefully?," *Daily Nation,* 21 June 1978, McMillan Memorial Library, Nairobi.
70. Street-food eateries were modern restaurants in the way theorized by Rebecca Spang in *The Invention of the Restaurant: Paris and Modern Gastronomic Culture* (Cambridge, MA: Harvard University Press, 2001). See the introduction for more on street-food eateries as restaurants.
71. The term *vibanda* was most commonly used in oral interviews, though rarely in written sources. Conversely, *kioski* was almost never used in interviews but regularly appeared in archival documents from the independence era.
72. Conclusions about gender and street food come from Street-Food Data, 1948–73, as well as numerous references in the UY files of KNA-Nairobi and KNA-Coast.
73. Conclusions about street-food cuisine were aggregated from Interviews, 2014–15, as well as numerous references throughout municipal minutes and reports found in KNA-Nairobi and KNA-Coast.
74. Interviews, 2014–15; Deverell, "Social Investigation in Mombasa," 79–80.
75. Sydney Mintz, *Sweetness and Power: The Place of Sugar in Modern History* (New York: Penguin, 1986), 8–14.
76. Interview: Temu.
77. Interviews: Ngotho and Miruka; Deverell, "Social Investigation in Mombasa," 65.
78. Interviews, 2014–15.
79. Street-Food Data, 1948–73; Interviews, 2014–15.
80. Interview: Miruka.

81. Interview: Ngotho.
82. Interview: Miruka.
83. Minutes of General Purposes Committee, 8 January 1968, KNA-Nairobi, UY/12/882.
84. Interview: Josephe, Mombasa, 24 November 2014.
85. The language of "pragmatic adjustments" is drawn from Choi and Peng, *Masculine Compromise,* 152–54.
86. Testimony of Kabatha wa Washomba, 1939, KNA-Nairobi, AG/8/119.
87. *Report of the Committee of Inquiry into Labour Unrest at Mombasa, Part I* (Nairobi: Government Printer, 1945), 26, KNA-Nairobi, ABK/18/82. For more evidence on these practices during the 1940s, see Deverell, "Social Investigation in Mombasa," 65, 92, and 97.
88. Interview: Onyango.
89. Justin Willis observed similar patterns in early-colonial Mombasa, though the argument here, drawing on Cooper's work on labor stabilization, is that they became more differentiated later in the colonial period. Willis, *Mombasa,* 97.
90. Interviews, 2014–15.
91. Stren, *Housing the Urban Poor,* 256–57, 264–66, 269–70.
92. "Social Services and Housing Department: Annual Report [Mombasa], 1975," 7, KNA-Coast, UY/2/252.
93. Interview: Gregory Osollo Omondi, Nyanza Province, 13 February 2015.
94. Interview: Barak Olela Abwao, Nyanza Province, 10 February 2015. The municipal housing estate in Changamwe opened in 1973. Originally the estate was envisioned as low-income housing for the city's population in general, but concessions to access land owned by Kenya Uganda Railways and Harbours (KURH), along with mounting financial pressures because of cost overruns, resulted in the entire estate being reserved for KURH employees, a process described in Stren, *Housing the Urban Poor,* 243–51.
95. Testimony of Robbins [no first name given], Public Works Department, 1939, KNA-Nairobi, AG/8/119.
96. Deverell, "Social Investigation in Mombasa," 65.
97. Interviews, 2014–15.
98. Interviews, 2014–15.
99. Interview: Martina Jera, Nyanza Province, 20 February 2015.
100. Interview: Appollo Nyinge Kithakwa, Mombasa, 3 December 2014.
101. Interview: Owiti.
102. Interview: Patrice Omollo Sweta, Nyanza Province, 17 February 2015.
103. This practice was not unique to Mombasa, as Turner points out in her study of working-class foodways in industrializing America in *How the Other Half Ate,* 50–51.
104. *Mombasa District Annual Report, 1930,* 12, KNA-Nairobi, DC/MSA/1/4.
105. Interviews, 2014–15; Deverell, "Social Investigation in Mombasa," 62, 65, 90, 92. The background on fish supplies in Mombasa comes from my research

project on the commercialization of Kenya's fisheries during the twentieth century.

106. Interviews, 2014–15; Street-Food Data, 1948–73; Minutes of Health Committee, 9 August 1957, 10 December 1957, and 4 September 1959, KNA-Nairobi, UY/12/693; Minutes of General Purposes Committee, 7 May 1962, KNA-Nairobi, UY/12/338; Deverell, "Social Investigation in Mombasa," 85.
107. Interview: Joshua Kalii, Mombasa, 8 December 2014.
108. Interview: Temu.
109. Interview: David Muywambu Kivindto and Alice Mutave, Mombasa, 16 January 2015.
110. Leys, *Underdevelopment in Kenya,* 180–81; Stren, *Housing the Urban Poor,* 267–68. For Zimbabwe, see Barnes, *"We Women Worked."*
111. Interviews, 2014–15.
112. Interview: Jacob M. Muli, Mombasa, 12 December 2014.
113. Street-Food Data, 1948–73.
114. Interview: Miruka; Deverell, "Social Investigation in Mombasa." References to these coffee hawkers appear regularly in Mombasa's municipal records, located in the UY series in KNA-Nairobi.
115. Gramsci scholar Kate Crehan describes "common sense" as "that accumulation of taken-for-granted 'knowledge' to be found in every human community. In any given time and place, this accumulation provides a heterogeneous bundle of assumed certainties that structure the basic landscapes within which individuals are socialized and chart their individual life courses." Common sense is not static, because it is subject to historical change as events and structural transformations unfold, but it can be durable and lasting. In this way, Antonio Gramsci's idea of common sense aligns well with David Schoenbrun's call that histories of African modernity be situated within the long-term "durabilities" as much as "ruptures" from the precolonial past. Kate Crehan, *Gramsci's Common Sense: Inequality and Its Narratives* (Durham, NC: Duke University Press, 2016), 43–58; David Schoenbrun, "Conjuring the Modern in Africa: Durability and Rupture in Histories of Public Healing between the Great Lakes of East Africa," *American Historical Review* 111, no. 5 (2006): 1403–39. For more on Gramsci's idea of common sense, see also Stuart Hall, "Gramsci's Relevance for the Study of Race and Ethnicity," *Communication Inquiry* 10, no. 2 (1986): 20–21. For Gramsci's original writings, see Quintin Hoare and Geoffrey Nowell Smith, eds., *Selections from the Prison Notebooks of Antonio Gramsci* (New York: International Publishers, 1973), especially 330n.
116. Interview: Mwangi.
117. Interview: Margaret Auma Ndolo, Nyanza Province, 6 February 2015.
118. Interview: Benike A. Owuir, Nyanza Province, 6 February 2015.
119. Choi and Peng, *Masculine Compromise,* 152–54.
120. Interview: Omondi.

CHAPTER 4: "MAKING FOOD VENDORS A REGULAR AND PERMANENT FEATURE IN THE TOWN"

Note: The quotation in the chapter title comes from Minutes of General Purposes Committee, 9 May 1966, Kenya National Archives, Nairobi (hereafter KNA-Nairobi), UY/12/353.

1. Interview: Sampson Kereu, Mombasa, 11 December 2014.
2. Padraic Burke, "Rolling Carts and Songs a Plenty: The Urban Food Vendor," *Journal of American Culture* 2, no. 3 (1979): 480–87; Daniel M. Bluestone, "'The Pushcart Evil': Peddlers, Merchants and New York City Streets, 1890–1940," *Journal of Urban History* 18, no. 1 (1991): 68–92; Jonathan Shapiro Anjaria, *The Slow Boil: Street Food, Rights, and Public Space in Mumbai* (Palo Alto, CA: Stanford University Press, 2016).
3. On labor stabilization in Mombasa, see Frederick Cooper, *On the African Waterfront: Urban Disorder and the Transformation of Work in Colonial Mombasa* (New Haven, CT: Yale University Press, 1987); and Richard E. Stren, *Housing the Urban Poor in Africa: Policy, Politics and Bureaucracy in Mombasa* (Berkeley: University of California Press, 1978). For other African cities, see Frederick Cooper, *Decolonization and African Society: The Labor Question in French and British Africa* (New York: Cambridge University Press, 1996); and Lisa Lindsay, *Working with Gender: Wage Labor and Social Change in Southwestern Nigeria* (Portsmouth, NH: Heinemann, 2003). For late-colonial campaigns to control urban trade in Nairobi, see Claire C. Robertson, *Trouble Showed the Way: Women, Men, and Trade in the Nairobi Area, 1890–1990* (Bloomington: Indiana University Press, 1997), 130–45; and in Dar es Salaam, Andrew Burton, *African Underclass: Urbanisation, Crime and Colonial Order in Dar es Salaam, 1919–1961* (Athens: Ohio University Press, 2005), 153–54, 158–62.
4. Such dynamics are not limited to urban Africa or the twentieth century. For the power of female food vendors in revolutionary Paris, see Katie Jarvis, *Politics in the Marketplace: Work, Gender and Citizenship in Revolutionary France* (New York: Oxford University Press, 2019), 4.
5. On ideas of citizenship and the politics of economic development in Kenya, see Kara Moskowitz, *Seeing Like a Citizen: Decolonization, Development and the Making of Kenya, 1945–1980* (Athens: Ohio University Press, 2019). For the importance of public housing to politics during the first decades of independence in Mombasa, see Stren, *Housing the Urban Poor.* See also Frederick Cooper, *Colonialism in Question: Theory, Knowledge, History* (Berkeley: University of California Press, 2005), 117–19; and Peter J. Bloom, Stephen F. Miescher, and Takyiwaa Manuh, eds., *Modernization as Spectacle in Africa* (Bloomington: Indiana University Press, 2014).
6. Stren, *Housing the Urban Poor,* 102–3, 138–40, 184–85. For a similar aesthetic vision of urban space in early-independence Nairobi, see Robertson, *Trouble Showed the Way,* 260. For tourism and economic development in independent Kenya, see Devin Smart, "'Safariland': Tourism, Development, and

the Marketing of Kenya in the Postcolonial World," *African Studies Review* 61, no. 2 (2018): 134–57.

7. For modernization at midcentury, see Cooper, *Colonialism in Question,* 117–19; and Bloom, Miescher, and Manuh, *Modernization as Spectacle.*
8. On the recent history of cost-recovery schemes, see David A. McDonald and John Pape, eds., *Cost Recovery and the Crisis of Service Delivery in South Africa* (London: Zed Books, 2002); and Myron Echenberg, *Africa in the Time of Cholera: A History of Pandemics from 1817 to the Present* (New York: Cambridge University Press, 2011), 148–53. Moskowitz has pointed to other areas of midcentury development in Kenya that operated on premises similar to those of later neoliberal policies, especially "self-help" Harambee programs in rural areas. Moskowitz, *Seeing Like a Citizen,* 226–27.
9. For these dynamics in rural land redistribution, see Colin Leys, *Underdevelopment in Kenya: The Political Economy of Neocolonialism, 1964–1971* (Berkeley: University of California Press, 1975), 28–62; in urban housing, see Stren, *Housing the Urban Poor,* 212, 220–52; and for urban mass transit, see Kenda Mutongi, *Matatu: A History of Popular Transportation in Nairobi* (Chicago: University of Chicago Press, 2017), 29–33, 43–47.
10. For stabilized wage labor as the form urban development took, see Cooper, *On the African Waterfront,* especially 274–75.
11. Conclusion aggregated from files in Kenya National Archives, Coast Province, Mombasa Records Centre (hereafter KNA-Coast), UY/5/74. For the establishment of food sanitation laws across urban Kenya during this period, see James Duminy, "Historical Urban Food Governance in Africa: The Case of Kenya, c. 1900–1950," in *Urban Food Systems Governance and Poverty in African Cities,* ed. Jane Battersby and Vanessa Watson (London: Routledge, 2018), 86–88.
12. D. S. Fraser, Town Clerk, Mombasa Municipality Eating House By-laws, 1930, 15 November 1930, KNA-Coast, UY/5/74.
13. Report of the Sub-Committee Appointed under Board Minute 938 to Reconsider the Mombasa Municipality (Inspection, Storage and Sale of Food) Bylaws, 1929, and Mombasa Municipality (Restaurant) Bylaws, 1931, 5 August 1936, KNA-Coast, UY/5/74.
14. Minutes of Meeting of Mombasa Municipal Board, 4 March 1947, and Minutes of African Affairs Committee, 20 May 1947, both in KNA-Nairobi, UY/12/309; "African Affairs: 10 Year Development Plan," ca. July 1947, and Native Trust Fund: Canteen, 1947, both in KNA-Nairobi, UY/12/310.
15. "African Affairs: 10 Year Development Plan."
16. Native Trust Fund: Canteen, 1947.
17. Minutes of Municipal Board of Mombasa, 19 September 1947, KNA-Nairobi, UY/12/310.
18. For the position of "liwali" in colonial-era coastal Kenya, see James R. Brennan, "A History of Sauti ya Mvita (Voice of Mombasa): Radio, Public Culture, and Islam in Coastal Kenya, 1947–1966," in *New Media and Religious*

Transformations in Africa, ed. Rosalind I. J. Hackett and Benjamin F. Soare (Bloomington: Indiana University Press, 2015), 21.

19. Minutes of Municipal Board of Mombasa, 6 January 1948, KNA-Nairobi, UY/12/310. Jetha made a similar defense that same year in June, and more than a decade later al-Hinawy was still advocating for vendors, in this case coffee hawkers who faced increasing restrictions on their trade. Minutes of General Purposes Committee (hereafter GPC), 1 June 1948, KNA-Coast, UY/5/85; Minutes of Health Committee, 5 June 1959, KNA-Nairobi, UY/12/698.
20. Minutes of Welfare Committee, Mombasa African Advisory Council, 19 June 1952, KNA-Nairobi, UY/12/27. For dock workers in Mombasa, see Cooper, *On the African Waterfront.*
21. John Burnett, *England Eats Out: A Social History of Eating Out in England from 1830 to the Present* (London: Routledge, 2004), 181, 260, 306, 317.
22. Minutes of Welfare Committee, Mombasa African Advisory Council, 18 September 1952, KNA-Nairobi, UY/12/27.
23. Minutes of GPC, 10 July 1961 and 11 September 1961, KNA-Nairobi, UY/12/338.
24. A. Z. Mahmud, Esquire, to Town Clerk, Mombasa, 20 August 1954, and Town Clerk, Mombasa, to A. Z. Mahmud, Esquire, 21 August 1954, both in KNA-Coast, UY/28/98.
25. F. P. B. Derrick, District Commissioner, Mombasa District, to East Africa Railway and Harbours, 26 September 1957, KNA-Nairobi, CQ/18/4.
26. H. S. Booker, "Report on the Economic and Social Background of Mombasa Labour Disputes," in *Report on the Social and Economic Background of Mombasa Labour Disputes* (1947), 1, KNA-Nairobi, ABK/11/6; G. M. Wilson, "Demographic Factors and Population," in *Mombasa Social Survey, Part I* (Nairobi: Cyclostyled, 1956), 146, Library of the Kenya National Archives, RW/301/SRE.
27. For the figure of C. D. Rosenwald and the significant power of the medical officer of health within the city administration, see Stren, *Housing the Urban Poor,* 138–40.
28. Minutes of Sub-Committee, Trade and Housing Committee, 18 April 1957, KNA-Nairobi, UY/12/53.
29. The initial arrests and other actions were explained well after the fact, without specifying exact dates for when they occurred. Minutes of Health Committee, 5 April 1957, KNA-Nairobi, UY/12/693.
30. Minutes of GPC, 11 August 1957, KNA-Nairobi, UY/12/318.
31. Minutes of GPC, 5 September 1957, KNA-Nairobi, UY/12/318.
32. District Commissioner, Mombasa District, to Town Clerk, Mombasa, 10 August 1957; Town Clerk, Mombasa, to District Commissioner, Mombasa District, 19 August 1957; both in KNA-Nairobi, CQ/18/4.
33. D. M. Korokoro, for Coast M.L.C., to Town Clerk, Mombasa, 30 August 1957, KNA-Nairobi, CQ/18/4.
34. F. P. B. Derrick, District Commissioner, Mombasa District, Circular, 10 September 1957, KNA-Nairobi, CQ/18/4.

35. C. J. MacGregor, Branch Manager, Shell Company of East Africa, to Medical Officer of Health, Mombasa, 20 September 1957, KNA-Nairobi, CQ/18/4.
36. Minutes of GPC, 5 September 1957.
37. F. J. Khamidi, African Elected Member of Legislative Council, Mombasa Area, to District Commissioner, 9 July 1958, KNA-Nairobi, CQ/18/4.
38. Memorandum for meeting in Town Clerk's Office: Relative to Food Vendors in Mombasa, 24 September 1957, KNA-Nairobi, CQ/18/4.
39. Mombasa Municipal Board to District Engineer, East African Railways and Harbours, 23 September 1957; F. P. B. Derrick, District Commissioner, Mombasa District, to East African Railway and Harbours, 26 September 1957; both in KNA-Nairobi, CQ/18/4.
40. Town Clerk, Mombasa, to District Commissioner, Mombasa District, 27 December 1957, KNA-Nairobi, CQ/18/4.
41. Minutes of GPC, 9 January 1958 and 1 May 1958, KNA-Nairobi, UY/12/318; Minutes of Health Committee, 9 May 1958, KNA-Nairobi, UY/12/693.
42. Minutes of GPC, 6 February 1958, KNA-Nairobi, UY/12/318.
43. Minutes of GPC, 27 January 1958, KNA-Nairobi, UY/12/318.
44. Minutes of GPC, 12 September 1958, KNA-Nairobi, UY/12/318.
45. Minutes of Health Committee, 5 September 1958, KNA-Nairobi, UY/12/698.
46. David Harvey, "The Right to the City," *New Left Review* 53 (2008): 33. For similar dynamics in urban India and Mexico, respectively, see Anjaria, *Slow Boil,* 49; and Sandra C. Mediola García, *Street Democracy: Vendors, Violence, and Public Space in Late Twentieth-Century Mexico* (Lincoln: University of Nebraska Press, 2017), 10–11.
47. Minutes of Health Committee, 10 October 1958, KNA-Nairobi, UY/12/693.
48. Minutes of Health Committee, 8 April 1960, KNA-Nairobi, UY/12/318.
49. Minutes of GPC, 12 February 1962 and 9 July 1962, KNA-Nairobi, UY/12/338.
50. Minutes of GPC, 10 October 1962, KNA-Nairobi, UY/12/338.
51. Minutes of GPC, 9 July 1962, KNA-Nairobi, UY/12/338.
52. For the history of local politics and governing institutions in Mombasa, see Stren, *Housing the Urban Poor,* especially 9–13. For a period of "accommodation" between government officials and street traders in Nairobi during the first years after independence, see Robertson, *Trouble Showed the Way,* 258–63.
53. Minutes of GPC, 10 February 1964, KNA-Nairobi, UY/12/338; Minutes of GPC, 9 November 1964, 19 November 1964, 8 March 1965, and 7 June 1965, all in KNA-Nairobi, UY/12/339.
54. Minutes of GPC, 7 June 1965.
55. C. D. Rosenwald, "Licensing of Food Hawkers," 15 June 1965, KNA-Nairobi, UY/12/339. For Rosenwald's professional biography and the medical officer of health's place in midcentury Mombasa's political structure, see Stren, *Housing the Urban Poor,* 138–40. Aesthetics was also part of why the Nairobi government repressed informal trade during this period. See Robertson, *Trouble Showed the Way,* 260.
56. Minutes of GPC, 21 June 1965, KNA-Nairobi, UY/12/339.

57. "A Curb on Hawkers," *Daily Nation,* 8 July 1965, Daily Nation Media Library–Nairobi (hereafter DNML).
58. Minutes of GPC, 9 August 1965, KNA-Nairobi, UY/12/339.
59. E. K. Cowen, "Municipal Inspector's Report on Hawkers Licenses and Zoning of Town," n.d., ca. November 1964, KNA-Nairobi, UY/12/339.
60. Memo from Town Treasurer, 4 December 1969, KNA-Nairobi, UY/12/884.
61. "Food Vendors: Mombasa Island," survey presented to General Purposes Committee, 10 May 1965; N. S. Rihal, Medical Officer of Health, to Town Clerk, 4 February 1966; both in KNA-Nairobi, UY/12/884.
62. Minutes of GPC, 21 June 1965, KNA-Nairobi, UY/12/339.
63. Minutes of GPC, 12 April 1965, KNA-Nairobi, UY/12/339.
64. Minutes of GPC, 9 August 1965, KNA-Nairobi, UY/12/339. Construction costs for canteens detailed in Minutes of GPC, 13 July 1964, KNA-Nairobi, UY/12/338.
65. N. S. Rihal, Policy in Respect of Unauthorised Foodvendors, 12 April 1966; Minutes of GPC, 12 April 1966; both in KNA-Nairobi, UY/12/353.
66. Minutes of GPC, 9 November 1964 and [date obscured by stamp] June 1965; Refusals: Addendum to Agenda of General Purposes Committee, 12 April 1965; C. D. Rosenwald, Medical Officer of Health, 15 June 1965; all in KNA-Nairobi, UY/12/339.
67. Minutes of GPC, 22 September 1965 and 7 February 1966, KNA-Nairobi, UY/12/339; Report of Foodvendors' Stalls Allocation Sub-Committee appointed under GPC Minute No. 1571/65, n.d., ca. March 1966, KNA-Nairobi, UY/12/339; Minutes of GPC, 13 June 1966 and 10 October 1966, KNA-Nairobi, UY/12/353.
68. Memo from Town Treasurer, 4 December 1969.
69. Minutes of GPC, 8 August 1966, 12 September 1966, and 7 November 1966, KNA-Nairobi, UY/12/353; Minutes of the GPC, 11 November 1968, KNA-Nairobi, UY/12/882.
70. Minutes of GPC, 11 November 1968, KNA-Nairobi, UY/12/882.
71. Minutes of GPC, 10 January 1966, KNA-Nairobi, UY/12/353; "Licenses," *Daily Nation,* 3 February 1966, DNML; Rihal to Town Clerk, 4 February 1966; Minutes of GPC, 7 March 1966, KNA-Nairobi, UY/12/339.
72. Rihal, Policy in Respect of Unauthorised Foodvendors, 12 April 1966.
73. Minutes of GPC, 12 April 1966, KNA-Nairobi, UY/12/353.
74. Minutes of the GPC, 9 May 1966, KNA-Nairobi, UY/12/353.
75. Paul Ocobock, *An Uncertain Age: The Politics of Manhood in Kenya* (Athens: Ohio University Press, 2017), 241.
76. "Marathon Tour for P.C.," *Daily Nation,* 13 May 1966, DNML.
77. "Destruction of Mombasa Food Stalls Condemned," *Daily Nation,* 25 May 1966, DNML.
78. "Destruction of Mombasa Food Stalls Condemned."
79. "Food-Vendors Suffering," *Daily Nation,* 16 June 1966, DNML.
80. Moskowitz, *Seeing Like a Citizen,* 98–109.

81. "Food Vendors Suffering."
82. Minutes of GPC, 11 November 1968, KNA-Nairobi, UY/12/882; A. A. Omar, Chief Health Inspectorate, Mombasa, to Chairman and Members of GPC, Mombasa, 13 April 1970, KNA-Nairobi, UY/12/884. During this period, there were also similar gendered dimensions to the claims that food traders in Nairobi made to city officials. See Robertson, *Trouble Showed the Way,* 260.
83. "Women Food Vendors in Mombasa Protest," *Daily Nation,* 26 March 1970, McMillan Memorial Library, Nairobi (hereafter MML).
84. "Plea to Allow Sale of Food in Streets," *Daily Nation,* 4 April 1970, MML.
85. Minutes of GPC, 13 April 1970, KNA-Nairobi, UY/12/882.
86. Ludwig Krapf gathered vocabularies for his Swahili dictionary during the 1840s; the vocabularies included the word *kipindupindu* for cholera. In Mijikenda languages, those predominant in the rural areas of what is now the Kenyan coast, cholera was specifically defined as *muandzala* during the mid-1800s, but by the end of the century a word that had previously meant a person "who is cold, spiritless; he is not sprightly as to his limbs, he resembles one who is sick," *peho,* had had its definition expanded to mean "epidemic"; in a modified form, *peho ya kumwaga* (diarrhea), it meant cholera. Ludwig Krapf, *A Dictionary of the Suahili Language* (London: Trübner, 1882), viii, 153; Ludwig Krapf and J. Rebmann, *Nika-English Dictionary* (London: Society for Promoting Christian Knowledge, 1887), v, 321; W. E. Taylor, *Giryama Vocabulary and Collections* (London: Society for Promoting Christian Knowledge, 1891). For cholera in nineteenth-century Zanzibar, see Echenberg, *Time of Cholera,* 50–64.
87. Echenberg, *Time of Cholera,* 50–64, 87–89; Dhiman Barua, "History of Cholera," in *Cholera,* ed. Dhiman Barua and William B. Greenough III (New York: Plenum Medical Book Company, 1992), 14–18. Cholera still posed a potential threat during the first half of the twentieth century, as in a 1912 outbreak in Zanzibar, but nothing occurred on the scale of mortality like during the epidemics of the 1800s. The 1912 Zanzibar outbreak seen from Kenya is covered in KNA-Nairobi, PC/Coast/1/15/91.
88. "No Cholera in Nairobi-Govt.," *Daily Nation,* 13 March 1971, MML.
89. Jane N. Zuckerman, Lars Rambo, and Alain Fisch, "The True Burden and Risk of Cholera: Implications for Prevention and Control," *Lancet* 7 (2007): 521–30.
90. Echenberg, *Time of Cholera,* 130–34.
91. Echenberg, 109, 141; Simukai Chigudu, *The Political Life of an Epidemic: Cholera, Crisis and Citizenship in Zimbabwe* (New York: Cambridge University Press, 2020), 35–62; Emily Brownell, *Gone to Ground: A History of Environment and Infrastructure in Dar es Salaam* (Pittsburgh: University of Pittsburgh Press, 2020), 130–31.
92. David Nilsson and Ezekiel Nyangeri Nyanchaga, "Pipes and Politics: A Century of Change and Continuity in Kenyan Urban Water Supply," *Journal of Modern African Studies* 46, no. 1 (2008): 139; Justus Kithiia and Gamoyo Majambo, "Motion but No Speed: Colonial to Post-colonial Status of Water and Sanitation Service Provision in Mombasa City," *Cities* 107 (2020): 2–12.

93. "Mombasa: Mainland North—An Urban Study, Project Report 3" (Nairobi: University of Nairobi, 1973), 36, map 4.5, KNA-Nairobi, UY/14/27. The sewage situation remained largely the same by the end of the century, except that the city's population had nearly doubled, with 70 percent of households using pit latrines, 17 percent with septic tanks, and 12 percent connected to the central sewage system. See Saheed M. Mwaguni, "Public Health Problems in Mombasa District: A Case Study on Sewage Management" (MA thesis, University of Nairobi, 2002), 26, 42. For the class and ethnic dynamics that shape the politics of excremental removal in another modern African city, see Tasha Rijke-Epstein, "The Politics of Filth: Sanitation, Work and Competing Moralities in Urban Madagascar, 1890s–1977," *Journal of African History* 60, no. 2 (2019): 229–56.
94. Annual Report of Medical Officer of Health, 1971, KNA-Coast, UY/14/249.
95. Annual Report of Medical Officer of Health, 1972, KNA-Coast, UY/4/247.
96. Annual Report of Medical Officer of Health, 1984, KNA-Coast, UY/4/328.
97. Chigudu, *Political Life,* 29. In Echenberg's survey of the history of cholera in Africa, he does not consider the dynamics of urban cholera control in any detail. Brownell does observe that in 1970s Dar es Salaam cholera control focused on "policing 'dirty' spaces of commerce" but does not take the analysis much beyond that. Brownell, *Gone to Ground,* 130–31.
98. M. C. Lim-Quizon et al., "Cholera in Metropolitan Malina: Foodborne Transmission via Street Vendors," *Bulletin of the World Health Organization* 72, no. 5 (1994): 745–49; David Griffith, Louise A. Kelley-Hope, and Mark A. Miller, "Review of Reported Cholera Outbreaks Worldwide, 1995–2005," *American Journal of Tropical Medicine and Hygiene* 75, no. 5 (2006): 973–77; F. Grandesso et al., "Risk Factors for Cholera Transmission in Haiti during Inter-peak Periods: Insights to Improve Current Control Strategies from Two Case-Control Studies," *Epidemiology and Infection* 142, no. 8 (2014): 1625–35.
99. For similar cholera control in 1970s Dar es Salaam, see Brownell, *Gone to Ground,* 130.
100. "Mombasa Council Lifts Its Ban on Hawkers," *Daily Nation,* 15 April 1971, MML; Robert F. Stock, *Cholera in Africa: Diffusion of the Disease, 1970–1975, with Particular Emphasis on West Africa* (London: International Africa Institute, 1976), 29.
101. Minutes of Health Committee, 26 March 1971, KNA-Nairobi, UY/12/527; "Kiosk Hawkers Protest Quit Notices," *Daily Nation,* 12 March 1971, MML; "Mombasa Food Ban Stays in Force," *Daily Nation,* 7 April 1971, MML.
102. "Mombasa Food Ban Stays in Force"; "Mombasa Now May Lift Tea Kiosk Ban," *Daily Nation,* 8 April 1971, MML; Minutes of Health Committee, 8 April 1971, KNA-Nairobi, UY/12/528; Minutes of GPC, 14 April 1971, KNA-Nairobi, UY/12/528.
103. Minutes of GPC, 14 April 1971; "Mombasa Council Lifts Its Ban on Hawkers."
104. Stock, *Cholera in Africa,* 29.
105. Minutes of (Special) Meeting of Health Committee, 26 March 1971, KNA-Nairobi, UY/12/527; Lance Jones Bengo, Director of Social Services and

Housing, Mombasa, to Chairman and Members of GPC, 19 July 1972, KNA-Coast, UY/18/17.

106. Lance Jones Bengo, Director of Social Services and Housing, Mombasa and Town Treasurer, Mombasa, Report on Markets and Food Vendors Canteens, sent to Chairman and Members of GPC, n.d., ca. July/August 1972, KNA-Coast, UY/18/17.
107. Social Services and Housing: Annual Report, 1974, KNA-Coast, UY/4/251.
108. Salim Omar, Health Inspector, Mombasa, to Chairman and Members of the Mombasa Municipal Commission, 16 March 1977, KNA-Coast, UY/30/25.
109. Bengo and Town Treasurer, Report on Markets and Food Vendors Canteens; Annual Report of the Director of Social Services and Housing, 1978, KNA-Coast, UY/4/260; Annual Report of the Director of Social Services and Housing, 1979, KNA-Coast, UY/4/266.
110. A. W. Mugenya, Medical Officer of Health, to Director of Social Services and Housing, 29 January 1980, KNA-Coast, UY/30/27.
111. Annual Report of the Medical Officer of Health, 1972, KNA-Coast, UY/4/247; Annual Report of the Medical Officer of Health, 1979, KNA-Coast, UY/4/264.
112. Annual Report of the Medical Officer of Health, 1971, KNA-Coast, UY/4/249; Annual Report of the Medical Officer of Health, 1972; and Social Services and Housing: Annual Report, 1975, KNA-Coast, UY/4/252.
113. Minutes of the Education, Public Health and Social Services Committee, 10 January 1975, KNA-Coast/UY/7/38; Minutes of the Education, Public Health and Social Services Committee, 7 February 1975, KNA-Coast, UY/7/45. The bacterium began to spread in Nyanza in December 1974, with the epidemic continuing until April 1975. Stock, *Cholera in Africa,* 29–30.
114. Meja Mwangi, *Going Down River Road* (Nairobi: East African Educational Publishers, 1993), 165.
115. "Setting Up a Tea Kiosk," *Daily Nation,* 25 January 1977, MML.
116. "Hospitals Clear Cholera Suspects," *Daily Nation,* 17 March 1978, MML; "New Moves as Cholera Hits More at Coast," *Daily Nation,* 17 April 1978, MML.
117. "Hospitals Clear Cholera Suspects."
118. Annual Report of Social Services and Housing, 1978; "New Moves as Cholera Hits More at Coast."
119. Conclusion aggregated from minutes of daily cholera meetings held at the Medical Officer of Health's office in Mombasa in KNA-Nairobi, UY/12/710. More-detailed information about these cholera control teams comes from Minutes of the Cholera Meeting, 29 April 1978, KNA-Nairobi, UY/12/710; and "New Moves as Cholera Hits More at Coast."
120. "Why Not Occupy These People More Usefully?," *Daily Nation,* 21 June 1978, MML.
121. Detailed in KNA-Nairobi, UY/12/710.
122. Minutes of the Daily Cholera Meeting, 8 June 1978 and 26 June 1978, KNA-Nairobi, UY/12/710. Numerous other documents in this file likewise indicate this strategy.

123. "180 Fined for Breaking Cholera Campaign Laws," *Daily Nation,* 12 May 1978, MML.
124. Minutes of the Cholera Meeting, 29 April 1978; Minutes of the Daily Cholera Meeting, 31 May 1978 and 8 June 1978, KNA-Nairobi, UY/12/710.
125. Minutes of the Daily Cholera Meeting, 6 May 1978, KNA-Nairobi, UY/12/710.
126. Minutes of the Daily Cholera Meeting, 15 June 1978, 24 June 1978, 26 June 1978, and 29 June 1978, KNA-Nairobi, UY/12/710.
127. Minutes of the Daily Cholera Meeting, 1 July 1978, KNA-Nairobi, UY/12/710.
128. A. W. Mugenya, Medical Officer of Health, Mombasa, to Chairman and Members of the Education, Public Health and Social Services Committee, 2 April 1980, KNA-Coast, UY/26/13.

CHAPTER 5: STREET FOOD AND URBAN LIFE AT THE END OF THE TWENTIETH CENTURY

1. Interview: John Omondi Onyango, Mombasa, 25 January 2015.
2. For urbanization across Africa in the late twentieth century and more recent past, see Organisation for Economic Co-operation and Development, *Africa's Urbanisation Dynamics, 2020: Afripolis, Mapping a New Urban Geography* (Paris: OECD Publishing, 2020). For examples of other historians exploring the socioeconomic and political history of this period of rapid urban growth in an East African context, see Kenda Mutongi, *Matatu: A History of Popular Transportation in Nairobi* (Chicago: University of Chicago Press, 2017); and Emily Brownell, *Gone to Ground: A History of Environment and Infrastructure in Dar es Salaam* (Pittsburgh: University of Pittsburgh Press, 2020).
3. See Kenya's annual *Economic Survey* from the 1980s and 1990s. Extensive data was recorded on urban informal economies across Kenya, but the government did not do large surveys of the sector in Mombasa. Instead, historians have to rely on qualitative descriptions of rapid growth, paired with these more aggregate numbers on urban Kenya, detailed in this chapter's section "The Business of Street Food at the End of the Twentieth Century."
4. These spatial constraints have been more common in rural areas. Consequently, worksite cafeterias and rationing have been more-regular features of waged employment in the countryside compared to urban centers, where commercial markets make it feasible for workers to buy their own food. For examples of employers provisioning food to their workers in rural colonial Kenya, see the descriptions throughout the "Labor Section" of the Native Affairs Department Annual Reports and those of the Labour Department (after 1945), accessed at the British Library as well as Commonwealth and African Collections at the University of Oxford. See also Priscilla M. Shilaro, *Failed Eldorado: Colonial Capitalism, Rural Industrialization, African Land Rights in Kenya, and the Kakamega Gold Rush, 1930–1952* (Lanham, MD: University Press of America, 2008), 167–69; and Godriver Wanga-Odhiambo, *The Political Economy of Sugar Production in Colonial Kenya: The Asian*

Initiative in Central Nyanza (New York: Lexington Books, 2016), 186–87. For these dynamics in other parts of Africa and the world, see Todd Cleveland, *Diamonds in the Rough: Corporate Paternalism and African Professionalism on the Mines of Colonial Angola, 1917–1975* (Athens: Ohio University Press, 2015), 80–81, 112–16; William Cronon, *Nature's Metropolis: Chicago and the Great West* (New York: Norton, 1991), 162–63; and Linda Carlson, *Company Towns of the Pacific Northwest* (Seattle: University of Washington Press, 2017), 50–55.

5. Historians have written little about the "staff meal" provided in restaurants and hotels, but these practices have been widespread in various parts of the world. The scholarly literature on meals for hotel employees is thin, but some research has been done in human resource and nutrition studies. See, for example, Eugene Tetteh Gorleku, "The Quality of Hotel Employee Meals, and Employees' Perception of the Quality" (MS thesis, Louisiana State University, 2002); and Luana Nanu, Cihan Cobanoglu, Ibrahim Hakan Yilmaz, and Timucin Dis, "Impact of Employee Meals on Employee Satisfaction and Hotel Financial Performance: An Experimental Study," *Journal of Hospitality Financial Management* 28, no. 2 (2020): 91–102. Though neither historians nor many other scholars have addressed the "staff" or "family" meals in restaurants, anyone who has worked in one can testify to their central place in the workday, while prominent chefs have even devoted whole cookbooks to these kinds of recipes and journalists have profiled the practice. See Ferran Adrià, *The Family Meal: Home Cooking with Ferran Adrià* (New York: Phaidon, 2011); and Derva First, "Chef's Table," *Boston Globe*, 5 May 2012.
6. By the 1980s, tourism represented more than 12 percent of Kenya's gross domestic product, earning nearly as much as coffee and tea combined, the country's next two top industries. John S. Akama, "The Role of Government in the Development of Tourism in Kenya," *International Journal of Tourism Research* 4, no. 1 (2002): 1–14; and Devin Smart, "'Safariland': Tourism, Development and the Marketing of Kenya in the Post-colonial World," *African Studies Review* 61, no. 2 (2018): 134–57.
7. For the trajectory of waged employment during the four decades after independence, see Charles Hornsby, *Kenya: A History since Independence* (New York: I. B. Taurus, 2012), 190–91, 419–24, 430–32, 567–71 (quotation from 431).
8. David Harvey, *A Brief History of Neoliberalism* (New York: Oxford University Press, 2005); Naomi Klein, *The Shock Doctrine: The Rise of Disaster Capitalism* (New York: Picador, 2008). In an African context, see Graham Harrison, *Neoliberal Africa: The Impact of Global Social Engineering* (London: Zed Books, 2010).
9. Robert Maxon and Peter Ndege, "The Economics of Structural Adjustment," in *Decolonization and Independence in Kenya, 1940–1993*, ed. B. A. Ogot and W. R. Ochieng'(Athens: Ohio University Press, 1995), 151–86; Hornsby, *Kenya*, 419–24, 430–32, 567–71.

10. Maxon and Ngege recognized this in their 1995 essay, cautioning against attributing all liberalizing tendencies in Kenya like those in the informal economy to the broader context of structural adjustment. See Maxon and Ngege, "Economics of Structural Adjustment," 169.
11. Republic of Kenya, *Sessional Paper No. 1 of 1986 on Economic Management for Renewed Growth* (Nairobi: Government Printer, 1986), 54, 58.
12. Analysts of "land-grabbing" in Kenya tend to focus on elite projects that secured vast tracts of public land for private accumulation, though the same political context also opened space for vendors to make small-scale claims on urban space. For elite land-grabbing, see Jacqueline M. Klopp, "Pilfering the Public: The Problem of Land Grabbing in Contemporary Kenya," *Africa Today* 47, no. 1 (2000): 7–26. Claire Robertson suggests that women in 1980s Nairobi after a demolition sought "political influence—a patron to protect them," but she does not push the point further. Claire C. Robertson, *Trouble Showed the Way: Women, Men, and Trade in the Nairobi Area, 1890–1990* (Bloomington: Indiana University Press, 1997), 270. Graeme Young has also detailed how such patrimonial relationships of protection between elected officials and informal vendors were present in Uganda during the late twentieth century. See Graeme Young, "From Protection to Repression: The Politics of Street Vending in Kampala," *Journal of Eastern Africa Studies* 11, no. 4 (2017): 714–33.
13. Interview: Thomas Mbeda Jura, Nyanza Province, 9 February 2015.
14. Interview: Rose Omwanda, Mombasa, 2014.
15. Interviews: Darshan Singh Wilkhu, Mombasa, 7 November 2014; Ken H. K. Sam, Mombasa, November 2014; Gurbachan Singh, Mombasa, November 2014.
16. Kathy Eldon, *Guide to Eating Out in Kenya* (Nairobi: Kenway Publications, 1987), 151–223.
17. Interview: Wilkhu.
18. Eldon, *Eating Out in Kenya,* 190.
19. Interviews: Julius Nzioka Nzonga, Mombasa, November 2014; Interview: Wilkhu.
20. Interview: Thomas Mbaja Minara, Nyanza Province, 13 February 2015.
21. Interview: Hezron Mupaghasa, Mombasa, 5 December 2014.
22. Interview: Vitalis Owiti, Nyanza Province, 19 February 2015.
23. Interview: Joseph Mariko Agwari, Nyanza Province, 11 February 2015.
24. Interview: Jacob M. Muli, Mombasa, 12 December 2014.
25. Interview: Patrick N. Kasau, Mombasa, 12 December 2014.
26. Interview: Benike A. Owuir, Nyanza Province, 6 February 2015.
27. Interview: Agwari.
28. This language is found throughout the archival record, especially in Kenya National Archives, Coast Province, Mombasa Records Centre (hereafter KNA-Coast), UY/20/147, CQ/18/10, CQ/20/55, and CQ/18/18.
29. By the 2000s, these processes had radically urbanized what had previously been a largely rural society. In 2018, an estimated 65 percent of Kenyans lived in cities. Organisation for Economic Co-operation and Development,

Africa's Urbanisation Dynamics, 2020, 138–40. See also *Kenya Population Census, 1962: Tables,* vol. 2, *Populations of Locations and County Council Wards by Race, Tribe and Sex* (Nairobi: Government Printer, 1965); and *1999 Population and Housing Census: Counting Our People for Development* (Nairobi: Government Printer, 2001), xxxiii.

30. Data on the urban informal economy in Kenya from the annual *Economic Survey* (1979–86), published by the Kenyan government. The average annual percentage from 1978 to 1985 does not include 1981 because the survey methodology changed to include more small towns/cities, causing an outlier increase in the percentage not representative of the actual rate of change.
31. Republic of Kenya, *Economic Survey, 1994* (Nairobi: Central Bureau of Statistics, 1995), 48–59.
32. M. K. Mumba, Acting Town Clerk, Mombasa, to Mayor, Councilor A. S. Mwidani, 23 February 1987, KNA-Coast, UY/20/147.
33. Meeting between His Worship the Mayor and the Coast Hawkers Association, 21 October 1988, KNA-Coast, CQ/20/55.
34. R. S. Maamiry, for Medical Officer of Health, to Town Clerk, 4 September 1986; Councilor William P. Karisa to Town Clerk, Mombasa, 29 December 1988; both in KNA-Coast, UY/20/147.
35. Report on Tea Kiosk for Mr. Mbwana Mohamed Musio, 21 September 1983; E. Mpate, Medical Officer of Health, to Municipal Engineer, Mombasa, 10 April 1986; F. G. Ndungu, Chief Building Inspector, care of Chief's Office, Likoni, 10 March 1986; E. Mpate, Medical Officer of Health, to Municipal Engineer, Mombasa, 7 August 1987; all in KNA-Coast, UY/20/147. For a discussion of building materials for working-class housing in Mombasa, similar to those used for vibanda, see Richard E. Stren, *Housing the Urban Poor in Africa: Policy, Politics and Bureaucracy in Mombasa* (Berkeley: University of California Press, 1978), 33–34. For coastal mangrove forests and their commercial use as building materials on the nearby Tanzanian coast, see Thaddeus Sunseri, *Wielding the Ax: State Forestry and Social Conflict in Tanzania, 1820–2000* (Athens: Ohio University Press, 2009).
36. Mpate to Municipal Engineer, 7 August 1987; Report on Tea Kiosk for Musio, 21 September 1983.
37. U. K. Nathwani, Medical Officer of Health, Mombasa, to Chairman and Members of Finance and General Purposes Committee, 12 April 1976, KNA-Coast, UY/30/26.
38. State of Likoni (Mainland) Open Air Market, 9 February 1987, KNA-Coast, UY/30/27.
39. Interview: Mary Nambui Chege, Mombasa, 12 December 2014. Sammy Syengo also shared his experiences selling curios and relying on vibanda for lunch during the 1970s. Interview: Sammy Syengo, Mombasa, 8 December 2014.
40. Interview: Emma Mudanya, Mombasa, 16 December 2014.

41. Interview: Catherine Muthoni, Mombasa, 18 December 2014. For similar dynamics of trust and credit between foodstuff traders and their customers in Mwanza, Tanzania, see Karen Coen Flynn, *Food, Culture, and Survival in an African City* (New York: Palgrave Macmillan, 2005), 50.
42. Interview: Mudanya.
43. Interview: Monica Mutiso, Mombasa, 17 December 2014.
44. Interview: Muthoni.
45. Interview: Mutiso.
46. Interview: Hadija Ali Gambere, Mombasa, 17 December 2014.
47. Conclusion aggregated from interviews, as well as extensive references to men running these kinds of eateries in UY and CQ files from the Kenya National Archives, Nairobi (hereafter KNA-Nairobi) and KNA-Coast.
48. Interview: Mohamed Amir Temu, Mombasa, 5 December 2014.
49. For observations on how women working in the informal economy in Nairobi also think about their earnings as a way to provide education for their children, see Mary Mjeri Kinyanjui, *Women and the Informal Economy in Urban Africa: From the Margins to the Centre* (London: Zed Books, 2014), 84–86.
50. Interview: Nuru Ibrahim Hajj, Mombasa, 20 December 2014.
51. Interview: Elizabeth Malleo, Mombasa, 22 December 2014.
52. Interview: Muthoni.
53. Interview: Sampson Kereu, Mombasa, 11 December 2014.
54. Interview: Josephe, Mombasa, 24 November 2014.
55. A. W. Mugenya, Medical Officer of Health, to Town Clerk, Mombasa, 30 August 1982, KNA-Coast, UY/12/147.
56. E. Mpate, Acting Medical Officer of Health, Mombasa, to Your Worship the Deputy Mayor, Councilor Samuel Ndoro, 25 June 1984, KNA-Coast, UY/30/21.
57. Interview: Hajj.
58. Interview: Muthoni.
59. Interview: Kereu.
60. Interview: Malleo.
61. Interview: Hajj.
62. Interview: Josephe.
63. Sylvester Obanda Ogwell to District Land Officer, 2 March 1988; [Name obscured], for District Commissioner, to Sylvester Obanda Ogwell, 2 March 1988; Sylvester Obanda Ogwell to Provincial State Council, 4 March 1988; all in KNA-Coast, CQ/20/55.
64. K. P. A. Langat, District Commissioner, Mombasa District to Principal State Council, Mombasa, 8 March 1988, NA-Coast, CQ/20/55.
65. The construction of ten food vendors' stalls in the Magongo Market during the early 1980s is the exception that proves the rule, the only example found in the archives of new stalls for street food built during a decade when the industry was expanding rapidly. K. Njendu, for Municipal Engineer, to Director of Social Services and Housing, 10 September 1980, KNA-Coast, UY/30/26.

66. Problems Facing Magongo Market. For other examples, see T. V. Mugusia, Acting Medical Officer of Health, to Acting Town Clerk, 25 September 1986; and T. V. Mugusia, Acting Medical Officer of Health, Mombasa, to Town Clerk, Mombasa, 15 October 1986; both in KNA-Coast, UY/30/25.
67. Meeting Held in the Mayor's Parlour, 24 October 1988, KNA-Coast, CQ/20/55.
68. E. Mpate, Medical Officer of Health, Mombasa, to Director of Social Services and Housing, Mombasa, 17 November 1986, KNA-Coast, UY/20/147; M. A. Skanda, Senior Public Health Officer, Report: Mainland South, Likoni Open Air Market, ca. early 1987, KNA-Coast, UY/30/27; Notes of a Meeting Held in the Town Clerk's Office, 19 February 1987, KNA-Coast, UY/30/8.
69. M. A. Skanda, Senior Public Health Officer, Report on the Public Health Inspection of Likoni Open Air Market, 20 November 1987, KNA-Coast, UY/30/27.
70. A. R. K. Odicoh, District Officer, Likoni, to District Commissioner, Mombasa, 3 March 1987, KNA-Coast, CQ/20/55.
71. Interview: Temu.
72. John Mbaria, "Why Kiosks in Mombasa Had to Go," *Daily Nation,* 27 December 2001, McMillan Memorial Library (hereafter MML).
73. L. G. Mwacharo, "Why Mombasa Kiosks Had to Go," *Daily Nation,* 1 January 2002, MML.
74. Priscilla Mwanake Murundi to Provincial Commissioner, Coast Province, 22 June 1984, KNA-Coast, CQ/20/55.
75. Priscilla Mwanake Murundi to Mombasa Municipal Council, 10 April 1985; Priscilla Mwanake Murundi to A. M. M. Nasser, Town Clerk, Mombasa, 14 May 1985; both in KNA-Coast, CQ/20/55.
76. A. M. M. Nasser, Town Clerk, Mombasa, to Priscilla Mwanake Murundi, 23 April 1985, KNA-Coast, CQ/20/55.
77. Murundi to Nasser, 14 May 1985.
78. James Kubai to Provincial Physical Planning Officer, Coast Province, 26 November 1984, KNA-Coast, CQ/20/55.
79. B. R. Maina, for Provincial Physical Planning Officer, Coast Province, to Commissioner of Lands, 14 May 1984; James Kubai to Provincial Physical Planning Officer, Coast Province, 26 November 1984; B. R. Maina, Provincial Physical Planning Officer, to Town Clerk, Mombasa, 27 November 1984; all in KNA-Coast, CQ/20/55.
80. D. T. A. Owino, District Land Officer, to J. K. Lulu, 3 December 1987, KNA-Coast, CQ/20/55.
81. B. W. Odour, Assistant Director of Fisheries, Mombasa, to Councilor Akoth Olang', Mombasa, 30 December 1988, KNA-Coast, CQ/20/55.
82. Councilor M. A. Olang' to B. W. Odour, Assistant Director of Fisheries, Mombasa, 16 June 1988; District Fisheries Officer, Mombasa, to District Commissioner, Mombasa, 18 October 1988, both in KNA-Coast, CQ/20/55.
83. Mwimbi Walikami, for the District Commissioner, Mombasa, to District Officer, Island, 25 January 1989, KNA-Coast, CQ/20/55.

Chapter epigraphs: David Makali, "Of Capital Gains and Hawker Losses," *Daily Nation,* 26 January 2002; K. K. Wales, "Election Link to Kiosk Destruction," *Daily Nation,* 29 January 2002; both accessed in Newspaper Collections, McMillan Memorial Library, Nairobi (hereafter MML).

1. Interview: Hadija Ali Gambare, 17 December 2014; "Tensions Rise over Demolitions," *Daily Nation,* 24 December 2001, MML. Kenneth Ombongi has noted that crews issued half-hour warnings to vendors, but my interviews indicate that this was not the case for everyone, and perhaps even most people. Kenneth Ombongi, "Radical Change in Mombasa," in *The Moi Succession: The 2002 Elections in Kenya,* ed. Hervé Maupeu, Musambayi Katamanga, and Winnie Mitullah (Nairobi: Transafrica Press, 2005), 318–19, 341n66.
2. Interview: Emma Mudanya, Mombasa, 16 December 2014.
3. Interview: Catherine Muthoni, Mombasa, 18 December 2014.
4. For Anjaria's critique, as well as historically rich ethnography of the politics of street food in Mumbai, see Jonathan Shapiro Anjaria, *The Slow Boil: Street Food, Rights, and Public Space in Mumbai* (Palo Alto, CA: Stanford University Press, 2016), 7, 39–63. The classic theory of neoliberal urbanism comes from David Harvey, focusing primarily on the West, though it is actually more historically informed than Anjaria's criticism of Harvey in particular allows. David Harvey, "The Right to the City," *New Left Review* 53 (2008): 23–40. For "World City" making as neoliberal urbanism, see David A. McDonald, *World City Syndrome: Neoliberalism and Inequality in Cape Town* (New York: Routledge, 2007). Examples of scholarship that situate the politics of vending in the recent past include Sandra C. Mediola García, *Street Democracy: Vendors, Violence, and Public Space in Late Twentieth-Century Mexico* (Lincoln: University of Nebraska Press, 2017); Graeme Young, "From Protection to Repression: The Politics of Street Vending in Kampala," *Journal of Eastern African Studies* 11, no. 4 (2017): 714–33; and Danielle Resnick, "The Politics of Crackdowns on Africa's Informal Vendors," *Comparative Politics* 52, no. 1 (2019): 21–41. For a deeper historical approach in East Africa, see Claire Robertson, *Trouble Showed the Way: Women, Men, and Trade in the Nairobi Area, 1890–1990* (Bloomington: Indiana University Press, 1997); and Andrew Burton, *African Underclass: Urbanisation, Crime and Colonial Order in Dar es Salaam, 1919–1961* (Athens: Ohio University Press, 2005).
5. Drawn from Devin Smart, "'Safariland': Tourism, Development and the Marketing of Kenya in the Post-colonial World," *African Studies Review* 61, no. 2 (2018): 134–57. For the experiences of street traders in such a context in postcolonial Nairobi, see Robertson, *Trouble Showed the Way,* 258–74.
6. Robertson, *Trouble Showed the Way,* 273.
7. Daniel Branch, *Kenya: Between Hope and Despair, 1963–2011* (New Haven, CT: Yale University Press, 2011), 195–215, 222–44; Jacqueline M. Klopp, "Remembering the Destruction of Muoroto: Slum Demolitions, Land and Democratisation in Kenya," *African Studies* 67, no. 3 (2008): 295–314.

8. Klopp, "Remembering the Destruction." See also Robertson, *Trouble Showed the Way,* 267–68.
9. Deborah Potts, "'Restoring Order'? Operation Murambatsvina and the Urban Crisis in Zimbabwe," *Journal of Southern African Studies* 32, no. 2 (2006): 276, 291.
10. For Nassir's biography and place in coastal and national politics in the later twentieth century, see Ombongi, "Radical Change in Mombasa," 300–306; and Mohamed Bakari, "A Place at the Table: The Political Integration of Muslims in Kenya, 1963–2007," *Islamic Africa* 4, no. 1 (2013): 18–19.
11. "Nassir Warns Hawkers," *Daily Nation,* 12 August 1991. Information about the life of Kennedy Kiliku is difficult to find in the scholarly literature, but short biographies of him were provided in the obituaries published after his 2010 death, the most comprehensive in "Kiliku: Life and Times of a Brave Politician," *Daily Nation,* 27 May 2010.
12. Bakari suggests that the spectacle of Nassir's constituents coming to his office to request (especially financial) support was key to how he projected his power and authority over the decades. Bakari, "Place at the Table," 21 and n. 10.
13. Patrick Mayoyo, "Traders Demonstrate," *Daily Nation,* 27 June 1996, Media Library, *Daily Nation* newspaper, Nairobi (hereafter DNML). For Nassir's power over various organs of government in Mombasa, see Ombongi, "Radical Change in Mombasa," 302.
14. Ombongi, "Radical Change in Mombasa," 305–22.
15. For the observation in a post-2002 election analysis that Mombasa's upcountry communities were "specifically known to be anti-KANU," see Mbaruku Vyakweli, "Civic Elections at the Coast," in Maupeu et al., *The Moi Succession,* 364.
16. Daniel Nyassy, "Kiosks: Nassir Backs Force," *East African Standard,* 24 December 2001.
17. "Kiosks: Nassir Sued," *Daily Nation,* 28 December 2001, MML.
18. Robert Odual, "Nassir's Role Queried," *Daily Nation,* 31 December 2001, MML.
19. Bensen Abele, "Minister's Men Demolish More Kiosks in City," *Daily Nation,* 14 January 2002, MML.
20. Conflicts over identity and space in coastal East Africa date to the history of slavery and other ideas of territory and belonging that in turn shaped how twentieth-century communities in the region interpreted the transformative processes of urbanization and migration during colonialism and decolonization, in ways that still affect politics today. For this process in Kenya, see James R. Brennan, "Lowering the Sultan's Flag: Sovereignty and Decolonization in Coastal Kenya," *Comparative Studies in Society and History* 50, no. 4 (2008): 831–61; Jeremy Prestholdt, "Politics of the Soil: Separatism, Autochthony, and Decolonization at the Kenyan Coast," *Journal of African History* 55, no. 2 (2014): 249–70; Devin Smart,

"Developing the Racial City: Conflict, Solidarity, and Urban Traders in Late-Colonial Mombasa," *Journal of Eastern African Studies* 11, no. 3 (2017): 425–41; and Ngala Chome, "Uses of Race: Moral Debate and Political Action in Mombasa" (PhD diss., Durham University, 2021). The topic has also been studied closely in Zanzibar and coastal Tanzania in, respectively, Jonathan Glassman, *War of Words, War of Stones: Racial Thought and Violence in Colonial Zanzibar* (Bloomington: Indiana University Press, 2011); and James R. Brennan, *Taifa: Making Nation and Race in Urban Tanzania* (Athens: Ohio University Press, 2012).

21. John Mbaria, "Why Kiosks Had to Go," *Daily Nation,* 27 December 2001, MML.
22. Interview: Mudanya.
23. "Nassir Starts Campaign to Flatten Slums in Mombasa," *Daily Nation,* 25 February 2002, MML.
24. "Tensions Rise over Demolitions," *Daily Nation,* 24 December 2001, MML; Odual, "Nassir's Role Queried"; "Nassir Backed by MPs," *East African Standard,* 31 December 2001.
25. "Kiosk Demolition Reflects Badly on Coast as Tourist Destination," *East African Standard,* 31 December 2001. Such representations of "instability" and violence can cause serious economic effects on the tourism industry. See Smart, "Safariland," 149–52.
26. Jaindi Kisero, "Election Goons Not the Answer," *Daily Nation,* 13 February 2002, MML.
27. Evelyn Kwamboka, "Kiosks: Church Pleads," *East African Standard,* 31 December 2001.
28. "So, What Is This City Mania All About?," *East African Standard,* 6 January 2002. See similar concerns in "Kiosk Demolition Reflects Badly"; and Haron Nyagah Amos, "Mombasa: Here's How to Make the New City Reflect Its Status," *East African Standard,* 4 January 2002.
29. "Nassir Goons Wreak Havoc," *East African Standard,* 25 December 2001; Mwahera Mwajefa, "Youths Beat Kiosk Owners in Scuffle at Town Hall," *Daily Nation,* 25 December 2001, MML.
30. "Protests as Kiosk Clear-Out Continues," *Daily Nation,* 26 December 2001, MML; "Chaos as Mombasa's Kiosk Riots Turn Tragic," *Daily Nation,* 27 December 2001, MML.
31. "Chaos as Mombasa's Kiosk Riots Turn Tragic." The tactic of using Mombasa's role as a key choke point in the regional economy resembles the workers' movements in the late-colonial era that made use of the city's strategic position in imperial trade networks to pressure employers and the state. See Frederick Cooper, *On the African Waterfront: Urban Disorder and the Transformation of Work in Colonial Mombasa* (New Haven, CT: Yale University Press, 1987). The spectacle of Nassir following demolition crews in a limousine was reported in "Tensions Rise over Demolitions."
32. Ombongi, "Radical Change in Mvita," 318–19.

33. Musikari Kombo, Letter to the Editor, "Violence against Hawkers Worrying," *Daily Nation,* 1 January 2002, MML.
34. "Outrage over Kiosk Demolitions," *East African Standard,* 26 December 2001.
35. Ombangi, "Radical Change in Mvita," 323–25; and Vyakweli, "Civic Elections."
36. "Council 'to Blame for Mushrooming Structures,'" *East African Standard,* 26 December 2001.
37. Photograph accompanying the article "After the Fanfair, It's Time to Act," *Daily Nation,* 10 January 2002, MML. The vast scale of informal structures in late-twentieth century Mombasa was also described in numerous interviews, including those with Josephe, Mombasa, 24 November 2014; Appollo Nyinge Kithakwa, Mombasa, 3 December 2014; Sampson Kereu, Mombasa, 11 December 2014; and David Muywambu Kivindto, Mombasa, 16 January 2015.
38. "Council 'to Blame for Mushrooming Structures.'"
39. Interviews: Mary Nambui Chege, Mombasa, 12 December 2014; Mohamed Amir Temu, Mombasa, 5 December 2014; Kereu.
40. Interview: Agnes Maweu, Mombasa, 3 December 2014.
41. Interview: Patrick N. Kasau, Mombasa, 12 December 2014.
42. Photograph accompanying the article "City Elevation Clamour Grips 2 Rift Towns: Clean Up Continues in Mombasa," *Daily Nation,* 17 January 2002, MML.
43. Interview: Temu.
44. Interview: Kasau.
45. Interview: Mueni Sammy, Mombasa, 11 December 2014.
46. Interview: Muthoni.
47. Interview: Mudanya.
48. For leisure and urban space in twentieth-century Kenya, see Caleb Edwin Owen, "Lands of Leisure: Recreation, Space, and the Struggle for Urban Kenya" (PhD diss., Michigan State University, 2016).
49. The "supermarket revolution" is a common conceptual term from the scholarship on supermarkets in Africa and the wider Global South; similar processes of corporatization have also been under way with fast food. For supermarkets, see Rosina Wanyama et al., "How Important Are Supermarkets for the Diets of the Poor in Africa?," *Food Security* (2019): 2. The recent establishment of individual American fast-food restaurants has been widely covered in the media; Kabugi Mbae provides a broad overview of this process in "When KFC Came to Kenya," *New Internationalist* (May–June 2021): 65–71.
50. "Supermarkets Opened 19 New Stores in 2021," *Business Daily,* 26 April 2022; "Naivas to Open New Store in Naivasha," *Business Daily,* 6 May 2022; "Carrefour Kenya Hires New Country Manager," *Business Daily,* 6 March 2023; Japhet Ruto, "List of Popular Supermarkets in Kenya, Their Owners and Branches," *Tuko,* 29 September 2023; Morris Kiruga, "Kenya's New Retail Giant Grows, but Risks Persist," *Kenyan Wall Street,* 15 December 2023.

51. Mbae, "When KFC Came to Kenya."
52. Jane Battersby and Vanessa Watson, eds., *Urban Food Systems Governance and Poverty in African Cities* (London: Routledge, 2018); Wanyama et al., "How Important Are Supermarkets?," 14–16.
53. Paul Otieno Opiyo and Harun Okello Ogindo, "The Characteristics and the Urban Food System in Kisumu, Kenya," in Battersby and Watson, *Urban Food Systems Governance,* 188–89; Wanyama et al., "How Important Are Supermarkets?," 14–16.
54. Wanyama et al., "How Important Are Supermarkets?," 14–16.
55. *Economic Survey, 2021* (Nairobi: Kenya National Bureau of Statistics, 2021), 51.

Bibliography

ARCHIVAL SOURCES

British Library (BL)
Commonwealth and African Collections, Bodleian Library, University of Oxford (CAC)
Kenya National Archives, Nairobi (KNA-Nairobi)
Kenya National Archives, Coast Province, Mombasa Records Centre (KNA-Coast)
McMillan Memorial Library, Nairobi (MML)
Media Library, *Daily Nation* newspaper, Nairobi (DNML)
National Archives (United Kingdom) (NA)

ORAL INTERVIEWS
LISTED CHRONOLOGICALLY

Rupen Dullabh Chauhan, Mombasa, 6 November 2014
Darshan Singh Wilkhu, Mombasa, 7 November 2014
Owner, Splendid View Café, Mombasa, 12 November 2014
Monica Mwende Njenga, Mombasa, 21 November 2014
Josephe (no last name given), Mombasa, Mombasa, 24 November 2014
Musa Okinda, Mombasa, 25 November 2014
Evans Nduati Gitonga, Mombasa, 28 November 2014
Julius Mambo, Mombasa, 29 November 2014
Maina Nduati, Mombasa, 29 November 2014
Julius Nzioka Nzonga, Mombasa, November 2014
Ken H. K. Sam, Mombasa, November 2014
Gurbachan Singh, Mombasa, November 2014
Peter Ninguna, Mombasa, 1 December 2014
Appollo Nyinge Kithakwa, Mombasa, 3 December 2014
Muema Maluki, Mombasa, 3 December 2014
Agnes Maweu, Mombasa, 3 December 2014
Jones Kingoo, Mombasa, 4 December 2014
Mohamed Amir Temu, Mombasa, 5 December 2014

Hezron Mupaghasa, Mombasa, 5 December 2014
Joseph Mwangi, Mombasa, 6 December 2014
Sammy Syengo, Mombasa, 8 December 2014
Joshua Kalii, Mombasa, 8 December 2014
Sampson Kereu, Mombasa, 11 December 2014
Mueni Sammy, Mombasa, 11 December 2014
Mary Nambui Chege, Mombasa, 12 December 2014
Patrick N. Kasau, Mombasa, 12 December 2014
Jacob M. Muli, Mombasa, 12 December 2014
Kilungua Kingangi Nzou, Mombasa, 13 December 2014
Joseph Kilaka Ndeti, Mombasa, 14 December 2014
Hassan Nyae, Mombasa, 14 December 2014
Emma Mudanya, Mombasa, 16 December 2014
Emily Mueni, Mombasa, 16 December 2014
Hadija Ali Gambere, Mombasa, 17 December 2014
Monica Mutiso, Mombasa, 17 December 2014
Agnes Gome, Mombasa, 18 December 2014
Catherine Muthoni, Mombasa, 18 December 2014
Damiras Nzalini, Mombasa, 19 December 2014
Fatuma Ali Enzi, Mombasa, 20 December 2014
Nuru Ibrahim Hajj, Mombasa, 20 December 2014
Elizabeth Malleo, Mombasa, 22 December 2014
Rose Omwanda, Mombasa, 2014
Kalutu Mutinda, Mombasa, 12 January 2015
Jackson Nthuli, Mombasa, 12 January 2015
Joyce Kiema, Mombasa, 13 January 2015
Paul Musili, Mombasa, 13 January 2015
David Muywambu Kivindto, Mombasa, 16 January 2015
Alice Mutave, Mombasa, 16 January 2015
Umi Mwandale, Mombasa, 24 January 2015
Alim Salim, Mombasa, 24 January 2015
John Omondi Onyango, Mombasa, 25 January 2015
Francisca Gakii, Mombasa, 28 January 2015
Jeremiah Mbunu, Mombasa, January 2015
Nzala Ngotho, Mombasa, January 2015
Asia Ahmed Omar, Nyanza Province, 4 February 2015
Ahmed Suelemann, Nyanza Province, 4 February 2015
James Okoth Mbayi, Nyanza Province, 5 February 2015
Michael Obat, Nyanza Province, 5 February 2015
Margaret Auma Ndolo, Nyanza Province, 6 February 2015
Benike A. Owuir, Nyanza Province, 6 February 2015
Thomas Mbeda Jura, Nyanza Province, 9 February 2015
Barak Olela Abwao, Nyanza Province, 10 February 2015
Peter Onyango Achienge, Nyanza Province, 11 February 2015

Joseph Mariko Agwari, Nyanza Province, 11 February 2015
Florence Ong'ong'a, Nyanza Province, 12 February 2015
Thomas Mbaja Minara, Nyanza Province, 13 February 2015
Gregory Osollo Omondi, Nyanza Province, 13 February 2015
Alice Ogola, Nyanza Province, 16 February 2015
James Hunnington Ogola, Nyanza Province, 16 February 2015
Patrice Omollo Sweta, Nyanza Province, 17 February 2015
James Miruka, Nyanza Province, 18 February 2015
Vitalis Owiti, Nyanza Province, 19 February 2015
Martina Jera, Nyanza Province, 20 February 2015

NEWSPAPERS AND ONLINE MEDIA

Boston Globe
Business Daily
Daily Nation
East African Standard
Kenyan Wall Street
New Internationalist
Tuko

BOOKS, ARTICLES, REPORTS, AND THESES

Adrià, Ferran. *The Family Meal: Home Cooking with Ferran Adrià.* New York: Phaidon, 2011.

Akama, John S. "The Role of Government in the Development of Tourism in Kenya." *International Journal of Tourism Research* 4, no. 1 (2002): 1–14.

Alozie, Bright. "'Sir, We Have the Honour Most Respectfully to Submit Our Humble Petition': Voices in Ink and the Politics of Petitions in Colonial Igboland." PhD diss., West Virginia University, 2021.

Ambler, Charles H. *Kenyan Communities in the Age of Imperialism: The Central Region in the Late Nineteenth Century.* New Haven, CT: Yale University Press, 1988.

Anjaria, Jonathan Shapiro. *The Slow Boil: Street Food, Rights, and Public Space in Mumbai.* Palo Alto, CA: Stanford University Press, 2016.

Atkins, Keletso. *The Moon Is Dead! Give Us Our Money! The Cultural Origins of an African Work Ethic, Natal, South Africa, 1843–1900.* Portsmouth, NH: Heinemann, 1993.

Babb, Florence E. *Between Field and Cooking Pot: The Political Economy of Marketwomen in Peru.* Austin: University of Texas Press, 1998.

Bakari, Mohamed. "A Place at the Table: The Political Integration of Muslims in Kenya, 1963–2007." *Islamic Africa* 4, no. 1 (2013): 15–48.

Barnes, Teresa. *"We Women Worked So Hard": Gender, Urbanization, and Social Reproduction in Colonial Harare, Zimbabwe, 1930–1956.* Portsmouth, NH: Heinemann, 1999.

Barua, Dhiman. "History of Cholera." In *Cholera,* edited by Dhiman Barua and William B. Greenough III, 1–36. New York: Plenum Medical Book Company, 1992.

Battersby, Jane. "Hungry Cities: A Critical Review of Urban Food Security Research in Sub-Saharan African Cities." *Geography Compass* 7, no. 7 (2013): 452–63.
Battersby, Jane, and Jonathan Crush. "Africa's Urban Food Deserts." *Urban Forum* 25, no. 1 (2014): 143–53.
———, eds. *Rapid Urbanisation, Urban Food Deserts and Food Security in Africa.* Basel, Switzerland: Springer, 2016.
Battersby, Jane, and Vanessa Watson, eds. *Urban Food Systems Governance and Poverty in African Cities.* London: Routledge, 2018.
Baur, P. T., and B. S. Yamey. "Economic Progress and Occupational Distribution." *Economic Journal* 61, no. 244 (1951): 741–55.
Bentley, Amy, ed. *A Cultural History of Food in the Modern Age.* New York: Bloomsbury, 2016.
Berman, Bruce, and John Lonsdale. *Unhappy Valley: Conflict in Kenya and Africa.* 2 vols. Athens: Ohio University Press, 1992.
Bhattacharya, Tithi, ed. *Social Reproduction Theory: Remapping Class, Recentering Oppression.* London: Pluto Press, 2017.
Bloom, Peter J., Stephen F. Miescher, and Takyikaa Manuh, eds. *Modernization as Spectacle in Africa.* Bloomington: Indiana University Press, 2014.
Bluestone, Daniel M. "'The Pushcart Evil': Peddlers, Merchants and New York City Streets, 1890–1940." *Journal of Urban History* 18, no. 1 (1991): 68–92.
Boyd, Robert. "Urbanization, Disadvantage and Petty Entrepreneurship: Street Peddling among African American Men in Southern and Northern Cities during the Early Twentieth Century." *Sociological Inquiry* 69, no. 2 (1999): 216–35.
Branch, Daniel. *Kenya: Between Hope and Despair, 1963–2011.* New Haven, CT: Yale University Press, 2011.
Brantley, Cynthia. "Kikuyu-Maasai Nutrition and Colonial Science: The Orr and Gilks Study in the Late 1920s." *International Journal of African Historical Studies* 30, no. 1 (1997): 49–86.
Brennan, James R. "A History of Sauti ya Mvita (Voice of Mombasa): Radio, Public Culture, and Islam in Coastal Kenya, 1947–1966." In *New Media and Religious Transformations in Africa,* edited by Rosalind I. J. Hackett and Benjamin F. Soare, 19–38. Bloomington: Indiana University Press, 2015.
———. "Lowering the Sultan's Flag: Sovereignty and Decolonization in Coastal Kenya." *Comparative Studies in Society and History* 50, no. 4 (2008): 831–61.
———. *Taifa: Making Nation and Race in Urban Tanzania.* Athens: Ohio University Press, 2012.
Brownell, Emily. *Gone to Ground: A History of Environment and Infrastructure in Dar es Salaam.* Pittsburgh: University of Pittsburgh Press, 2020.
Bruegel, Martin. *A Cultural History of Food in the Age of Empire.* New York: Bloomsbury, 2016.
Burke, Padraic. "Rolling Carts and Songs a Plenty: The Urban Food Vendor." *Journal of American Culture* 2, no. 3 (1979): 480–87.
Burke, Timothy. *Lifebuoy Men, Lux Women: Commodification, Consumption, and Cleanliness in Modern Zimbabwe.* Durham, NC: Duke University Press, 1996.

Burnett, John. *England Eats Out: A Social History of Eating Out in England from 1830 to the Present.* London: Routledge, 2004.

———. *Plenty and Want: A Social History of Diet in England from 1815 to the Present Day.* London: Thomas Nelson, 1989.

Burton, Andrew. *African Underclass: Urbanisation, Crime and Colonial Order in Dar es Salaam, 1919–1961.* Athens: Ohio University Press, 2005.

Calaresu, Melissa, and Danielle van den Heuvel, eds. *Food Hawkers: Selling in the Streets from Antiquity to the Present.* London: Routledge, 2016.

Callanan, J. C. J. "Notes on the Foodstuffs of the Luo Tribes." *Kenyan Medical Journal* 3 (1926): 58–60.

Carlson, Linda. *Company Towns of the Pacific Northwest.* Seattle: University of Washington Press, 2017.

Carman, John A., and M. A. W. Roberts. "Social and Health Conditions among the Jaluo, with Special Reference to Maternal and Infant Welfare." *East Africa Medical Journal* 11 (1934): 107–24.

Carroll, Abigail. *Three Squares: The Invention of the American Meal.* New York: Basic Books, 2013.

Chauncy, George, Jr. "The Locus of Reproduction: Women's Labour in the Zambian the Copperbelt, 1927–1953." *Journal of Southern African Studies* 7, no. 2 (1981): 135–64.

Chigudu, Simukai. *The Political Life of an Epidemic: Cholera, Crisis and Citizenship in Zimbabwe.* New York: Cambridge University Press, 2020.

Choi, Susanne Y. P., and Yinni Peng. *Masculine Compromise: Migration, Family, and Gender in China.* Berkeley: University of California Press, 2016.

Chome, Ngala. "Uses of Race: Moral Debate and Political Action in Mombasa." PhD diss., Durham University, 2021.

Clark, Carolyn M. "Land and Food, Women and Power, in Nineteenth-Century Kikuyu." *Africa: Journal of the International Africa Institute* 50, no. 4 (1980): 357–70.

Clark, Gracia. *Onions Are My Husband: Survival and Accumulation by West African Market Women.* Chicago: University of Chicago Press, 1994.

Clayton, Anthony, and Donald Savage. *Government and Labour in Kenya, 1895–1963.* London: Cass, 1974.

Cleveland, Todd. *Diamonds in the Rough: Corporate Paternalism and African Professionalism on the Mines of Colonial Angola, 1917–1975.* Athens: Ohio University Press, 2015.

Cohen, David William. "Food Production and Food Exchange in the Precolonial Lakes Plateau Region." In *Imperialism, Colonialism and Hunger: East and Central Africa,* edited by Robert I. Rotberg, 1–18. Lexington, MA: Lexington Books, 1983.

Cohen, Deborah. "From Peasant to Worker: Migration, Masculinity, and the Making of Mexican Workers in the US." *International Labor and Working-Class History* 69 (2006): 81–103.

Colony and Protectorate of Kenya. *Atlas of Kenya.* Nairobi: Survey of Kenya, 1962.

———. Labour Department Annual Reports.

———. Native Affairs Department Annual Reports.
Cooper, Frederick. *Colonialism in Question: Theory, Knowledge and History.* Berkeley: University of California Press, 2005.
———. "Colonizing Time: Work Rhythms and Labor Conflict in Colonial Mombasa." In *Colonialism and Culture,* edited by Nicholas Dirks, 209–45. Ann Arbor: University of Michigan Press, 1992.
———. *Decolonization and African Society: The Labor Question in French and British Africa.* New York: Cambridge University Press, 1996.
———. *From Slaves to Squatters: Plantation Labor and Agriculture in Zanzibar and Coastal Kenya, 1890–1925.* New Haven, CT: Yale University Press, 1980.
———. *On the African Waterfront: Urban Disorder and the Transformation of Work in Colonial Mombasa.* New Haven, CT: Yale University Press, 1987.
———. *Plantation Slavery on the East Coast of Africa.* Portsmouth, NH: Heinemann, 1977.
———. "Work, Class, and Empire: An African Historian's Retrospective on E. P. Thompson." *Social History* 20, no. 2 (1995): 235–41.
Counihan, Carole. "Gendering Food." In Pilcher, *Oxford Handbook of Food History,* 99–116.
Crawshay, Richard. "Kikuyu: Notes on the Country, People, Fauna and Flora." *Geography Journal* 20, no. 1 (1902): 24–49.
Crehan, Kate. *Gramsci's Common Sense: Inequality and Its Narratives.* Durham, NC: Duke University Press, 2016.
Cronon, William. *Nature's Metropolis: Chicago and the Great West.* New York: Norton, 1991.
Crosby, Alfred. *Columbian Exchange: The Biological and Cultural Consequences of 1492.* Westport, CT: Praeger, 2003.
Dalgleish, A. G. *Survey of Unemployment.* Colony and Protectorate of Kenya, 1960.
Davies, Julia, Corrie Hannah, Zack Guido, Andrew Zimmer, Laura McCann, Jane Battersby, and Tom Evans. "Barriers to Urban Agriculture in Sub-Saharan Africa." *Food Policy* 103 (2021): 1–14.
Denning, Michael. "Wageless Life." *New Left Review* 66 (2010): 79–97.
Deutsch, Tracey. "Labor Histories of Food." In Pilcher, *Oxford Handbook of Food History,* 61–80.
Dickson, B. "The Eastern Borderlands of Kikuyu." *Geographical Journal* 21, no. 1 (1903): 36–39.
Drouard, Alan. "'*Escoffier, Bocuse et (surtout) les autres . . .*': Towards a History of Cooks in France in the Nineteenth and Twentieth Centuries." In Jacobs and Scholliers, *Eating Out in Europe,* 215–28.
Duis, Perry R. *Challenging Chicago: Coping with Everyday Life, 1837–1920.* Urbana: University of Illinois Press, 1998.
Duminy, James. "Historical Urban Food Governance in Africa: The Case of Kenya, c. 1900–1950." In Battersby and Watson, *Urban Food Systems Governance,* 86–88.
———. "Urban Change and the Multi-Scalar Politics of Food Systems in Colonial Africa." In *Routledge Handbook of Urban Food Governance,* edited by Ana

Moragues-Faus, Jill K. Clark, Jane Battersby, and Anna Davies, 35–47. New York: Routledge, 2022.

East Africa Protectorate. *Native Labour Commission: Evidence and Report, 1912–1913.* Nairobi: Government Printer, ca. 1913.

Echenberg, Myron. *Africa in the Time of Cholera: A History of Pandemics from 1817 to the Present.* New York: Cambridge University Press, 2011.

Eldon, Kathy. *Guide to Eating Out in Kenya.* Nairobi: Kenway Publications, 1987.

Fair, Laura. *Pastimes and Politics: Culture, Community, and Identity in Post-Abolition Urban Zanzibar, 1890–1945.* Athens: Ohio University Press, 2001.

Ferguson, James. *Expectations of Modernity: Myths of Meanings of Urban Life on the Zambian Copperbelt.* Berkeley: University of California Press, 1999.

Flynn, Karen Coen. *Food, Culture, and Survival in an African City.* New York: Palgrave Macillan, 2005.

Frayne, Bruce, Cameron McCordie, and Helena Shilomboleni. "The Myth of Urban Agriculture." In Crush and Battersby, *Rapid Urbanisation,* 19–31.

Freund, Bill. *The African Worker.* New York: Cambridge University Press, 1988.

Gabaccia, Donna R., and Jeffrey Pilcher. "'Chile Queens' and Checkered Tablecloths: Public Dining Cultures of Italians in New York City and Mexicans in San Antonio, Texas, 1870s–1940s." *Radical History Review* 110 (2011): 109–26.

García, Sandra C. Mediola. *Street Democracy: Vendors, Violence, and Public Space in Late Twentieth-Century Mexico.* Lincoln: University of Nebraska Press, 2017.

George, Abosede A. *Making Modern Girls: A History of Girlhood, Labor and Social Change in Colonial Lagos.* Athens: Ohio University Press, 2014.

Glassman, Jonathon. *War of Words, War of Stones: Racial Thought and Violence in Colonial Zanzibar.* Bloomington: Indiana University Press, 2011.

Glenn, Evelyn Nakono. "From Servitude to Service Work: Historical Continuities in the Racial Division of Paid Reproductive Labor." *Signs* 18, no. 1 (1992): 1–43.

Goody, Jack. *Cooking, Cuisine, and Class: A Study in Comparative Sociology.* New York: Cambridge University Press, 1982.

Gorleku, Eugene Tetteh. "The Quality of Hotel Employee Meals, and Employees' Perception of the Quality." MS thesis, Louisiana State University, 2002.

Gottlieb, Robert, and Anupama Joshi. *Food Justice.* Cambridge, MA: MIT Press, 2010.

Grandesso, F., M. Allan, P. S. J. Jean-Simon, J. Boncy, A. Blake, R. Pierre, K. P. Alberti et al. "Risk Factors for Cholera Transmission in Haiti during Inter-peak Periods: Insights to Improve Current Control Strategies from Two Case-Control Studies." *Epidemiology and Infection* 142, no. 8 (2014): 1625–35.

Griffith, David, Louise A. Kelley-Hope, and Mark A. Miller. "Review of Reported Cholera Outbreaks Worldwide, 1995–2005." *American Journal of Tropical Medicine and Hygiene* 75, no. 5 (2006): 973–77.

Guyer, Jane, ed. *Feeding African Cities: Studies in Regional Social History.* Bloomington: Indiana University Press, 1987.

Hall, Stuart. "Gramsci's Relevance for the Study of Race and Ethnicity." *Communication Inquiry* 10, no. 2 (1986): 5–27.

Hamilton, Shane. *Supermarket USA: Food and Power in The Cold War Farms Race.* New Haven, CT: Yale University Press, 2018.
Harries, Patrick. *Work, Culture and Identity: Migrant Laborers in Mozambique and South Africa, c. 1860–1910.* Portsmouth, NH: Heinemann, 1994.
Harrison, Graham. *Neoliberal Africa: The Impact of Global Social Engineering.* London: Zed Books, 2010.
Hart, Keith. "Informal Income Opportunities and Urban Employment in Ghana." *Journal of Modern African Studies* 11, no. 1 (1973): 61–89.
Harvey, David. *A Brief History of Neoliberalism.* New York: Oxford University Press, 2005.
———. *Paris: Capital of Modernity.* New York: Routledge, 2006.
———. "The Right to the City." *New Left Review* 53 (2008): 23–40.
Hay, Douglas, and Paul Craven, eds. *Masters, Servants, and Magistrates in Britain and the Empire, 1562–1955.* Chapel Hill: University of North Carolina Press, 2014.
Hay, Margaret J. "Economic Change in Luoland: Kowe, 1890–1945." PhD diss., University of Wisconsin, Madison, 1972.
Hayer, Judith. "Some Problems in the Valuation of Subsistence Output." Center for Economic Research: Discussion Paper no. 14. University College, Nairobi, 1965.
Hoare, Quintin, and Geoffrey Nowell Smith, eds. *Selections from the Prison Notebooks of Antonio Gramsci.* New York: International Publishers, 1973.
Hobley, C. W. *Eastern Uganda: An Ethnological Survey.* London: Anthropological Institute of Great Britain and Ireland, 1902.
———. "People, Places and Prospects in British East Africa." *Geographical Journal* 4, no. 2 (1894): 97–123.
Holtzman, Jon. "In a Cup of Tea: Commodities and History among Samburu Pastoralists in Northern Kenya." *American Ethnologist* 30, no. 1 (2003): 136–55.
———. *Uncertain Tastes: Memory, Ambivalence, and the Politics of Eating in Samburu, Northern Kenya.* Berkeley: University of California Press, 2009.
Hornsby, Charles. *Kenya: A History since Independence.* London: I. B. Taurus, 2012.
Humphrey, N. *The Kikuyu Lands: The Relationship of Population to the Land in South Nyeri.* Nairobi: Government Printer, 1945.
International Labour Office. *Employment, Incomes and Equality: A Strategy for Increasing Productive Employment in Kenya.* Geneva, Switzerland, 1972.
Ivaska, Andrew. *Cultured States: Youth, Gender, and Modern Style in 1960s Dar es Salaam.* Durham, NC: Duke University Press, 2011.
Jacobs, Marc, and Peter Scholliers, eds. *Eating Out in Europe: Picnics, Gourmet Dining and Snacks since the Late Eighteenth Century.* New York: Bloomsbury, 2003.
Janmohamed, Karim. "A History of Mombasa, c. 1895–1939: Some Aspects of Economic and Social Life in an East African Port Town during Colonial Rule." PhD diss., Northwestern University, 1978.
Jarvis, Katie. *Politics in the Marketplace: Work, Gender and Citizenship in Revolutionary France.* New York: Oxford University Press, 2019.

Judt, Tony. *Postwar: A History of Europe since 1945.* New York: Penguin, 2005.

Kanogo, Tabatha. *Squatters and the Roots of Mau Mau, 1905–1963.* Athens: Ohio University Press, 1987.

Kelley, Victoria. *Cheap Street: London's Street Markets and the Cultures of Informality, c. 1850–1939.* Manchester: Manchester University Press, 2019.

Kenyatta, Jomo. *Facing Mount Kenya.* New York: Vintage, 1965.

Killingray, David, and Richard Rathbone, eds. *Africa and the Second World War.* New York: St. Martin's Press, 1986.

King, Kenneth. *Jua Kali Kenya: Change and Development in an Informal Economy, 1970–1995.* Athens: Ohio University Press, 1996.

Kinyanjui, Mary Mjeri. *Women and the Informal Economy in Urban Africa: From the Margins to the Centre.* London: Zed Books, 2014.

Kitching, Gavin. *Class and Economic Change in Kenya: The Making of an African Petite-Bourgeoisie, 1905–1970.* New Haven, CT: Yale University Press, 1980.

Kithiia, Justus, and Gamoyo Majambo. "Motion but No Speed: Colonial to Post-colonial Status of Water and Sanitation Service Provision in Mombasa City." *Cities* 107 (2020): 2–12.

Klein, Naomi. *The Shock Doctrine: The Rise of Disaster Capitalism.* New York: Picador, 2008.

Klopp, Jacqueline M. "Pilfering the Public: The Problem of Land Grabbing in Contemporary Kenya." *Africa Today* 47, no. 1 (2000): 7–26.

———. "Remembering the Destruction of Muoroto: Slum Demolitions, Land and Democratisation in Kenya." *African Studies* 67, no. 3 (2008): 295–314.

Krapf, Ludwig. *A Dictionary of the Suahili Language.* London: Trübner, 1882.

Krapf, Ludwig, and J. Rebmann. *Nika-English Dictionary.* London: Society for Promoting Christian Knowledge, 1887.

Kümin, Beat. "Eating Out before the Restaurant: Dining Culture in Early-Modern Inns." In Jacobs and Scholliers, *Eating Out in Europe,* 71–87.

Laslett, Barbara, and Johanna Brenner. "Gender and Social Reproduction: Historical Perspectives." *Annual Review of Sociology* 15 (1989): 381–404.

Leys, Colin. *Underdevelopment in Kenya: The Political Economy of Neocolonialism, 1964–1971.* Berkeley: University of California Press, 1975.

Leys, Norman. *Kenya.* London: Hogarth Press, 1925.

Lim-Quizon, M. C., R. M. Benabaye, F. M. White, M. M. Dayrit, and M. E. White. "Cholera in Metropolitan Malina: Foodborne Transmission via Street Vendors." *Bulletin of the World Health Organization* 72, no. 5 (1994): 745–49.

Lindblom, Gerhard. *The Akamba in British East Africa: An Ethnological Monograph.* Uppsala, Sweden: Appelbergs, 1920.

Lindsay, Lisa A. *Working with Gender: Wage Labor and Social Change in Southwestern Nigeria.* Portsmouth, NH: Heinemann, 2003.

Lonsdale, John. "The Depression and the Second World War in the Transformation of Kenya." In *Africa and the Second World War,* edited by David Killingray and Richard Rathbone, 97–142. New York: St. Martin's Press, 1986.

———. "The Moral Economy of Mau Mau: Poverty, Wealth and Civic Virtue in Kikuyu Political Thought." In Berman and Lonsdale, *Unhappy Valley,* 2:315–504.

Lonsdale, John, and D. A. Low. "Towards the New Order." In *History of East Africa, Part III,* edited by John Lonsdale and D. A. Low, 1–64. Oxford: Clarendon Press, 1976.

Luissier, Anne. "Eating Out during the Workday: Consumption and Working Habits among Urban Laborers in France in the Second Half of the Nineteenth Century." In Jacobs and Scholliers, *Eating Out in Europe,* 337–50.

Madan, A. C. *Swahili-English Dictionary.* Oxford: Clarendon Press, 1903.

Mandala, Elias C. *The End of Chidyerano: A History of Food and Everyday Life in Malawi, 1860–2004.* Portsmouth, NH: Heinemann, 2004.

Martin, Phyllis. *Leisure and Society in Colonial Brazzaville.* New York: Cambridge University Press, 1996.

Maupeu, Hervé, Musambayi Katamanga, and Winnie Mitullah, eds. *The Moi Succession: The 2002 Elections in Kenya.* Nairobi: Transafrica Press, 2005.

Maxon, Robert, and Peter Ndege. "The Economics of Structural Adjustment." In *Decolonization and Independence in Kenya, 1940–1993,* edited by B. A. Ogot and W. R. Ochieng', 151–86. Athens: Ohio University Press, 1995.

McCann, James C. *Maize and Grace: Africa's Encounter with a New World Crop.* Cambridge, MA: Harvard University Press, 2007.

———. *Stirring the Pot: A History of African Cuisine.* Athens: Ohio University Press, 2009.

McDonald, David A. *World City Syndrome: Neoliberalism and Inequality in Cape Town.* New York: Routledge, 2007.

McDonald, David A., and John Pape, eds. *Cost Recovery and the Crisis of Service Delivery in South Africa.* London: Zed Books, 2002.

McMahon, Elisabeth. "Developing Workers: Coerced and 'Voluntary' Labor in Zanzibar." *International Labor and Working-Class History* 92 (2017): 114–33.

Meager, Kate. "Cannibalizing the Informal Economy: Frugal Innovation and Economic Inclusion in Africa." *European Journal of Development Research* 30 (2018): 17–33.

Mintz, Sidney. *Sweetness and Power: The Place of Sugar in Modern History.* New York: Penguin, 1986.

Mirza, Sarah, and Margaret Strobel, eds. *Three Swahili Women: Life Histories from Mombasa.* Bloomington: Indiana University Press, 1989.

Monsutti, Alessandro. "Migration as a Rite of Passage: Young Afghans Building Masculinity and Adulthood in Iran." *Iranian Studies* 40, no. 2 (2007): 167–85.

Moskowitz, Kara. *Seeing Like a Citizen: Decolonization, Development and the Making of Kenya, 1945–1980.* Athens: Ohio University Press, 2019.

Murillo, Bianca. *Market Encounters: Consumer Cultures in Twentieth-Century Ghana.* Athens: Ohio University Press, 2017.

Mutongi, Kenda. *Matatu: A History of Popular Transportation in Nairobi.* Chicago: University of Chicago Press, 2017.

Mwaguni, Saheed M. "Public Health Problems in Mombasa District: A Case Study on Sewage Management." MA thesis, University of Nairobi, 2002.

Mwangi, Meja. *Going Down River Road.* Nairobi: East African Educational Publishers, 1993.

Nanu, Luana, Cihan Cobanoglu, Ibrahim Hakan Yilmaz, and Timucin Dis. "Impact of Employee Meals on Employee Satisfaction and Hotel Financial Performance: An Experimental Study." *Journal of Hospitality Financial Management* 28, no. 2 (2020): 91–102.

Nilsson, David, and Ezekiel Nyangeri Nyanchaga. "Pipes and Politics: A Century of Change and Continuity in Kenyan Urban Water Supply." *Journal of Modern African Studies* 46, no. 1 (2008): 133–58.

Northcote, G. A. S. "The Nilotic Kavirondo." *Journal of the Royal Anthropological Institute of Great Britain and Ireland* 37 (1907): 58–66.

Ocobock, Paul. *An Uncertain Age: The Politics of Manhood in Kenya.* Athens: Ohio University Press, 2017.

Okia, Opolot. *Communal Labor in Kenya: The Legitimation of Coercion.* New York: Palgrave Macillan, 2012.

Ombongi, Kenneth. "Radical Change in Mombasa." In Maupeu et al., *The Moi Succession,* 300–325.

Opiyo, Paul Otieno, and Harun Okello Ogindo. "The Characteristics and the Urban Food System in Kisumu, Kenya." In Battersby and Watson, *Urban Food Systems Governance,* 182–194.

Organisation for Economic Co-operation and Development. *Africa's Urbanisation Dynamics, 2020: Afripolis, Mapping a New Urban Geography.* Paris: OECD Publishing, 2020.

Orr, J. B., and J. L. Gilks. *Studies of Nutrition: The Physique and Health of Two African Tribes.* London: His Majesty's Stationary Office, 1931.

Orwell, George. *Down and Out in Paris and London.* London: Harvest, 1963.

Osborn, Emily Lynn. "Casting Aluminium Cooking Pots: Labour, Migration and Artisan Production in West Africa's Informal Sector, 1945–2005." *African Identities* 7, no. 3 (2009): 373–86.

Osei-Opare, Nana. "'If You Trouble a Hungry Snake, You Will Force It to Bite You': Rethinking Postcolonial African Archival Pessimism, Worker Discontent, and Petition Writing in Ghana, 1957–1966." *Journal of African History* 62, no. 1 (2021): 59–78.

Oswald, Felix. *Alone in Sleeping Sickness Country.* London: Trübner, 1915.

Owen, Caleb Edwin. "Lands of Leisure: Recreation, Space, and the Struggle for Urban Kenya." PhD diss., Michigan State University, 2016.

Philip, C. R. "Nutrition in Kenya: Notes on the State of Nutrition of African Children." *East African Medical Journal* 20, no. 7 (1943): 227–34.

Pilcher, Jeffrey, ed. *The Oxford Handbook of Food History.* New York: Oxford University Press, 2012.

Pillsbury, Richard. *From Boarding House to Bistro: The American Restaurant Then and Now.* Boston: Unwin Hyman, 1990.

Potts, Deborah. "'Restoring Order'?: Operation Murambatsvina and the Urban Crisis in Zimbabwe." *Journal of Southern African Studies* 32, no. 2 (2006): 273–91.

Prestholdt, Jeremy. *Domesticating the World: African Consumerism and the Genealogies of Globalization.* Berkeley: University of California Press, 2008.

———. "Politics of the Soil: Separatism, Autochthony, and Decolonization at the Kenyan Coast." *Journal of African History* 55, no. 2 (2014): 249–70.

Procter, R. A. W. "The Kikuyu Market and Kikuyu Diet." *Kenya Medical Journal* 3, no. 1 (1926): 15–22.

Rawson, Katie, and Elliott Shore. *Dining Out: A Global History of Restaurants.* London: Reaktion Books, 2019.

Republic of Kenya. Economic Surveys.

———. *Kenya Population Census, 1962: Tables, Volume II,* vol. 2, *Populations of Locations and County Council Wards by Race, Tribe and Sex.* Nairobi: Government Printer, 1965.

———. *1999 Population and Housing Census: Counting Our People for Development.* Nairobi: Government Printer, 2001.

———. *Sessional Paper No. 1 of 1986 on Economic Management for Renewed Growth.* Nairobi: Government Printer, 1986.

Resnick, Danielle. "The Politics of Crackdowns on Africa's Informal Vendors." *Comparative Politics* 52, no. 1 (2019): 21–41.

Rich, Jeremy. *A Workman Is Worthy of His Meat: Food and Colonialism in the Gabon Estuary.* Lincoln: University of Nebraska Press, 2007.

Richards, Audrey. *Land, Labour and Diet in Northern Rhodesia.* London: Oxford University Press, 1939.

Richter, Reynolds. "Food Rationing, Labor and Citizenship in Kenya during World War II." MA thesis, Yale University, 2006.

Rijke-Epstein, Tasha. "The Politics of Filth: Sanitation, Work and Competing Moralities in Urban Madagascar, 1890s–1977." *Journal of African History* 60, no. 2 (2019): 229–56.

Robertson, Claire C. *Trouble Showed the Way: Women, Men, and Trade in the Nairobi Area, 1890–1990.* Bloomington: Indiana University Press, 1997.

Rockel, Stephen J. *Carriers of Culture: Labor on the Road in Nineteenth-Century East Africa.* Portsmouth, NH: Heinemann, 2006.

Rotberg, Robert I., ed. *Imperialism, Colonialism and Hunger: East and Central Africa.* Lexington, MA: Lexington Books, 1983.

Routledge, W. Scoresby, and Katherine Routledge. *With a Prehistoric People: The Akikuyu of British East Africa.* London: Frank Cass, 1968.

Sacleux, C. S. *Dictionnaire Swahili-Français.* Paris: Institut d'Ethnologie, 1939.

Savage, Anthony, and Donald C. Clayton. *Government and Labour in Kenya, 1895–1963.* London: Frank Cass, 1974.

Schoenbrun, David. "Conjuring the Modern in Africa: Durability and Rupture in Histories of Public Healing between the Great Lakes of East Africa." *American Historical Review* 111, no. 5 (2006): 1403–39.

Scholliers, Peter. "Eating Out." In Bruegel, *Cultural History of Food,* 107–22.

———. "Workers' Time for Cooking and Eating in Nineteenth- and Twentieth-Century Western Europe." *Food and Foodways: Explorations in the History and Culture of Human Nourishment* 6, no. 3–4 (1996): 243–60.

Shilaro, Priscilla M. *Failed Eldorado: Colonial Capitalism, Rural Industrialization, African Land Rights in Kenya, and the Kakamega Gold Rush, 1930–1952.* Lanham, MD: University Press of America, 2008.

Skinner, Caroline. "Contributing yet Excluded? Informal Food Retail in African Cities." In Battersby and Watson, *Urban Food Systems Governance,* 104–115.

Smart, Devin. "Developing the Racial City: Conflict, Solidarity, and Urban Traders in Late-Colonial Mombasa." *Journal of Eastern African Studies* 11, no. 3 (2017): 425–41.

———. "'Safariland': Tourism, Development and the Marketing of Kenya in the Post-colonial World." *African Studies Review* 61, no. 2 (2018): 134–57.

Spang, Rebecca. *The Invention of the Restaurant: Paris and Modern Gastronomic Culture.* Cambridge, MA: Harvard University Press, 2001.

Stichter, Sharon. *Migrant Labour in Kenya: Capitalism and African Responses, 1895–1975.* London: Longman, 1982.

Stock, Robert F. *Cholera in Africa: Diffusion of the Disease, 1970–1975, with Particular Emphasis on West Africa.* London: International Africa Institute, 1976.

Stoll, Steven. "The Captured Garden: The Political Ecology of Subsistence under Capitalism." *International Labor and Working-Class History* 85 (2014): 75–96.

Stren, Richard E. *Housing the Urban Poor in Africa: Policy, Politics and Bureaucracy in Mombasa.* Berkeley: University of California Press, 1978.

Strobel, Margaret. *Muslim Women in Mombasa, 1890–1975.* New Haven, CT: Yale University Press, 1979.

———. "Slavery and Reproductive Labor in Mombasa." In *Women and Slavery in Africa,* edited by Claire Robertson and Martin Klein, 111–29. Portsmouth, NH: Heinemann, 1997.

Styrbæk, Ole Mouritsen Klavs. *Mouthfeel: How Texture Makes Taste.* New York: Columbia University Press, 2017.

Sugrue, Thomas J. *The Origins of the Urban Crisis: Race and Inequality in Postwar Detroit.* Princeton: Princeton University Press, 2014.

Sunseri, Thaddeus. "Labour Migration in Colonial Tanzania and the Hegemony of South African Historiography." *African Affairs* 95, no. 381 (1996): 581–98.

———. *Vilimani: Labor Migration and Rural Change in Early Colonial Tanzania.* Portsmouth, NH: Heinemann, 2001.

———. *Wielding the Ax: State Forestry and Social Conflict in Tanzania, 1820–2000.* Athens: Ohio University Press, 2009.

Szabo, Michelle, and Shelly Koch, eds. *Food, Masculinities, and Home: Interdisciplinary Perspectives.* London: Bloomsbury, 2017.

Tate, H. R. "Further Notes on the Kikuyu Tribe of British East Africa." *Journal of the Royal Anthropological Institute* 34 (1904): 255–65.

———. "Notes on the Kikuyu and Kamba Tribes of British East Africa." *Journal of the Anthropological Institute of Great Britain and Ireland* 34 (January–June 1904): 130–48.

Taylor, D. R. F. "Changing Food Habits in Kikuyuland." *Canadian Journal of African Studies/Revue Canadienne des Études Africaines* 4, no. 3 (1970): 333–49.

———. "The Markets of Mombasa." *African Urban Notes* 5, no. 2 (1970): 175–84.
Taylor, W. E. *Giryama Vocabulary and Collections.* London: Society for Promoting Christian Knowledge, 1891.
Thompson, E. P. *Customs in Common: Studies in Traditional Popular Culture.* New York: New Press, 1993.
———. *The Making of the English Working Class.* New York: Vintage, 1966.
———. "Time, Work-Discipline, and Industrial Capitalism." *Past and Present* no. 38 (1967): 56–97.
Thoms, Ulrike. "Industrial Canteens in Germany, 1850–1950." In Jacobs and Scholliers, *Eating Out in Europe,* 351–72.
Tinker, Irene. *Street Foods: Urban Food and Employment in Developing Countries.* New York: Oxford University Press, 1997.
Trubeck, Amy B. "Kitchen Work, 1920–Present." In *A Cultural History of Food in the Modern Age,* edited by Amy Bentley, 127–44. New York: Bloomsbury, 2016.
Turner, Katherine Leonard. *How the Other Half Ate: A History of Working-Class Meals at the Turn of the Century.* Berkeley: University of California Press, 2014.
Twagira, Laura Ann. *Embodied Engineering: Gendered Labor, Food Security, and Taste in Twentieth-Century Mali.* Athens: Ohio University Press, 2021.
Vyakweli, Mbaruku. "Civic Elections at the Coast." In Maupeu et al., *The Moi Succession,* 349–73.
Wanga-Odhiambo, Godriver. *The Political Economy of Sugar Production in Colonial Kenya: The Asian Initiative in Central Nyanza.* New York: Lexington Books, 2016.
Wanyama, Rosina, Theda Gödecke, Christine G. K. Chege, and Matin Qaim. "How Important Are Supermarkets for the Diets of the Urban Poor in Africa?," *Food Security* (2019): 1–26.
White, Luise. *Comforts of Home: Prostitution in Colonial Nairobi.* Chicago: University of Chicago Press, 1990.
———. *Speaking with Vampires: Rumor and History in Colonial Africa.* Berkeley: University of California Press, 2000.
Willis, Justin. "'Men on the Spot': Labor, and the Colonial State in British East Africa: The Mombasa Water Supply, 1911–1917." *International Journal of African Historical Studies* 28, no. 1 (1995): 25–48.
———. *Mombasa, the Swahili, and the Making of the Mijikenda.* Oxford, UK: Clarendon, 1993.
Winders, Jamie, and Barbara Ellen Smith. "Social Reproduction and Capitalist Production: A Genealogy of Dominant Imaginaries." *Progress in Human Geography* 43, no. 5 (2019): 871–89.
Wolpe, Harold. "Capitalism and Cheap Labor-Power in South Africa: From Segregation to Apartheid." *Economy and Society* 1, no. 4 (1972): 425–56.
Wood, Ellen Meiksins. *The Origin of Capitalism: A Longer View.* New York: Verso, 2017.

Wylie, Diana. *Starving on a Full Stomach: Hunger and the Triumph of Cultural Racism in Modern South Africa.* Charlottesville: University Press of Virginia, 2001.

Young, Graeme. "From Protection to Repression: The Politics of Street Vending in Kampala." *Journal of Eastern African Studies* 11, no. 4 (2017): 714–33.

Zuckerman, Jane N., Lars Rambo, and Alain Fisch. "The True Burden and Risk of Cholera: Implications for Prevention and Control." *Lancet* 7 (2007): 521–30.

Index

The letter *f* following a page number denotes a figure.

Abwao, Barak Olela, 99
African Affairs Department's "Ten Year Development Plan," 109
African Retail Price Index, 61
agrarian societies: food systems in East Africa, 35–41; foodways, 6, 9, 34; variety in diet, 34
Agwari, Joseph Mariko, 81, 140
al-Hinawy, Mbarak, 110, 112, 205n19
Amethis Finance of France, 171
Angote, David E. L., 91, 130
Associated Vehicle Assemblers (AVA), 138
Atkins, Keletso, 7, 16, 176n25

Bakari, Mohamed, 218n12
Balala, Najib, 163, 166
Bamburi Cement Factory, 138
Barnes, Teresa, 5, 175n17
Bemba, 8, 10
Bengo, Lance Jones, 127–28
Berman, Bruce, 20
bin Mohamed, Abdul Kader, 90
bin Mohamed, Shariff, 17
Blue Room, 142
Bondo, 81
Booker, H. S., 65
borrowing networks, 63, 67
Brazzaville, 179n57
breakfast, 16, 77, 148; foods, 86–89, 89f, 144–45; gendered roles, 86, 88–89; rural Kenya, 79–82, 86; street vendors, 79, 86–89
Brennan, James R., 61
Britain, 58, 73; industrialization, 7–8; social reproduction, 8, 42–43, 106; working-class food system, 33, 51, 182n2
British Library, 28
Burudi, Nabwera, 62

Cannon Towers, 163
canteens, 109, 111, 130, 151; dock, 62; at hotels, 139–40; and kitchens, 109; liquor, 109; state-run, 113–16, 118, 120–22, 127, 129; subsidies for, 120–21, 124
capitalism, 2, 4–5, 19–20, 59, 75, 132, 173n5, 192n49; "choice" and, 53; colonial, 78; globalization and, 13; kitchen labor and, 76–104; time-discipline of industrial, 16–17, 196n5; urban, 7, 13–15, 83
caravan trade, 42
Carrefour, 74, 171
Castle Road Hotel, 143
Catholic Church, 166
Chamber of Commerce and Agriculture, 111
Changamwe Market, 70
Chege, Mary Nambui, 143
Chicago, Illinois, 14
Chigudu, Simukai, 126
China, 6, 104
Choi, Susanne Y. P., 6, 104
cholera, 23, 124–31, 136, 167, 208nn86–87; El Tor strain, 124–25; Harare's 2008–9 epidemic, 126
Coast General Hospital, 100
Cohen, Deborah, 6
colonial labor theory, 8
"common sense," 103, 202n115
conjugal family households, 65; gendered division of labor, 78–79, 99–100
Conservancy Department, 46f, 49
Cooke, S. V., 59
cooking fuel, 71–73; charcoal, 72, 73; firewood, 72–73; paraffin oil, 72, 73

Cooper, Frederick, 7, 15, 20, 29, 50, 53, 58, 65, 78, 175n25, 189n14, 192n39, 201n89
Crehan, Kate, 202n115
curio vendors, 102, 140, 143, 167

Daily Nation, 28, 92, 119, 123, 127, 129, 153, 158, 163, 164, 166, 167
Dar es Salaam, 61, 178n49, 209n97
Debonairs, 171
Democratic Party, 162
Denning, Michael, 19, 192n49
Department of Social Services and Housing, 128
Derrick, F. P. B., 113
Desai, R. K., 57
Deverell, N. M., 62, 63, 87, 88
Digo, 88
Dingley, Zebulon, 181n77
dinner/supper, 16, 77, 97–103; rural Kenya, 79, 81–82; street vendors and, 79
District Fisheries Office, 156
domestic labor: cooks, 78, 144–45; gendered division, 15, 56–57, 83, 97, 103, 174–75n15; non-cash compensation, 57
Dominos, 171
Duis, Perry, 14

E. A. Mercantile Company, 77
East African Breweries, 111
East African Legislative Assembly, 124
East African Power and Lighting, 193n67
East African Railway and Harbours (EARH), 114
East African Standard, 164, 167
Eating Out in Kenya (Eldon), 138–39
Eldon, Kathy, 139
Embu, 35
Express Handling Services Building, 130

factory system, 17
Fair, Laura, 191n30
fast food, 170–71, 220n50
Ferunzy, Juma, 124
food deserts, 53
FORD-Kenya, 166
Fort Hall, 1

Gabon, 6
Gambere, Hadji Ali, 145–46, 149
Gazi, 45
Gazi-Gogoni Estate, 47
General Post Office, 147f
General Purposes Committee, 118–19, 122
George, Abosede A., 19
Ghana, 6
githeri, 1, 39, 66, 80–82, 86, 93, 94, 167, 197n11
Gitonga, Evans Nduati, 1–2
Glassman, Jonathon, 191n30
Gome, Agnes, 4
Goody, Jack, 18
Gramsci, Antonio, 103, 202n115
Great Depression, 29, 53, 55–56, 58
Guyer, Jane, 4, 182n6

Hajj, Nuru Ibrahim, 146, 149
Harries, Patrick, 8
Harrison, Giddeon, 60
Harvey, David, 21, 115, 217n4
Hay, Janet, 37
Hayer, Judith, 82
Health Department, 119
Hobley, C. W., 36–37, 46, 48
Holy Ghost Cathedral, 164
Hornsby, Charles, 136
hotels, staff meals, 139–40, 212n5
household eateries, 88–89, 96

Ikumi, David, 90, 91
industrial paternalism, 111, 138; gendered, 8, 33; racial, 8, 33, 140–41, 169
Industrial Revolution, 13
informal economy, 14, 23, 84, 107–8, 123, 132, 147, 149, 157, 171–72, 180n64, 180n66, 214n30; crackdowns on, 159; politics of, 20–21, 110, 141–50; in the twenty-first century, 158–72
inns, 18, 180n59
irio, 8, 39–40, 82, 93, 105
isio, 7, 39–40, 82

Jera, Martina, 100
Jetha (councilor), 110–12
Jones, Lance, 90, 91
Josephe, 96, 147–49
Jubilee Square, 116
Jura, Thomas Mbeda, 138

kahawa chungu, 102–3
Kajembe, Rhamadhan, 165
Kakali, David, 158
Kalii, Joshua, 101
Kamau, John, 164
Kamba, 8, 35, 184n34; agriculture, 36, 82; animal husbandry, 37–38; diet, 7, 9, 34, 39–41, 47, 50, 60, 81–82, 183–84n23, 185n40; gender roles, 36–38; trade networks, 37–38

Kasau, Patrick, 140, 143, 167–68
Kashere, Maganga, 87
Kenya: agrarian foodways, 6, 9; Central Province, 29, 35, 80–82, 85, 100; colonial era, 8, 32–51, 73; decolonization, 105–32; food costs, 59–67; food rations and labor, 41–45; food shortages, 58; Highlands, 1, 7, 42; independence, 22–23, 81, 91–92, 107, 117–24, 141, 151, 181n76; land consolidation and distribution, 55, 153–54, 213n12; land ownership, 123; mealtime routines in rural areas, 79–83; migration in early-colonial period, 32–51; Nyanza Province, 29, 35, 81, 85, 96, 97, 100, 129; political economy, 20; resettlement schemes, 123; rural cuisines, 1, 7, 8, 11, 32–51, 79–83, 175n17; subsistence agriculture, 54; Tana River District, 125, 127; widows' rights, 123–24; working class, creation of, 34, 42
Kenya African National Union (KANU), 123–24, 157, 161–62, 166
Kenya Bus Service, 193n67
Kenya Landing and Shipping Company, 61, 193n67
Kenya Medical Journal, 44
Kenya National Archives (KNA), 28, 31, 181n76
Kenya National Traders Association, 123
Kenya Ports Authority (KPA), 54, 91
Kenyatta, Jomo, 36, 38, 122
Kenyatta Conference Center, 159–60
Kenya Uganda Railways and Harbours, 193n67, 201n94
Kereu, Sampson, 81, 105, 108, 146–47, 149
KFC, 171
Khamisis, F. J., 115
Kibaki, Mwai, 160, 162
Kikuyu, 7–8, 35, 64, 96, 105, 184n34; agriculture, 35, 36, 40–41; animal husbandry, 37–38, 71; diet, 9, 34, 39–41, 44, 48, 50–51, 71, 81–82, 93, 185n40; gender roles, 36–39, 93; rainy seasons, 40; trade networks, 37
Kilifi, 45, 48, 49
Kiliku, Kennedy, 162
Kilindini Harbour, 133
Kilindini Labour Office, 110
Kilindini Port, 90, 91, 91f, 92, 110, 156; canteens, 111; street vendors, 90, 110–11
Kimani, Jackson, 152
Kinyozi Road Food Canteen, 121
Kisauni, 84, 109
Kisero, Jaindi, 164
Kisumu, 30, 80
kitchen labor, 4–7, 13; commodified, 13, 169; gender division of, 4–7, 18–19, 78–79, 85, 97, 99–100, 103–4; social and economic dynamics of, 5; urban households and, 5–6; and the working day, 76–104
Kitching, Gavin, 84
Kithakwa, Appollo Nyinge, 100
Kivindto, David Muywambu, 102
Koch, Shelly, 5, 174n15
Kombo, Msanitu, 119
Kombo, Musikari, 166
Kongowea Market, 67, 143, 167
Kosoki, Ratas, 64
Krapf, Ludwig, 41–42, 50, 185n49, 208n86
Kubai, James, 155
Kwale, 146

labor migration, 5, 8, 10, 25, 35–36, 55; cuisine of, 44–45, 50
labor scarcity, 45–46, 49, 83, 187n80; workers' leverage of, 50, 186n67
labor stabilization, 53, 78, 106, 201n89
labor strikes, 20–21, 29, 50, 106, 192n39; 1939 general strike, 29, 53, 57, 189n14; 1947 general strike, 53
Lake Victoria, 35, 54–55; fishing, 55, 101, 184n26
Langat, K. P. A., 150
Legislative Council, 113, 115
Leys, Colin, 180n66
Libreville, 16
Likoni Market, 70, 152
Likoni Police Station, 152
Lindblom, Gerhard, 36
Lindsay, Lisa, 15, 19, 65, 78, 180n64
Liyali, Luyai, 165
Lonsdale, John, 20
Lory, J. J., 45
Luhya, 35
Lulu, J. K., 156
lunch, 16, 77, 90–96, 105, 148, 179n57, 180n59; foods, 93–94, 98f; rural areas, 17, 77, 80–82; working class, 16–18
Luo, 35, 184n34; agriculture, 36–37; animal husbandry, 37–38; diet, 9, 37, 40, 50, 67, 81, 101, 176n32; diet, seasonality of, 40; fishing, 37, 101; gender roles, 36–38; trade networks, 37

Machakos, 102, 167
MacKinnon Market, 67–71

maduka/duka, 2, 53–54, 65f, 66, 74, 83, 169; bulk breaking, 63; credit, 61–64, 67, 75, 144, 171; food sold, 87, 199n47; South Asian traders, 54
Madumadu, George G., 90, 91
Magnum International, 130
Magongo Market, 70, 151, 215n65
Maina, B. R., 155
maize meal, 1–2, 49, 66, 176n32, 192n52; cash purchases of, 9–10, 66; as rations, 9–10, 34, 43, 47; and relishes, 2, 34
Makadara Gardens, 163
Makupa Market, 69, 70, 87, 101; breakfast sold at, 87; canteens, 114; fee-paying vendors, 68
Malawi, 6
Mali, 6, 11
Malleo, Elizabeth, 146, 149
marital migrancy, 5–6, 175n17
"market women," 15
Martin, Phyllis, 179n57
masculine compromise, 6
Maseno, 55
Masha, Ali, 89f
"master and servant" laws, 8–9, 34, 43, 48–49, 56, 57
Mathange, I. M., 122
Maweu, Agnes, 167
Mbaria, John, 153, 163
MBC Equity Fund, 171
Mbeda, Thomas, 89
McCann, James C., 6, 10, 176n32
McMillan Memorial Library, 28
Medical Officer of Health, 119
Meru, 35
Mexico, 6
migrant/contract laborers: access to meat, 70–71; cash purchases of food, 1–2, 45, 48, 54–67, 72, 111, 169, 211n4; labor strikes, 20–21, 29, 50, 53, 57, 106, 189n14, 192n39; *posho* system, 43–50, 53, 56; rumor networks, 46, 186n67; wages, 14, 49, 52–53, 56, 58, 60–61, 65–67, 72, 78, 111, 187n80, 192n39; women, 65–66
Mijikenda, 34, 208n86
Minara, Thomas Mbaja, 139
Ministry of Health, 122
Ministry of Local Government, 119, 122
Mintz, Sidney, 8, 11, 34, 40, 93
Miruka, James, 74, 88, 96
Mkamba, 62
Mohamed, Abdulla, 61
Moi, Daniel arap, 161
Mombasa: 1848 map, 3f; 1900, 14; 1930s, 20, 58; 1940s, 88; 1947 survey, 87–88; 1963 map, 3f; Airport Road, 165; Bondeni, 88; Central Business District (CBD), 135, 139, 141–43, 150, 163, 167, 169–70; Changamwe, 84, 88, 92, 99, 109, 138, 142, 162, 201n94; Coast Province, 122; colonial era, 4, 20, 30, 64, 67–68, 71, 73, 78, 83, 85, 105–32, 175n25, 201n89; commercialization of daily life, 52–75; Dar es Salaam Road, 92; Digo Road, 142; food provisioning in midcentury period, 52–75; food system, 53–54; High-Level, 90, 91, 114; Jomo Kenyatta Avenue, 142; Kilindini High Ground, 114; Kilindini Road, 68; Kongowea, 73; labor politics, 58, 97, 175n25; Likoni, 84, 99, 104, 133–34, 142–43, 161; Magongo Road, 142; Majengo, 61, 68–69, 88, 97, 109, 114, 122; Makupa, 58; Makupa Road, 68; Mama Ngina Drive, 154; Mbaraki, 58, 72, 91; Mikindani Street, 150, 170; Moi Avenue, 135, 142, 148, 163, 167, 170; Mombasa-Nairobi Road, 138; Mozambique Road, 114; Mwembe Tayari, 139, 142, 145f, 148, 155; Nkrumah Road, 170, 171; Old Town, 67–69, 163, 170; population, 83–84, 193n69, 209n97; produce and protein in modern food system, 67–71; rural food systems, 30; sanitation, 125–26, 128, 151, 209n93; Shimanzi, 58, 113–14; social inequality, 67; the Station, 90–91; street food and the political economy, 19–24, 105–32; Tudor Estate, 97, 99; unemployment, 22, 84, 150–51; urban development, 162–64; water, access to, 125–26; working day, 13–19, 83–103
Mombasa African Advisory Council, Welfare Committee, 111
Mombasa Beach Hotel, 140
Mombasa Social Survey, 62, 66
Mombasa Technical College, 145
Moskowitz, Kara, 123, 204n8
Mount Kenya, 81
Mouritsen, Ole, 11
Mpate, F., 148
Mritini, 138
Mudanya, Emma, 66, 143, 158–59, 168
Mugenya, A. W., 131
Muli, Jacob, 102, 140
Mumba, M. K., 141
Municipal Board of Mombasa, 29, 113
Municipal Council of Mombasa, 29

municipal-run markets, 68–69; fees, 69
Muon, Wambogu, 102
Mupaghasa, Hezron, 139–40
Murundi, Priscilla Mwanake, 154–56
Musio, Mbwana Mohamed, 142
Mutave, Alice, 102
Muthoni, Catherine, 144–46, 148, 159, 168
Mutiso, Monica, 144–45, 148
Mutua, Onemus, 29, 133–34
Mwacharo, L. G., 153–54
Mwangi, Joseph, 80, 103
Mwangi, Mwai, 129
Mwaruwa, Salim I., 124
Mwembe Tayari Market, 67–68, 70, 83, 113, 143, 148; breakfast sold at, 87; canteens at, 114; street vendors at, 112
Mzungu, Umazi, 95f

Nairobi, 1, 7, 28, 31, 35, 81, 84, 107, 114, 119, 172, 206n55, 208n82, 213n12; Central Business District, 129, 160; Haile Selassie Avenue, 129; Kibra, 172; Mathare, 172
Naivas, 74, 171
Nakumatt, 170
Nasser, A. M. M., 155
Nassir, Shariff, 123–24, 157, 159, 161–66, 169–70, 218n12
Natal, 7, 16
Nathwani, U. K., 126
National Archives at Kew, 28
National Traders Association, Coast Province branch, 120, 123
Ndolo, Margaret Auma, 88–89, 103
Ndonyo, Musomi, 76–77
Ndoro, Samuel, 148
neoliberalism, 22–24, 108, 132, 204n8, 217n4
Neptune Beach Hotel, 140
New Lady Grigg Hospital, 91
Ngala, Ronald, 112–13, 123
Ngotho, Joseph, 142
Ngotho, Nzalu, 85, 96
Nigeria, 66, 78
Northcote, G. A. S., 36
Nthuli, Jackson, 54, 92
Ntinda, Nicholas, 123
Nyambok, Mercy, 29
Nyoka, Hamisi, 145f
Nzonga, Julius Nzioka, 139

Ocobock, Paul, 122
Ogola, James Hunnington, 55
Ogwell, Sylvester Obanda, 150, 153, 155–56
Olang', Akoth, 156
Omar, A. A., 123
Omar, Mohammed, 147f
Omar, Salim, 128
Ombongi, Kenneth, 166, 217n1
Omondi, Gregory Osollo, 81, 99, 104
Omwanda, Rose, 138
Onyango, John Omondi, 97, 134
open-air markets, 2, 54, 67
Operation Murambatsvina, 161
Organisation for Economic Co-operation and Development (OECD), 5
Orwell, George, 192n52
Osborn, Emily Lynn, 19
Osei-Opare, Nana, 31
Owen, Caleb Edwin, 181n77
Owino, D. T. A., 156
Owiti, Vitalis, 55, 80, 100, 140
Owuir, Benike, 54, 103, 140

Paris, nineteenth century, 21
Peng, Yinni, 6, 104
petty commerce, 14, 21, 29, 101, 104, 106, 110, 111, 167; expansion of, 143; monitoring of, 128; women and, 66
Philip, C. R., 71
Pizza Hut, 171
plantation slavery, 42
posho rationing system/standard, 9, 12, 32–33, 57, 60, 62, 67, 75, 83, 169; in 1910s, 32–33, 43, 45, 48; in 1920s, 35, 45, 48; cash in lieu of, 51, 56, 58–59; on the coast of East Africa, 41–45; end of, 9, 49, 52; migrant/contract laborers and, 43–50; monotony of, 34–35, 44, 45, 47–48, 51, 53, 59, 176n32; origins of word, 41–42, 185n48; precolonial, 42; racialization of, 191nn29–30; in wartime, 12, 48, 58–59
Potts, Deborah, 161
Powysland Estate, 45, 49
Prestholdt, Jeremy, 163
Procter, R. A., 44, 51
produce vendors, 53–54, 67, 74, 104, 115, 158
proletarian/proletarianization, 2, 19, 169; definition of, 19
Provincial Administration, 122
Public Works Department (PWD), 47, 56, 60, 99

railway housing, 100
restaurants, 18, 149; definition of, 109; gendered division of, 19; legality of, 108–9; structures of, 108–9
Rich, Jeremy, 16

Richards, Audrey, 8, 10–11
Rift Valley, 66, 143, 147, 161
Rihal, N. S., 120, 121, 122, 151
roadside eateries/kiosks, 79, 101, 114, 153–54, 172, 200n71; licenses, 118–19
Robertson, Claire, 160, 213n12
Rockel, Stephen, 42
roommates/housemates, 64, 75; division of labor in, 78, 97, 99, 104
Rosenwald, C. D., 112, 118–19, 121, 151
rubber plantations, 32, 45
Rwandan genocide, 125
Rydon, A. H. B., 84

Sakarani, Omar M., 123
Sammi, Mueni, 168
Schoenbrun, David, 202n115
Sessional Paper No. 1 of 1986, 137
sex workers, 15, 178n51
Shell Company of East Africa, 56, 113
Shimba Hills, 73
Siaya, 54, 81, 99, 134
sikuma wiki, 2, 93
Silver Beach Hotel, 139–40
sima, 10, 50, 66, 146
Simpson, W. J., 44
Singh Restaurant, 139
sisal plantations, 32, 45
Skanda, M. A., 152
Social Democratic Party of Kenya, 165
social reproduction, 173n5, 174n8; commodification, 4, 15, 197n10; employers' responsibilities toward workforce, 34, 41–45, 47, 49–50, 182n6; limits of postwar development, 109–11; street vendors, 106, 112–13, 179n52; work, gendered, 33, 44–45
Social Services and Housing, 128
Sokoke Estate, 48
South Africa, 6, 34
starch/staple-and-relish framework, 11, 40–42, 93–94; supplement to, 45
state-run eateries, 109–10
Steers, 171
Stevens, John Josiah, 61
Stoll, Steven, 47
street-food industry, 2, 13–19, 79, 83, 96–97, 98f, 103–4, 179n52; 1950s, 76; 1965 survey, 85; 1978 campaign to shut down industry, 23; alternatives, 137–41; benefits of ownership, 145–47; breakfast, 86–89; contradictory politics, 111–17; credit, 18, 144, 171; destruction / shutting down, 106, 108, 110, 112–13, 122–23, 127, 129–31, 137, 149, 150, 155, 159, 161–69, 213n12, 217n1; dinner, 101–2; employees, 148–49; end of the twentieth century, 133–57; gendered divisions, 19, 84–85, 100; household cooking, 101; independence, 117–24; legal issues and laws, 23, 109, 152, 205n19; lunch, 90–96; Mombasa's political economy, 19–24, 105–32; operating costs, 14–15, 106; pandemic politics, 124–25; political power, 106–8, 117, 123, 137, 162; politics, 150–56; practicality, 17–18, 106; prices, 14, 109–10, 113, 143–44, 171–72; sanitation, 21, 23, 106, 115, 118, 120–22, 124, 126–27, 129–31, 150, 160; snacks, 94–95; social life, 102; structures, 24, 106, 118, 142; twenty-first century, 158–72; vendor arrests, 20, 21, 24, 105, 108, 115, 118, 149, 152; vendors, licenses, 106, 115–16, 118–19, 121, 127, 130, 150, 153–56; vendors, unlicensed/illicit, 77, 85, 106, 109–10, 112, 115–16, 118–19, 122, 128–29, 141–49, 162; water, access to, 21, 106, 128, 150
Strobel, Margaret, 179n52
structural adjustment packages, 136, 213n10
Styrbæk, Klavs, 11
suburbanization, 137–41
Subway, 171
sugar plantations, 176n32
supermarkets, 220n49; Mombasa, 74, 170–71; United States, 53
Sweta, Patrice Omollo, 100
Szabo, Michelle, 5, 174n15

Taita, 35
Tanzania, 129, 186n67
tea carts (*gari ya chai*), 87, 90–93, 103, 130, 146, 199n47, 205n19; destruction of, 116; gendered roles at, 87–88, 96; licenses for, 90, 120
temporary occupation license (TOL), 153, 155–56
Temu, Mohamed Amir, 91, 101–2, 146, 153, 167
Texaco Oil Company, 17, 56
Thompson, E. P., 7, 16, 196n5
Tieta, 64
tourism, 107, 118, 121, 135, 140, 159, 163–64, 212n6, 219n25
Town Hall, 165

Tudor Market, 70
Tulk, Alfred William, 17
Tuskys, 170
Twagira, Laura Ann, 11
typhoid, 112

ubwali, 10–11
Uchumi, 170
uchuru, 39–40, 80
ugali, 10, 50, 62, 64, 81–82, 94, 98f, 139, 145f, 167–68; definition, 50; grains used in, 81
Uganda, 73
Uganda Railway, 43–44, 76, 90
uji, 80–82, 86, 168, 197n11; grains used in, 82
Ukambani, 29, 54, 64, 81–82, 85, 92, 139
University of Oxford, Commonwealth and African Collections at, 28
urban food sharing, 18
urbanization, 2, 5, 10, 13, 218n20; industrial, 13
usu, 39, 80

Vacuum Oil Co., 56, 193n67
Vegetable Growers Association, 57
vibanda/kibanda, 91–92, 93, 101, 102, 105, 142, 145–47, 149, 200n71; breakfast at, 143–44; destruction of, 130, 159, 163; dinner at, 101; foods served at, 93–95, 144–45, 167; gender roles in, 91–92, 123–24, 146; licenses, 118, 123–24; lunch at, 103, 167
vibarua, 42

Wadigo, 67
Wales, K. K., 158
Washomba, Kabatha wa, 57, 64, 97
water: access to, 21, 106, 128, 150; commodification of, 73–74; delivery, 73–74
welfarism, 50
White, Luise, 15
Wilkhu, Darshan Singh, 139
Willis, Justin, 73, 179n52, 187n80, 201n89
Wilson, G. M., 84
Wolpe, Harold, 197n10
Wood, Ellen Meiksins, 173n5
World Bank's International Finance Corporation, 171
World War I, 46, 111
World War II, 12, 22, 58, 109, 112
Wylie, Diana, 10

Zambia, 11, 47
Zanzibar, 42, 191n30, 208n87
Zimbabwe, 126, 161, 175n17
Zimbabwe African National Union–Popular Front, 161
Zulu, 7, 10, 16